CHARLES AND ADA

CHARLES AND ADA

THE COMPUTER'S MOST PASSIONATE PARTNERSHIP

JAMES ESSINGER

The
History
Press

This book is dedicated with admiration and affection
to Briony Kapoor, queen of Romney Marsh.

Cover illustration: Part of the Analytical Engine (Chris Howes/Wild
Places Photography/Alamy Stock Photo)

Every effort has been made to contact the holders of copyright.
First published 2019

The History Press
97 St George's Place, Cheltenham
Gloucestershire, GL50 3QB
www.thehistorypress.co.uk

British Library Cataloguing in Publication Data.
A catalogue record for this book is available from the British Library.

ISBN 978 0 7509 9095 0

Typesetting and origination by The History Press
Printed and bound in Great Britain by TJ International Ltd

MIX
Paper from
responsible sources
FSC® C013056

CONTENTS

'It has done me harm, my friend. It has aged me, tired me, vexed me, disappointed me. It does no man any good to have his patience worn out, and to think himself ill-used.'

Daniel Doyce in *Little Dorrit* (1857), by Charles Dickens

'We may say most aptly, that the Analytical Engine *weaves algebraical patterns* just as the Jacquard loom weaves flowers and leaves.'

Ada Lovelace, 1843 (her own emphasis)

FOREWORD
BY LISA NOEL BABBAGE

I remember my parents telling me when I was little that we had a famous ancestor. That knowledge only became meaningful for me, though, in the 1980s, when in sixth grade I commuted to the Virginia Highlands area of Atlanta, Georgia, to attend Inman Middle School. During a history class we were told about Charles Babbage, who had designed a computer made out of cogwheels. From that moment I was immensely proud to have Charles Babbage as my forebear (he is, in fact, my great-great-great-great-grandfather), and it's thrilling that so many people know about him today. Nowadays he is a daily inspiration to me.

It was due to him that I discovered who I could be. In the face of huge odds, Charles (I like to think of him by his first name) faced his dream, staring it down day after day for the better part of a lifetime. And he did this, not solely for himself, but very much for everyone – to make people's lives better. It is this habitual force of seeing beyond the everyday and maintaining a vision of sublimity that I draw on in my own life as an invaluable insight for how I want to live.

The world we live in today is, I think, much shaped by Charles' work. To that end I count it a joy to have to explain the peculiarity of my last name to people who don't know me and who mistakenly call me 'Lisa Baggage' or some other inaccurate rendition of our family surname. The Babbage Connection, as my mother calls it, is the stuff of dreams.

To me, the Babbage Connection means that I was born into a lineage that helped me reach beyond the walls of ghetto life in America to what the possibility of living empowered could be. And it was the constant reminder of Charles' 'stick-to-it-tiveness' – his determination never to give up on pursuing his dream – that helped me hold on to my own desires and dreams.

Both my grandparents were well travelled, having served in the Royal Air Force of the United Kingdom during the Second World War. Stuart Barton Babbage, my grandfather, was actually born in New Zealand in 1916. When I visited him in Sydney, Australia, in the 1990s, I found he had lots of family memorabilia in his house, including a copy of the old, yellowing newspaper from 1871 that announced Charles Babbage's death. Stuart was a remarkable man, who also spent three years in comparative humility as a vicar at an African American church in Decatur, Georgia. It was there in Atlanta that his son, my father Christopher Charles Babbage, married an African American, LaNell Johnson – my mother.

We, within ourselves, are the ultimate drivers of destiny; complexion and gender do not constrain what is inside us nor do the external forces around us ultimately contain it. My great-great-great-great-grandfather gave me that destiny-driven vision and I have held on to it with all I am.

Ada Lovelace, like Charles, has always been a constant figure in my mind. Knowing that her efforts not only supported Charles' inventions but pushed them beyond what was initially predicted gave me a sense of pride as a woman and as a member of the Babbage bloodline.

I've always imagined what their dynamic friendship must have been like, and I have on many occasions tried to put myself in Ada's shoes. She is a hero's heroine because she didn't shy away from doing her best to have an intellectual life, even when it would have been much easier for her to abandon that aim. She and I share a common struggle, both being daughters of a broken marriage. Yet neither of us chose to give up pursuing a dream of wanting to have a significant positive impact on humanity – in that respect, Ada is most deservedly and understandably a role model for millions of women today, worldwide.

AUTHOR'S NOTES

We need to have an accurate idea of the modern value of nineteenth-century monetary sums. A useful rule of thumb is that we should multiply nineteenth-century monetary amounts by about a hundred to give an approximate idea of what the sums would be worth today. There was little price inflation in Britain during the nineteenth century; indeed, prices sometimes actually went down.

Inevitably, it is only an approximation. Food, drink and in particular the cost of domestic service were disproportionately cheaper in Charles Babbage's time than they are in the second decade of the twenty-first century. In the nineteenth century, even middle-class people who were far from wealthy would have typically had one or more live-in servants. These servants would have been given their board (i.e. food and drink) and accommodation, but only a tiny salary that might have been no more than £20 per year.

In letters I use italics where in the manuscript the word was underlined by the writer. Ada Lovelace was a particularly keen emphasiser.

I have sometimes broken up the paragraphing of source material, both printed and manuscript, in order to make the material more readable. In the case of the printed material, the excessively long paragraphs were usually designed to make the material shorter to save money, rather than done with any concern for readability or posterity.

PREFACE

Charles Babbage, an English mechanical engineer, mathematician and polymath, designed the world's first programmable computer. He did this not in our century, or even in the twentieth, but back in the 1830s.

His great friend Ada Lovelace, born Ada Byron, encouraged him and supported him emotionally in his endeavours, and her insights into his work – insights that not even Charles had – help posterity understand just how far ahead of its time his thinking really was. In particular, Ada saw that Charles had in fact invented a general-purpose machine that could govern all sorts of processes, including even the composition and playing of music, whereas Charles thought that he was only designing machines for carrying out mathematical calculations. Charles and Ada were both geniuses and their talents existed in a kind of symbiosis with each other, although neither of them fully understood this at the time. I choose to use their first names because it seems more friendly – and more respectful – than 'Babbage and Lovelace'.

After first inventing a revolutionary machine he called the Difference Engine, devised to print accurate mathematical and navigational tables, Charles, in 1834, realised that a much more general machine, which he christened the Analytical Engine, was possible. Programs (to use modern terminology) and data were to be furnished to the Analytical Engine by means of punched cards, which were already being used at the time to govern the operation of the Jacquard loom, a remarkable and inspired automatic loom for weaving complex images and patterns.

The Analytical Engine's output would be a printer, a curve plotter and a bell, and the machine would also be able to punch numbers on to cards to be read into the machine later. The Analytical Engine was the world's first ever general-purpose computer. Many of the great inventions that have made the modern world possible were devised in the nineteenth century rather than the twentieth, but of these none is more important than the computer. Unfortunately, at the time, hardly anyone recognised the importance of Charles' computer, apart from Ada Lovelace.

Charles and Ada is the first book to make maximum use of the extensive collection of material in the British Library Babbage Archive in London. Anthony Hyman's 1982 biography, *Charles Babbage: Pioneer of the Computer*, uses some material from that remarkable archive but curiously omits – or perhaps overlooks – abundant personal material which reveals extensive information about Charles' personality and his feelings towards many of the events of his life, including his tragic private life and the rejection he felt at the hands of the world.

Posterity can be grateful to Charles for many reasons: one is that he had a habit of making handwritten copies of important letters he was sending or of important documents. They may also have been early drafts and it often impossible to know whether an ostensible copy is that or an early draft.

By definition, someone's archive usually only consists of letters or other documents sent *to* them, but because Charles made these crucial copies, we have this additional material available. He was a brilliant writer, and while he expressed his own emotions rarely, when he did it was often with deeply moving intensity. Also – and this is by no means a trivial consideration when one sees just how many of the letters he received from others are written in handwriting that is close to, if not completely, unreadable – his own handwriting is usually very legible and there are only a few instances where I have been unable to decipher crucial words.

Anyone seeking to write Charles and Ada's story ought to be humbled by the task; indeed, if they were not it is difficult to imagine that the resulting biography could have any merit. This biography, like any other, can only ever aspire to offer an approximate idea of what Charles was like when he lived. Still, it is at least a consolation that – with perhaps only two exceptions: his beloved wife Georgiana, who died at a tragically early age in September 1827, and his close friend Ada Lovelace, who also died young – nobody who knew him when he was alive had very much idea of what to make of him either. Today, we do at least have the privilege of being able to look back on Charles' life in its entirety and to do our best to try to fathom what made this remarkable genius the man he was, and what he was really like.

What is incontestable is that Charles was a far more emotional and deeply feeling man than he has so far been regarded by posterity. Still, if posterity doesn't usually get him right in this respect, that's to a large extent his own fault; by all accounts, he wasn't much of a communicator in private about his personal emotional state, and in public he was even less so, even by nineteenth-century standards.

For example, in his 1864 autobiography *Passages from the Life of a Philosopher* (meaning 'scientist'), there is much excellent material about his plans and aims for the machines he called Difference Engine 1 and Difference Engine 2. There is also some first-rate material about the Analytical Engine, but even given the reticence we habitually expect to encounter in autobiographies written during the latter years of the nineteenth century, *Passages* contains almost no material whatsoever relating to Charles' personal life. He does not once mention his beloved wife Georgiana by name, although he does refer to her indirectly:

The Queen of Sardinia was the sister of the Grand Duke of Tuscany (Leopold II) from whom I had, many years before, when under severe affliction from the loss of a large portion of my family, received the most kind and gratifying attention.

That 'large portion of my family' certainly includes his wife Georgiana. As for Ada Lovelace, Charles only mentions her once in a passage which is explored later.

·A major problem with the autobiography is that it has helped to give later generations the impression that Charles was a hard and unfeeling, mathematically minded man without much in the way of emotions. Ada, on the other hand, is popularly regarded as being someone who wore her emotions on her sleeve and was passionate about her work.

At the start of his autobiography, Charles employs a quotation from Lord Byron's *Don Juan* (1824). Byron was Ada Lovelace's father. The quotation, which is completely at odds with the reticence and indeed deliberate evasion surrounding emotional topics in the autobiography, is:

> I'm a philosopher. Confound them all.
> Birds, beasts and men; but no, not womankind.

In fact, Charles misquotes Byron here: Byron wrote, 'Bills, beasts and men' rather than 'Birds, beasts and men' – Charles, with an enormous inheritance, was not so preoccupied with money on a day-to-day basis as Byron was.

The misquotation may be due to Charles confusing the lines in *Don Juan* with an extract from Byron's poem *Darkness* (1816), which reads:

> ... and kept
> The birds and beasts and famish'd men at bay.

This misquotation suggests that Charles was a man for whom women were a spiritually vital part of his life, yet it's impossible to be certain what they really meant to him. He was capable of very strong attachments and there is no doubt that he and Ada did indeed have a close romantic friendship, but there is no proof as to whether this ever became physical.

Generally, there is very little extant evidence in the documentation that allows much to be written of Charles' feelings about women other than his devotion to his wife Georgiana and all his children, his terrible distress when his daughter Georgiana died, and his great fondness for Ada.

The Sirens of Machinery

In Greek mythology, the Sirens are dangerous temptresses, who sang charmingly and lured nearby sailors to their deaths on dangerous rocks. Machines can be Sirens too.

Charles and Ada were fascinated by the possibility of what mechanisms could do. Charles once remarked, when talking about a machine he'd seen in the industrial north, how extraordinary it was that every single time the machine operated, a particular part of its mechanism would reach up to exactly the same place as before. This might seem a commonplace observation, but to Charles it was something akin to poetry. As for Ada, she once went on a tour of England's north with her mother, and enjoyed it very much.

Charles loved mechanical figures and toys that were able to move about by themselves. He grew extremely enthusiastic about them, and when he bought one for his house he would beg his close friends to come and see it and he would introduce it to a wider circle of friends at his regular social soirées. Indeed, its regularity was itself a kind of manifestation of Charles' love of order, precision and the relentless progression of mechanism. He loved machinery of all kinds, being fascinated by it beyond its own utility. He loved devices for their own sake. Charles was the kind of person who liked to play around with machinery to see what would happen. As we'll see, he even confesses in his autobiography to having the fundamental problem as a child of being far more interested in what was inside a machine than in what it could do for him.

In his love of and appreciation for machinery, Charles is not only a Victorian genius, but, in a very real sense, a modern genius too. Researching into his life and writing about him, one is so often overwhelmed with a sense that this was a man who was, to a large extent, timeless.

The trouble with loving machines, though, is that they don't usually love us back. What is true of physical machines generally is especially true of inventions. It's never enough merely to conceptualise the invention; you need to build one if you're going to be an inventor of any importance. That can be a task that often requires superhuman persistence and patience. For example, in the 1970s and 1980s, James (now Sir James) Dyson, the inventor of the revolutionary cyclonic bagless vacuum cleaner, made more than 5,000 prototypes of the vacuum cleaner he dreamed of building before he finally got it right.

Indeed, machines often have a tendency to turn into Sirens who break inventors' hearts. The reason for this is that physical materials need to do complex things very accurately and reliably if the invention is going to work.

Most of the technical problems Charles faced throughout his career stemmed from his decision to try to construct his computation machines from cogwheels. These were designed to function in the engines to represent numbers, which in modern computers would be embodied in microchip circuitry.

Charles did not give serious consideration to using any other technology for his machines than cogwheels. Electrical science was nowhere near sophisticated enough in his time to make an electrical Difference Engine or Analytical Engine even remotely feasible. Cogwheels, on the other hand, had an excellent tried-and-tested pedigree within a meticulous, highly commercial, practical science that spanned the globe: the manufacture of clocks and watches. Cogwheels allowed a weight to fall in regular, measured increments and so brought the passage of time – which, until the invention of the cogwheel in the Middle Ages, had been only tracked by sundials and clumsy estimates – under the precise dominion of human awareness and observation.

Charles wanted to extend that same precision to arithmetical and mathematical calculation. With the help of the engineers he employed, he was able to produce the cogwheels he needed for the required accuracy – indeed, there is evidence that his level of accuracy was actually in excess of what was required to make the machines work.

But Charles needed to do more than just produce a handful of cogwheels. The Difference Engine, if it were to be completed, required about 20,000 essentially identical cogwheels at a time when the only way of making them was by hand; this was simply too big an undertaking even for someone as ambitious and wealthy as Charles. The Analytical Engine would need even more. As Doron Swade explains in his book *The Cogwheel Brain* (2000): 'The lesson from Babbage's unhappy fate was that unless he could produce the hundreds of near-identical parts in an incredibly short time and at low cost, the world at large – and bank managers in particular – would lose patience.'

The point is that brilliant ideas are dreams, and dreams need to be made to come true with the investment of time, expertise and hard cash. In imagination things may work perfectly, but making an invention work in reality can be a much more difficult matter.

While heartbreak is the swansong of many an inventor, Charles at least had the defence against the Sirens that he lived very much inside his own mind and to some extent in his own world as well, which could make reality less painful for him. In January 1832, for example, the geologist Charles Lyell travelled to Hendon, today a northern suburb of London but at that time a village separate from the capital, and visited his friends Dr William Fitton and William Conybeare, who were also both geologists. Charles was there as well. As Lyell recalled:

We have had great fun in laughing at Babbage, who unconsciously jokes and reasons in high mathematics, talks of the 'algebraic equation' of such a one's character in regard to the truth of his stories etc. I remarked that the paint of Fitton's house would not stand, on which Babbage said, 'no: painting a house outside is calculating by the index minus one,' or some such phrase, which made us stare; so that he said gravely by way of explanation, 'That is to say, I am assuming revenue to be a function.' All this without pedantry, and he bears well being well quizzed by it.

Lyell found his evening in this stimulating company delightful:

Fitton's carriage brought us from Highwood House to within a mile of Hampstead, and then Babbage and I got out and preferred walking. Although enjoyable, yet staying up till half-past one with three such men, and the continual pelting of new ideas, was anything but a day of rest.

It was in the summer of 1821 that Charles is definitely known to have started working on automatic calculating machines, though it is possible he might have thought of them before then. In *Passages* he states:

> The earliest idea that I can trace in my own mind of calculating arithmetical tables by machinery arose in this manner:
>
> One evening I was sitting in the rooms of the Analytical Society, at Cambridge, my head leaning forward on the table in a kind of dreamy mood, with a table of logarithms lying open before me. Another member, coming into the room and seeing me half asleep, called out, 'Well, Babbage, what are you dreaming about?' to which I replied, 'I'm thinking that all these tables (pointing to the logarithms) might be calculated by machinery.'

However, Charles adds immediately after this: 'I am indebted to my friend, the Rev. Doctor Robinson, the Master of the Temple, for this anecdote. The event must have happened either in 1812 or 1813.'

If Charles did mention to a fellow student his plans for using machinery to calculate mathematical tables back in the days when he was at Cambridge University, it seems unlikely that he – a man with a prodigious memory – would not have remembered this himself. This particular anecdote therefore is probably apocryphal, although the fact that Charles put it in his autobiography shows how significant in his intellectual development he saw his notion of mechanising calculations.

Robert Pirsig, in his autobiographical philosophical memoir *Zen and the Art of Motorcycle Maintenance* (1974), characterises two kinds of attitudes towards technology. Pirsig depicts himself as interested in the details of maintenance in order that his machine will have the best chance of delivering excellent performance during the trip: the 'Classical' approach to technology. His friend John Sutherland, conversely, is shown as having little or no interest in the details of motorcycle maintenance. He basically just hopes for the best and that his own motorcycle won't break down. Pirsig calls this the 'Romantic' approach, suggesting that most people tend to fall into one category or the other when it comes to technology.

Employing this terminology, Charles could be said to have held the 'Classical' and 'Romantic' attitudes simultaneously. We might say that he was both a Classical and Romantic inventor, capable of being a superb engineer while simultaneously maintaining an idealistic and passionate attitude towards his inventions and remaining deeply excited about the benefits they might bring to humanity, even while behaving much of the time in ways that were fundamentally inimical to any chance of that happening. This, essentially, was the nature of the tragedy of his life.

In time to come, Ada understood this fundamentally self-destructive aspect of his personality, and did all she could to help him overcome it. With what effect, we shall see.

1

BRITAIN TRANSFORMED

'I can think of nothing else but this machine.'
James Watt, in a letter to Dr James Lind,
29 April 1765, writing about the steam engine

The Britain into which Charles was born on 26 December 1791 was the richest country in the world by aggregate wealth, but a land in which the distribution of wealth was fantastically unequal.

The economist Joseph Massey estimated in the late 1750s that the bottom 40 per cent of the British population, wealth-wise, had to live on 14 per cent of the nation's wealth. Massey also produced an estimate of Britain's social structure for 1759, which is still regarded as accurate by modern historians.

According to Massey, only about 310 families in Britain had an annual income in 1759 of more than £5,000; this made them peers and grand landowners. The next category comprised about 1,000 families with an annual income of more than £1,000; these were also gentry, though not quite as elevated as the first category. Next came wealthy merchants and squires; there were about 3,400 families fitting into this category, and they had an annual income of £600 or above. It is important to bear in mind that in those days when industrialisation, while burgeoning, had not been burgeoning for long, most of the wealth of the nation still came from farming. If you owned substantial land, you were rich; if you didn't, by and large you weren't.

Next along came small landowners, clergy, traders and professionals who had an annual income of about £100 or more. There were about 105,000 of these families. Then there were about 160,000 families whose annual income was between £50 and £100. These were small traders, lesser clergy and moderately prosperous farmers.

The rest of the population, about 1.1 million families, had an income of below £50 a year and were impoverished and often also malnourished, though this was a time before the discovery of vitamins or any other elements of nutrition, so people tended to measure nourishment according to how full their bellies were. The overall population of Britain was about 6 million in 1750 and had risen to about 8 million by 1790.

It was a Britain hard to imagine today. Until the 1730s, only six decades before Charles was born, there had still been laws in force condemning witches to be burnt at the stake. The first half of the eighteenth century also saw the beginning of what is now known as the Industrial Revolution. The term – believed to have been coined by a Frenchman, the diplomat Louis-Guillaume Otto, who on 6 July 1799 had written to a friend to say that '*une revolution industrielle*' had started in France – has come to be used to describe the enormous acceleration in the application of steam technology and mass manufacture throughout British industry.

The Industrial Revolution was well entrenched by the time Charles was born. In 1718, businessmen John and Thomas Lombe had set up a silk mill in Derby, five storeys high and powered by water from the River Derwent. The Lombe manufactory employed about 300 people and is regarded as one of the world's first factories.

The factories of the eighteenth and nineteenth centuries have generally acquired a bad press today, having come to be regarded and thought of by many as ugly, cramped, noisy places of excessively strict rules. Cramped and noisy they often were, but when they were first built they weren't as bad as they became. They were once new, after all. It's true that the rules prevailing in them were draconian – for example, in some factories workers were routinely fined more than a day's pay for being even slightly late, and were sometimes fined the following day's pay too. Yet we need to bear in mind that, at the time, for many people who went to work in the factories of the Industrial Revolution, the alternative was solitary toil, such as at handlooms up muddy country lanes in damp, miserable cottages for unpredictable and starvation pay. For such people, going to work in a factory at least offered the advantages of regular wages, reasonable working conditions and new social possibilities.

George Eliot, in her inspired novel *Silas Marner* (1861), tells the story of a solitary weaver of linen who lives in a little cottage and grows half-demented (and extremely miserly) from loneliness until he accidentally becomes the guardian of a little girl on whom he dotes, and who eventually comes to regard him as her father. Mary Essinger, somewhat more recently, worked in clothing factories in the British Midlands city of Leicester in the 1950s and writes, in her memoir *Mary, Quite Contrary* (2016), about the difference between how factories are often perceived today and what it was like to work in them back then:

> The Leicester knitwear industry has all but vanished and I thought of the generations of skilled workers making dresses, jumpers, underwear and socks … Factory workers were considered 'common'. It made me think of all the beautiful girls who worked alongside me in the factory and the fun we had. And none of them were common.
>
> Factories were not dark, satanic mills, sewing needs daylight and factories had lots of windows. Leicester's vibrant and creative industry once helped to clothe the world with high-quality knitted outerwear and underwear.

While factory regulations of the early Industrial Revolution do often seem draconian and indeed outrageous to modern sensibilities, the rules were thought necessary at the time to try to create reliable factory workers out of people who had never worked in those places before. Not that this excuses what the regulations were like. In due course, government legislation curtailed much of the excessive strictness inflicted on factory workers – who were usually referred to as 'hands', as if that were the only part of their anatomy that really mattered.

Even though most people in eighteenth-century Britain lived in savage poverty, many families were growing more prosperous. Sometimes insights into what a particular period was really like are gleaned from, on the face of it, relatively trivial statistical information that suggests a significant new pattern of behaviour. To take one example, the sale of wallpaper in Britain rose from 197,000 yards in 1713 to more than 2 million yards in 1785, a more than tenfold increase in a little over seventy years.

Inevitably, as the infrastructure slowly became better, this had a beneficial effect on the poor as well as the wealthy. It is, after all, a common -sense fact that if (say) wealthy people install streetlights on a road, then the impoverished can benefit from those lights as well as the rich who installed them. This helps to explain why improvements in infrastructure tend to benefit the whole community, not only the instigators. Moreover, infrastructure improvements, by speeding up social and economic processes and making the process itself more efficient, tend to increase economic prosperity anyway.

The Britain into which Charles was born was going through a revolution in physical communications as well as of industry. Before the middle of the eighteenth century, long-distance travel in Britain was rare. Roads were sometimes little more than dirt tracks, often with deep ruts that would have broken the wheel of a horse-drawn carriage. Often the only reliable way of travelling was on foot. In July 1618, the English playwright Ben Jonson wanted to go to Scotland from London; he did so by the simple but laborious expedient of walking there. It took him two weeks.

In the early eighteenth century the idea of travelling a long distance for pleasure was still generally a contradiction in terms. For example, the fastest journey between London and Cambridge, a distance of about 60 miles, took a long day in a horse-drawn coach that would travel at an average of 5 miles an hour, with the horses usually being changed at every coaching inn for fresh, watered ones. Travelling the 160 miles from London to Shrewsbury by horse-drawn coach could take more than three days. The journey to Edinburgh by coach still took around ten days, not much shorter than Jonson's walk. Some travellers even made their wills before starting on a journey; this wasn't at all an irrational thing to do, as coaches often overturned on bad roads, or encountered swollen rivers, often with fatal consequences.

But by the middle of the eighteenth century, things were getting better. Roads were being improved. Privately financed turnpike roads had spread from London and around the capital to major English cities including Bristol, Manchester, Newcastle, Leeds and Birmingham. In the 1770s, these private turnpike roads spread further into Wales and Scotland.

Yet people still braved the old Roman roads and bridle paths, which were often the only routes available in many parts of the country. Some journeys were remarkably ambitious. For example, every year, tens of thousands of cattle from the Scottish Highlands were driven southwards until they reached the Smithfield meat market in London. More and more demand for manufactured goods fostered the spread of inland trade, as did increasing industrial specialisation in British regions.

Altogether, the Industrial Revolution created opportunities for wealth and technological advancement and personal enrichment that were close to unimaginable until it got under way. In May 1733, a singularly ingenious inventor, John Kay, had been granted a patent for his 'flying shuttle'. This did not literally fly – instead the shuttle was shot very rapidly through a loom along wheels in a track by a weaver, who pulled a cord to operate it. Kay's invention speeded up the weaving process enormously, and increased yarn consumption so much that the flying shuttle spurred the invention of new machines that would spin yarn from cleaned and combed wool more rapidly than ever before.

The next most significant invention in the fabric-processing industry was the invention by James Hargreaves in 1764 of the 'spinning jenny', named after his daughter. The jenny was the first major breakthrough in textile machinery that comprehensively met the challenge set by John Kay. It greatly increased the rate at which yarn could be spun, though the thread produced by Hargreaves' machine was coarse and lacked strength, making it suitable only for use as weft: that is, the threads woven at right angles across a warp when making fabric.

In 1771, Richard Arkwright, a former barber who had become interested in textiles while carrying on a sideline as a wig maker, patented his 'water frame', a water-powered spinning frame that produced a yarn of a superior quality to that yielded by the spinning jenny. Arkwright built a five-storey mill at Cromford, Derbyshire, in the English Midlands. The mill operated round the clock in two twelve-hour shifts, one starting at

6 a.m. and the other at 6 p.m. Arkwright needed 200 workers for his factory, which was far more than the locality of Cromford could provide, so he built housing for his workers nearby, being one of the first employers ever to do so.

Most of Arkwright's workers were women and children, the youngest being only 7 years old. Later, the minimum age of child workers was raised to 10 – even at the time, many people were uneasy about children working in factories and Arkwright arranged for his employees' children to be given six hours of education per week. He did this, however, not so much for idealistic humanitarian reasons but so that the children could do the factory's record-keeping that their largely illiterate parents could not. Arkwright's factory was the first to be ruled by the clock rather than by daylight hours, and it eventually used hundreds of water frames. His Cromford mill grew to employ about 1,000 people, and later in life he became known as the 'father of the modern industrial factory system'. Other mills using Arkwright's machines and employment principles were built under licence, including one at Pawtucket, Rhode Island. When Arkwright died in 1792, he was the richest non-aristocratic person in Britain.

In 1779, Samuel Crompton's 'spinning mule' or 'mule jenny' had combined the main benefit of the water frame (the quality of its yarn) with the speed of the spinning jenny. The name Crompton chose for his machine exploited the pun that the name for a female donkey – mules are horse/donkey hybrids – is a 'jenny', though in fact a mule has a male donkey for a father and a female horse for a mother. Since around 1790, most of the yarn-spinning machines in Britain had been Crompton's mules. Meanwhile, Edward Cartwright had in 1784 invented the first steam-powered loom. By 1833, almost all the garments produced in Britain were woven on powered looms.

Steam power – the first practical way of producing motive force from heat – was rightly seen as the practical and mystical catalyst of the Industrial Revolution. Steam power was the wonder of the age, offering the ability to get work completed more quickly and much more reliably than the old energy sources: people, horses and running water.

In the steam engine, iron, coal, water and fire were used to create a noisy, smoky and smelly machine that at first produced up and down motion, but then was ingeniously adapted so that it could also produce rotary movement. Heat produced steam that pushed against pistons to produce reliable power even if there was no source of running water nearby, or if it had dried up.

The man who had made steam the supreme force of the British Industrial Revolution was a Scottish instrument maker and inventor named James Watt. Watt didn't, in fact, invent the first steam engine – that had been achieved by Thomas Savery, who patented an inefficient steam pump in 1698. But Watt's engines were much better than Savery's, and better even than the steam engines of an inventor called Thomas Newcomen, which were themselves a significant improvement on Savery's.

Watt's successes at making the Newcomen steam engine more efficient came to the attention of Matthew Boulton, a Birmingham-based industrialist who manufactured decorative items and who engaged Watt to build him a steam engine. Boulton grasped that steam engine manufacture itself could be a highly successful commercial venture, and in 1775 Watt and Boulton went into business together. Their collaboration made Watt rich and Boulton even richer. By 1800, their factory in Birmingham had produced more than 500 steam engines. Boulton liked to bustle influential guests around his factory, boasting that he sold 'what every man desires: POWER'.

Charles Babbage, as he grew up in the nineteenth century, had an ingenuous – and, on occasion, even naive – fascination with machinery and its reliability, and how it seemed to him to offer human beings a level of control over their environment, and over processes, which was unprecedented. Charles was not so much fascinated by machinery as obsessed with it.

The British postal service was also greatly improved in this period, although it remained far from adequate, mainly because recipients of letters had to pay for them and the postage was expensive; often recipients didn't want to pay.

London's first daily newspaper appeared in 1702. By 1760 there were four daily newspapers in London and six evening papers, published three times a week, which circulated in the capital. The provinces were still relatively autonomous culturally and generated their own newspapers, their own books, dictionaries, magazines, printed advertisements and primers.

In 1695, Parliament had passed legislation allowing printing presses to be established outside London; between 1700 and 1750, printing presses were founded in fifty-seven English provincial towns. In 1755, Dr Samuel Johnson's famous *Dictionary*, while too expensive for anyone who wasn't rich, nonetheless set down for the first time a reliable spelling standard which, while it has been superseded since then in the cases of some individual words, is generally still the standard.

As the eighteenth century came to a close, despite the poverty and want that afflicted far too many people and shortened their lives, the new century, the nineteenth, seemed full of potential. And indeed it proved to be so. Inventions devised in the nineteenth century include international telecommunications (the first successful transatlantic telegraph cable was laid in 1865), the telephone, the typewriter, the camera and, thanks to Charles Babbage, the computer. In a very real sense, we are all to some extent, at least in a technological sense, children of the 1800s.

At the beginning of the nineteenth century, London was the largest city in the world, with more than 650,000 citizens. For sheer size, the capital easily dwarfed other British towns. In 1750, its nearest rival in terms of population, Norwich, had been recorded as having fewer than 50,000 people. Even so, the provincial towns, while nowhere near as big as London itself in terms of population, were also growing in size and importance. In 1700, only ten of Britain's provincial cities contained more than 10,000 people, but by 1750 there were seventeen towns with populations of that size, and by 1800 more than fifty.

As London and the provincial towns and cities grew, they became better organised, better run, and more pleasant to live in.

No other capital in the world was remotely as populous. The UK census started in 1801 and that year the population of London was recorded as 864,845, so we can reasonably assume that in 1791 – the year Charles Babbage was born – the population of London was about 750,000, an enormous number of people by the standards of the world of the late eighteenth century. It was not only the location of the courts and of parliament, but also Britain's chief port, its financial centre, and the hub of its printing industry and of its communications network.

In London, Britain's rulers were brought into contact – perhaps not always necessarily willingly – with powerful economic lobbies from all parts of Britain and with a large, constantly fluctuating portion of their subjects. It has been estimated that, in the eighteenth century, about one in six Britons spent part of their working life in London.

And so it was into this world – one of power and machinery, of riches and poverty, of iron, steam engines, enterprise and fortune seeking – that Charles was born, a little over eight years before the end of the eighteenth century. When he came into the world, Ada's father-to-be Lord Byron, himself born on 22 January 1788, was 3 years old. At that tender age, the future lord, who had a slightly deformed foot (there is no conclusive evidence which foot it was), is recorded by his mother as having reprimanded a lady neighbour who said it was a pity that such a 'handsome little lad should be born lame' with the words 'dinna ye speak of it!' in the Scots dialect his mother had taught him, and little Byron even struck out at the neighbour with his toy whip. The Byrons had always had a distinct tendency towards self-assertion.

2

BOYHOOD

My heart leaps up when I behold
A rainbow in the sky:
So was it when my life began;
So is it now I am a man;
So be it when I shall grow old,
Or let me die!
The Child is father of the Man;
And I could wish my days to be
Bound each to each by natural piety.

William Wordsworth (26 March 1802)

In *Passages from the Life of a Philosopher*, Charles remarks on the supposed origins of his surname. He observes that some have believed 'Babbage' to have been 'derived from the cry of sheep … Others have supposed it is derived from the name of a place called Bab or Babb, as we have in the west of England Bab Tor, Babbacombe, et cetera.' Charles, though, maintains that he doesn't believe these rumours. He continues:

The name of Babbage is not uncommon in the west of England. One day during my boyhood [in fact, he seems to have been about 14 or 15 when this happened] I observed it over a small grocer's door, whilst riding through the town of Chudley. I dismounted, went into the shop, purchased some figs, and found a very old man of whom I made enquiry of his family. He had not a good memory himself, but his wife told me that his name was Babb when she married him and it was only during the last twenty years he adopted the name of Babbage, which, the old man thought, sounded better. Of course, I told his wife that I entirely agreed with her husband and thought him a very sensible fellow.

Charles' father Benjamin was born in 1753 and was by profession a goldsmith and banker. These two occupations were closely allied in those days; it was sensible and practical for people to keep their valuables in the safes run by goldsmiths, where the valuables would obviously be much more secure than if kept at home and could be used as collateral for loans from the same goldsmith. Whether Benjamin Babbage actually worked as a practising goldsmith is not known for certain. In the goldsmith-turned-banker we have two of his son Charles' great interests combined: precision manufacture and a quantitative approach to economic and social problems.

Charles, born in the heyday of the Industrial Revolution, grew up at a time when the reduction of considerations to quantitative terms was not only an imperative for many professions but was increasingly a cultural imperative too. In 1854, Charles Dickens, in his novel *Hard Times*, parodied the Industrial Revolution mindset of focusing on hard facts that had by the middle of the nineteenth century made Britain the wealthiest country in the world per capita:

'Now, what I want is, Facts. Teach these boys and girls nothing but Facts. Facts alone are wanted in life. Plant nothing else, and root out everything else. You can only form the minds of reasoning animals upon Facts: nothing else will ever be of any service to them. This is the principle on which I bring up my own children, and this is the principle on which I bring up these children. Stick to Facts, sir!'

The scene was a plain, bare, monotonous vault of a school-room, and the speaker's square forefinger emphasised his observations by underscoring every sentence with a line on the schoolmaster's sleeve. The emphasis was helped by the speaker's square wall of a forehead, which had his eyebrows for its base, while his eyes found commodious cellarage in two dark caves, overshadowed by the wall. The emphasis was helped by the speaker's mouth, which was wide, thin, and hard set. The emphasis was helped by the speaker's voice, which was inflexible, dry, and dictatorial. The emphasis was helped by the speaker's hair, which bristled on the skirts of his bald head, a plantation of firs to keep the wind from its shining surface, all covered with knobs, like the crust of a plum pie, as if the head had scarcely warehouse-room for the hard facts stored inside.

Yet, powerful as the parody undoubtedly is – and *Hard Times* brilliantly stigmatises the folly of founding on hard facts an emotional philosophy of life – it's undeniable that the hard-fact approach to economics and culture had successfully brought in remarkable new technologies that were building the nineteenth-century world, such as the railway locomotives in which Dickens loved to travel and which also carried the instalments of his novels (all of which were first published in weekly or monthly instalments) to his millions of readers around Britain. In precision engineering, such as that which enables a railway locomotive to be built, nothing works properly unless the calibrations are precise.

The Babbage family had been well established since the late seventeenth century in Totnes, a small town in the county of Devon. The first documentary mention of the Babbage family there dates from 12 November 1600, when a William Babbage, who died in 1633, is recorded as having married one Elinora Ashellaye. In a document dated 18 April 1628, a Roger 'Babbidge' is listed as a payer of rates. Benjamin was the latest in a long line of Babbages who had distinguished themselves in commerce. Charles' grandfather, also a successful goldsmith and also called Benjamin, had been mayor of Totnes in 1754.

Totnes today is a bustling, amiable little market town, particularly beloved by people living New Age lifestyles. Its population has remained much the same at about 8,000 since the end of the eighteenth century, when the town was prosperous from wool provided by the numerous sheep that spent their lives munching the grass of the meadows on the surrounding hills. This wool was turned into a cloth called kersey.

Named after the village of Kersey in Suffolk, where it appears to have originated, kersey was a thick, sturdy fabric popular throughout Britain and abroad for workmen's breeches and trousers.

Benjamin Babbage certainly wore the trousers in the Babbage household. The archetypal *paterfamilias* of a nineteenth-century family, his three major passions were money, cash and gold. He gradually built up his activities in the town and the surrounding district. Benjamin did not open a bank, but traded more informally, lending out sums, transacting business under his own name, and acting as an agent for some London banks. Business was excellent.

By the start of the 1790s, though, the Totnes cloth trade was visibly fraying. Machines powered by steam were making an impact on weaving and all aspects of fabric making. The new form of power provided what seemed unlimited energy as long as the fuel supply lasted. Coal-fuelled steam engines were the future, and in this new industrial world Totnes couldn't compete, Devon having no coal. In the whirl of the Industrial Revolution, all Totnes had to offer were waterwheels, which can only run as fast as the rivers that power them. In the new world, Totnes was being left behind.

Benjamin, alive to what was going on, made plans to transfer his business activities to London, a big change indeed in those days, when the vast majority of the population lived out their lives in the village or town where they had been born. He moved in 1791. His wife Elizabeth (Betty), who was born on 17 August 1760, went with him. The timing of the master banker was perfect, though doubtless he knew it would be; the London banking business at that time of rapid economic growth was golden with opportunity for canny lenders.

The sole surviving portrait of Benjamin shows a jovial man who has the look of having a precise understanding of his importance in the world and his success. If his son Charles can be relied on, we can be fairly sure that Benjamin's joviality was due to him thinking about money.

The world of Charles Babbage scholarship owes a significant debt to his first biographer, Anthony Hyman, who proved for the first time that Charles, previously believed to have been born in Totnes, did in fact come into this world in London. He was born at his father's house, 44 Crosby Row, Walworth, Surrey, about 500 yards from the famous hostelry of the Elephant and Castle, which gives its name to a district of South London. The earliest surviving record of this name relating to the area appears in the Court Leet (a historical manorial court) book of the Manor of Walworth which met at 'Elephant and Castle, Newington' on 21 March 1765. The house where Charles was born no longer exists, though Crosby Row, surprisingly perhaps, still does.

Benjamin and Betty had probably married in 1790, but the date of their marriage is not known for certain. Charles was born on Monday, 26 December 1791; it's important to emphasise the correct year, because many encyclopaedia entries have it, incorrectly, as 1792.

Charles was baptised at St Mary Newington Church on 6 January 1792: there is an entry in the baptismal register for 'Charles, son to Benjamin and Betty Plumleigh Babbage'. The church was built in 1721 and no longer exists; it was replaced by a new building in 1876, which was subsequently badly damaged in the Second World War and itself replaced by a modern church built in 1958.

Benjamin and Betty had a second son, Henry, who was born in October 1794 but who died in infancy. Another son was born in May 1796, also named Henry: it was quite common in those days, when a large proportion of children did not survive childhood, for parents to give the name of a deceased baby to a new baby in the hope that this one would live, although in this case that approach unfortunately didn't work, for the second Henry also died while a small child.

Then, in March 1798, Benjamin and Betty had a baby girl, christened Mary Anne, who remained on warm terms with Charles for life and who outlived him. There are surprisingly few extant letters to and from Charles and his sister, but I found one at the British Library that indicates clearly that Mary Anne was left with much less money than Charles; she actually writes to him to try to borrow some money so that one of her sons could have an apprenticeship. There is no record of whether Charles helped her, but his relations with his sister appear to have been cordial, if reserved, in the familiar nineteenth-century manner.

Charles developed his fascination with machinery and its reliability from a very early age, and seemed to understand intuitively how it could offer human beings a level of control over their environment, and over processes, which was unprecedented. In his autobiography, he speaks fondly of the enquiring nature of his mind:

> From my earliest years I had a great desire to enquire into the causes of all those little things and events which astonish the childish mind. At a later period I commenced the still more important enquiry into those laws of thought and those aids which assist the human mind in passing from our received knowledge to that other knowledge then unknown to our race. Truth only has been the object of my search, and I am not conscious of ever having turned aside in my enquiries from any fear of the conclusions to which they might lead.

Charles also recalled how as a child he loved to take things apart to find out how they worked:

> My invariable question on receiving any new toy, was 'Mamma, what is inside of it?' Until this information was obtained those around me had no repose, and the toy itself, I have been told, was generally broken open if the answer did not satisfy my own little ideas of the 'fitness of things'.

He also recalls:

> Two events which impressed themselves forcibly on my memory happened, I think, previously to my eighth year.
> When about five years old, I was walking with my nurse, who had in her arms an infant brother of mine, across London Bridge holding [her], as I thought by her apron. I was looking at the ships in the river. On turning round to speak to her, I found that my nurse was not there, that I was alone upon London Bridge. My mother had always impressed upon me the necessity of great caution in passing any street-crossing: I went on, therefore, quietly until I reached Tooley

Street, where I remained watching the passing vehicles in order to find a safe opportunity of crossing that very busy street.

One imagines the little child, confronted with a wide street full of people on horseback, and carriages with one, two or more horses pulling them, animals that would have been at least as dangerous to a childhood frame as modern internal combustion engine vehicles.

Charles continues:

In the meantime, the nurse, having lost one of her charges had gone to the crier, who proceeded immediately to call, by the ringing of his bell, the attention of the public to the fact that a young philosopher was lost, and to the still more important fact that five shillings would be the reward of his fortunate discoverer. I well remember sitting on the steps of the door of the linen draper's shop on the opposite corner of Tooley Street, when the gold-lace crier was making proclamation of my loss; but I was too much occupied with eating some pears to attend to what he was saying ...

The fact was that one of the men in the linen draper's shop, observing a little child by itself, went over to it and asked what it wanted. Finding that it had lost its nurse, he brought it across the street, gave it some pears, a place on the steps of the door: having asked my name, the shopkeeper found it to be that of one of his own customers. He accordingly sent off a messenger who announced to my mother the finding of young Pickle before she was aware of his loss.

Presumably 'Pickle' was a childhood name either for Charles or for children generally, or an allusion to *The Adventures of Peregrine Pickle*, the 1751 novel by Tobias Smollett.

A couple of paragraphs later, Charles recalls:

I was walking with my nurse and my brother in a public garden, called Montpelier Gardens, in Walworth. On returning through the private road leading to the gardens, I swallowed some dark berries very like blackcurrants – these were poisonous.

On my return home, I recollect being placed between my father's knees, and his giving me a glass of caster-oil, which I took from his hand.

These anecdotes also unintentionally reveal something about Charles that hints at one aspect of what he could be like emotionally. The brother he mentions in both the recollection about getting lost and the one about accidentally eating poisonous berries must have been one of the Henrys who died while still a child. It is strangely typical of Charles that he does not refer to this. Instead, he recalls:

Several years ago when the houses in Tooley Street were being pulled down, I believe to make room for the new railway terminus, I happened to pass along the very spot on which I'd been lost in my innocence. A slate of the largest size, called a Duchess, was thrown from the roof of one of the houses, had penetrated into the earth close to my feet.

So Charles doesn't seem particularly moved by the memory of his dead infant brother but instead is more interested in the name of the tile which came quite close to injuring him or even killing him. Indeed, he gives a footnote in his autobiography and remarks: 'There exists an aristocracy even amongst slates, perhaps when they're occupying the most *elevated* position in every house. Small ones are called Ladies, larger size Countesses, and the biggest of all are Duchesses.'

The rather feeble pun he essays in this footnote says something about how feeble his puns frequently were, how pedantic Charles could sometimes be, and how analytical his mind often was. Certainly, he seems much more interested in the tiles than the memory of his long-dead younger brother.

In another anecdote from Charles' autobiography, he recalls how when he was a schoolboy, he discovered that plunging into intellectual pleasure could actually restore him to health:

One day, when uninterested in the sports of my little companions, I had retired into the shrubbery and was leaning my head, supported by my left arm, upon the lower branch of a thorn tree. Listless and unoccupied, I *imagined* I had a headache. After a time I perceived, lying on the ground just under me, a small bright bit of metal. I instantly seized the precious discovery, and turning it over, examined both sides. I immediately concluded that I had discovered some valuable treasure, and running away to my deserted companions, showed them my golden coin.

The little company became greatly excited, and declared that it must be gold, that it was a piece of money of great value. We ran off to get the opinion of the usher [this was a usual term at the time for a schoolmaster, and in fact the term is still used at the famous British public school Eton College to denote a master]; but whether he partook of the delusion or we acquired our knowledge from the higher authority of the master, I know not. I only recollect the entire dissipation of my headache, and then my ultimate great disappointment when it was pronounced, upon the undoubted authority of the village doctor, that the square piece of brass I had found was a half-dram weight which had escaped from the box of a pair of medical scales.

This little incident had an important effect upon my after-life. I reflected upon the extraordinary fact, that my headache had been entirely cured by the discovery of the piece of brass. Although I may not have put into words the principle, *that occupation of the mind is such a source of pleasure that it can relieve even the pain of a headache* … Some few years after, when suffering under a form of toothache, not acute though tediously wearing, I often had recourse to a volume of *Don Quixote* and still more frequently to one of *Robinson Crusoe*.

Although at first it required a painful effort of attention, it had almost always happened, after a time, that I had forgotten the moderate pain in the overpowering interest of the novel.

The restorative power Charles derived from concentration of thought was fortunate, for he was a somewhat sickly child. In his autobiography he mentions an unspecified illness which struck him at the age of just 5 and, at 10, he was hit by what he describes as 'violent fevers' which necessitated his removal to the countryside. He was sent to a school in Alphington, near Exeter, then a village but nowadays a suburb of Exeter. It had two schools at the time, but it is not known for certain which one

Charles attended; it's likely that both were similar in the education they offered. Charles was placed under the care of a clergyman.

One of the Alphington schools was presided over by a Mr Halloran and known as Alphington Academy, which – for £20 per year and a one-guinea entrance fee – gave sons of gentlemen 'instruction in English, Latin and Greek languages as well as in such branches of education as are necessary qualifications for trade or the sea service'. It's likely that these 'branches of education' would include accountancy and navigation, which were subjects frequently taught at schools located near the English ports.

When his health had recovered completely, he was moved by his parents to a small school of about thirty pupils in Enfield, which was then not a suburb of London but a village north of the capital. Charles didn't take to the institution immediately, finding the other pupils too noisy for him, but he soon began to enjoy his schooling. He was under the tutelage of one Stephen Freeman, who combined his schoolmasterly duties with a keen amateur interest in astronomy. Freeman introduced Charles to a great many books, including a mathematical treatise which particularly captured his imagination. As Charles recalls:

> Amongst the books was a treatise on Algebra, called 'Ward's Young Mathematician's Guide.' I was always partial to my arithmetical lessons, but this book attracted my particular attention. After I had been at this school for about a twelve-month, I proposed to one of my school-fellows, who was of a studious habit, that we should get up every morning at three o'clock, light a fire in the schoolroom, and work until five or half past five. We accomplished this pretty regularly for several months.

It is, perhaps, difficult to imagine many of today's schoolboys aged 10 or 11 agreeing with each other as readily as this to get up in the depths of the night and work for two or two and a half hours, even after they'd lighted a fire in the schoolroom. Yet it appears that this nocturnal studying attracted a certain amount of kudos among the boys of the school, for, according to young Charles:

Our plan had, however, become partially known to a few of our companions. One of these, a tall boy, bigger than ourselves, having heard of it, asked me to allow him to get up with us, urging that his sole object was to study, and that it would be of great importance to him in after-life. I had the cruelty to refuse this very reasonable request. The subject has often recurred to my memory, but never without regret.

News of the early morning study club led by Charles spread quickly among the boys, including Frederick Marryat, who became a close friend of young Charles and went on to become a Royal Navy officer, a novelist, and an acquaintance of Dickens. Young Marryat begged Charles to join the study club, but Charles found it fun to prevent him from doing so. There is a touch of malice about Charles' recollection here, too. Charles recalls in his autobiography how he 'threaded' his way through the 'devious course' of the night-time school building, creeping across landings, up and down staircases and down the 'long passage to the schoolroom' silently, padding with caution past the room where the schoolmaster and his wife slept. Marryat shared a room with Charles, and so keen was he to join him that each night he would tie pack-thread between his bed and the door, so that Charles couldn't leave without waking him up. Charles tried to foil Marryat by untying the cord, but Marryat was determined. As Charles recalls:

> A few nights later I found it impossible to untie the cord, so I cut it with my pocket-knife. The cord then became thicker and thicker for several nights, but still my pen-knife did its work.
>
> One night I found a small chain fixed to the lock, and passing thence into Marryat's bed. This defeated my efforts for that night, and I retired to my own bed. The next night I was provided with a pair of pliers, and unbent one of the links, leaving two portions attached to Marryat's arm to the lock of the door.
>
> This occurred several times, varying by stouter chains, and by having a padlock which I could not pick in the dark.
>
> At last one morning I found a chain too strong for the tools I possessed; so I retired to my own bed, defeated. The next night, however, I provided myself with a ball of pack-thread. As soon as I

heard by his breathing that Marryat was asleep, I crept over to the door, drew one end of my ball of pack-thread through a link of the two-powerful chain and bringing it back with me to bed, gave it a sudden jerk by pulling both ends of the pack-thread passing through the link of the chain.

Marryat jumped up, put out his hand to the door, found his chain all right, then lay down.

As soon as he was asleep again I repeated the operation. Having awakened him for the third time, I let go one end of the string, and drew it back by the other, so that he was unable at daylight to detect the cause.

In order to keep the peace, Charles finally allowed Marryat and some other friends to join them, but they were soon discovered, due in part to their propensity to let off fireworks during their night-time escapades.

One morning, Freeman, with a serious expression, told the boys gravely of the injurious effects such actions could have on their health, and added that he could tell, due to their pallid expressions, who the boys behind the event were. Charles would recall wryly that it was rather strange that Freeman hadn't noticed their sleepless countenances in the weeks and months before, when they had been studying in the twilight hours.

Reading about Charles' childhood, one forms an irresistible image of an intellectually precocious boy, who spent a great deal of time thinking about abstract ideas and who also liked winning an advantage over others, even if the consequences were that the other people might end up feeling humiliated. The adult Charles never entirely ceased being that kind of person.

At around this time, when Charles was in London with his parents, his mother took him to several exhibitions of machinery, including one in Hanover Square, organised by a man who called himself 'Merlin':

I was so greatly interested in it, that the exhibitor remarked the circumstance, and after explaining some of the objects to which the public had access, proposed to my mother to take me up to his workshop, where I should see still more wonderful automata. We accordingly ascended to the attic. There were two uncovered female figures of silver, about twelve inches high.

One of these walked or rather glided along a space of about four feet, when she turned round and went back to her original place. She used an eye-glass occasionally, and bowed frequently, as if recognising her acquaintances. The motions of her limbs were singularly graceful.

The other silver figure was an admirable *danseuse*, with a bird on the forefinger of her right hand, which wagged its tail, flapped its wings, and opened its beak. This lady attitudinised in a most fascinating manner. Her eyes were full of imagination, and irresistible.

These silver figures were the chef d'oeuvres of the artist: they had cost him years of unwearied labor, and were not even then finished.

Charles' description of the automata in his autobiography seems very modern; reading his account, we need to remember that he was writing about automata built at around the turn of the eighteenth and nineteenth century at a time when machinery, while certainly sophisticated enough, would not in truth have been able to evoke life in the way that Charles describes it.

There is the clearest sense, here in this recollection, that Charles yearned so much to see a truly sophisticated, realistic automaton – the kind of device, in fact, that is not even technologically possible *today* – that he imagined he was seeing something like that. His imagination had to some extent taken over his memory.

Charles delicately admired the appearance of the automata – their 'singularly graceful movement' – and marvelled at the 'unweary labour' of the artist who had created them. Years later, he recalled the event with perfect clarity in his autobiography, and it is clear how intensely the experience had moved him.

Later in his life, Charles, by an intriguing coincidence, actually had the opportunity of buying one of the two silver ladies. He succumbed to the temptation right away. As he writes in his autobiography:

I mentioned in an early chapter, my boyish admiration of an automaton in the shape of a silver lady, who attitudinized in the most graceful manner. Her fate was singular: at the death of her maker she was sold with the rest of his collection of mechanical toys, and was purchased by Weekes, who had a mechanical exhibition in Cockspur Street. No attempt appears to have been made to finish the automaton; and it seems to have been placed out of the way in an attic uncovered and utterly neglected.

On the sale by auction of Weeke's Museum, I met again the object of my early admiration. Having purchased the silver figure, I proceeded to take to pieces the whole of the mechanism, and found a multitude of small holes which had been stopped up as not having fulfilled their intended object. In fact, it appeared tolerably certain that scarcely any drawings could have been prepared for the automaton, but that the beautiful result arose from a system of continual trials.

Charles also records:

I myself repaired and restored all the mechanism of the Silver Lady, by which title she was afterwards known to my friends. I placed her under a glass case on a pedestal in my drawing room, where she received, in her own silent but graceful manner, these valued friends who so frequently honoured me with their society on certain Saturday evenings.

This piece of mechanism formed a striking contrast with the unfinished portion of the Difference Engine, No. 1, which was placed in the adjacent room: the whole of the latter mechanism existed in drawings upon paper before any portion of it was put together.

Among the other boyhood reminiscences in Charles' autobiography is a recollection of how he once tried to walk on water. As he explains:

One day an idea struck me, that it was possible, by the aid of some simple mechanism to walk upon the water, or at least to keep at a vertical position, and have head, shoulders, and arms above water.

My plan was to attach to each foot two boards closely connected together by hinges, themselves fixed to the sole of the shoe. My theory was that in lifting up my leg, as if in the act of walking, the two boards would close up towards each other; while on pushing down my foot, the water would rush between the board, causing them to open out into a flat surface, and thus offer greater resistance to my sinking in the water.

I took the pair of boots for my experiment, and cutting up a couple of old useless volumes with very thick binding, I fixed the boards by hinges in the way I proposed. I placed an obstacle between the two flaps of each book to prevent them from approaching too nearly to each other so as to impede their opening by the pressure of the water.

I now went down to the river, and thus prepared, walked into the water. I then struck out to swim as usual, and found little difficulty. Only it seemed necessary to keep the feet further apart. I now tried the grand experiment. For a time, by active exertion of my legs, I kept my head and shoulders above water and sometimes also my arms. I was now floating down the river with the receding tide, sustained in a vertical position with a very slight exertion of force.

So the plan to walk on water was conveniently forgotten by Charles the moment he found that he sank into the water, but all the same, the boot and old useless volumes contrivance managed to keep him vertical in a sort of comfortably floating aspect.

Or maybe the truth was that he came very close to drowning but was too proud to have admitted this.

From his autobiography and from some other incidental details, we have abundant insights into what Charles was like as a boy: a resourceful, sometimes pedantic but always inventive young fellow, rather given to doing his best to come out tops in situations, and who was utterly fascinated by machinery and mechanisms and what they could achieve. What of his teenage years? They, alas, remain a mystery, for he says nothing about them in his autobiography and there is no useful documentary evidence about them. They are the least well-documented phase of an otherwise reasonably well-documented life.

All we can be sure of is that Charles worked hard at his studies and did well at them. Did he have any teenage flings with, or crushes on, girls he met? We will probably never know. He certainly doesn't reveal anything along these lines in his autobiography and there is absolutely no evidence one way or the other. One suspects, perhaps, that during his teenage years, with his remarkable mind developing fast, he would have continued to indulge his rich inner life with thoughts of inventions; perhaps this left room for little else. Or perhaps he fell in love often.

In 1810, when Charles was 18 years old, he won a place at Trinity College, Cambridge University; the very same college which Ada's father Lord Byron had attended. Charles' formal education had, even by the educational standards of the schools of the day, been haphazard. After attending the school in Enfield, he studied with a clergyman tutor in Cambridge before returning to Devon to be educated at Totnes Grammar School. The final step in his pre-university education was a period spent studying Classics under an Oxford tutor, also in Totnes. The path to admission may have been smoothed by the fact that his Cambridge clergyman tutor had contacts at the university.

All the same, it's difficult to imagine that a boy as intellectually precocious as Charles Babbage wouldn't have been an irresistible choice for the university, particularly as Benjamin's success in business meant that the Babbage family was wealthy, and could afford the fees. And so Charles went off to Cambridge University, where he knew that great things were already expected of him. He hoped he would not disappoint.

3

CAMBRIDGE DAYS, AND ADA IS BORN

As lightly I came,
I lightly wave goodbye
To the sunlit clouds in the western sky.
The golden willows of that riverside
Are brides in the setting sun,
Their glimmering reflections in the water
Ripple in the depth of my heart.
The waterlilies in the soft mud
Sway splendidly under the water
In the gentle waves of the Cam.

From 'Saying goodbye to Cambridge again' (1928)
by Xu Zhimo, trans. Silas S. Brown

The University of Cambridge is a collegiate university in the city of Cambridge, which lies about 50 miles north of London. The city - on the River Cam as the name suggests - is close by an area of Britain known as the Fens, or Fenland. This is a naturally marshy region famed for its great beauty and numerous natural and artificial waterways.

As a collegiate university, the only way to access Cambridge University in Charles' day, and also today, is via one of its various picturesque and highly esteemed colleges. An undergraduate joins a particular college and thus becomes a member of the university. Migrations from one college to another were possible in Charles' day and still are.

This college system was inherited from Oxford University, where formal teaching dates back to 1096 and which is the oldest university in the English-speaking world; Cambridge is the second oldest. Oxford University was originally a collection of religious houses that gradually formed together into a university but which, as at Cambridge, retained their independent status. The university in Cambridge grew out of an association of scholars who left Oxford University back in 1209, after a dispute with the townspeople of Oxford that had led to a great deal of violence in Oxford itself.

Studying mathematics was once compulsory at Cambridge University for all the graduates reading for (this is academic terminology for 'studying') any Bachelor of Arts degree.

When Charles went up to Cambridge, the most famous alumnus of Trinity College was Isaac Newton, widely recognised even today as one of the most influential scientists of all time. The poet Alexander Pope aptly wrote of Newton:

Nature and nature's laws lay hid in night,
God said, 'Let Newton be,' and all was light.

Though Newton himself made fewer claims about his own achievements, remarking with moving modesty, not long before his death:

I do not know what I may appear to the world, but to myself I seem to have been only like a boy playing on the seashore, and diverting myself in now and then finding a smoother pebble or a prettier shell than ordinary, whilst the great ocean of truth lay all undiscovered before me.

Much of that great ocean of truth is now mapped and surveyed, though there is an even more remote region of the ocean containing truths that may not be understood for a millennium or more.

From Newton's time until the middle of the nineteenth century, Cambridge University maintained an especially strong emphasis on applied mathematics, particularly mathematical physics. The mathematics exam at Cambridge was and is known as the Tripos, and it was in Charles' day the only way to obtain an Honours degree. The word's origins are obscure but possibly may be traced to a three-legged stool on which university candidates once used to sit when taking oral examinations.

Despite Charles' varied and rather informal schooling, by the time he went up to Trinity College, in October 1810, he was able to handle mathematical questions in the three different types of mathematical notation then current: those used by the great mathematicians Newton, Leibniz and Lagrange. Later in his university career Charles would migrate to Peterhouse College to take his degree.

Cambridge University had and has an illustrious reputation for deep thinking, but despite the fame of the Tripos, the teaching of mathematics there in Charles' day was not especially brilliant. Mathematics was too often seen not as a practical subject that might have a key role to play in the world, but as mental training for future clergyman, lawyers and gentlemen who would live lives of genteel, but unspectacular, and for the most part unproductive, learning.

The emphasis was on intensive coaching to train students to solve problems that would be set in the examinations held at the end of the year (in practice, many examinations actually took place in January). These problems were frequently extremely difficult, but they did not have any intrinsic value other than to hone mental agility. They were essentially mathematical crossword puzzles: ingenious, arduous, mentally stimulating, but ultimately a trifle pointless.

Here is an example, from the Cambridge Tripos examination held on Monday, 17 January 1814. It must surely rank as one of the most tortuous questions ever inflicted on an examination candidate in any subject in any period of human history. Charles himself very likely tackled this very question, for he graduated with a BA in 1814 and would consequently probably have sat the paper on which this question appeared. It was only one of several similar problems which the unfortunate candidates were expected to answer on that Monday morning, before lunch:

From the vertex of a paraboloid of given dimensions, a part equal to one-fourth of the whole is cut off by a plane parallel to the base; and the frustrum being then placed in a fluid with its smaller end downwards, sinks till the surface of the fluid bisects the axis which is vertical.

It is required to determine the specific gravity of the paraboloid, that of the fluid in which it is immersed and the density of the atmosphere being given.

Charles had never seen, and never saw, mathematics as a mere exercise in solving frightful problems like this. Instead, what *he* dreamed of was using mathematics, the great science of quantity, to achieve practical improvements in the processes that mattered in everyday life.

Certainly, the time for such an attitude to mathematics had never been riper. As we've seen, Britain was in the midst of an unprecedented technology revolution. Transport, communications and above all the application of steam power to industry were giving humankind the opportunity to use levels of power thousands of times greater than that which the horse, or the human hand, could produce. Charles desperately wanted to take part in it, so he withdrew from his formal curriculum at Cambridge and pursued his own mathematical and scientific agenda. At the time, gentlemen scholars were permitted to do this.

It was at Cambridge that Charles met John Herschel, son of the illustrious German-born self-taught astronomer Sir William Herschel, who had discovered Uranus in 1781, the first new planet found since antiquity. Charles, along with Herschel and some other students, started what he called the 'Analytical Society'. Its main objective was to overhaul the study of calculus at Cambridge and replace the notation of Newton with what Charles and his friends regarded as the much more efficient notation invented by Leibniz. The campaign was, in the end, successful, although it would not be won until after Charles graduated from Cambridge in 1814. But the vigour of the arguments put forward to support the change forced the outside mathematical world to start to take notice of the founders of the Analytical Society, and particularly of Charles Babbage and John Herschel.

The friendship between the two men was the first serious intellectual attachment for either. They were touchingly good companions. They addressed each other as 'Dear Herschel' or 'Dear Babbage' in letters: an extremely intimate salutation by the formal standards of the time. The informality of their letters (which usually contained abundant mathematical formulae as well as more personal material) is in effect neatly summarised by a comment Herschel made at the start of a letter he wrote to Charles on 25 February 1813: 'When men with common pursuits in which they are deeply interested, correspond on the subject of those pursuits, the trifling ceremonials of an ordinary correspondence may in great measure be waived.' Herschel became Charles' closest male friend for the rest of their lives; they both lived until old age and died in the same year, 1871.

Another good friend Charles met at Cambridge was Edward Ryan, who became part of Charles' family. Ryan was subsequently appointed to be a judge of the Supreme Court in Calcutta, in 1826, and was later Chief Justice of Bengal. He was there at the end of Charles' life to help him sort out his affairs when his health was failing. Ryan outlived both Herschel and Charles by about four years, dying on 22 August 1875.

On 13 December 1814, Ryan married Louisa Whitmore, the daughter of William Whitmore and Frances Barbara Lyster. Charles would later marry Louisa's younger sister Georgiana, who was born in 1792 – the precise date is not known – and was about three years younger than Louisa. But he was not in marrying mode just yet.

Intelligent, inventive, charming Ada Byron was infinitely the best product of a disastrous marital liaison between Lord Byron, one of the greatest poets in history but not known for his paternal skills or indeed for his uxorious tendencies, and a well-born young woman named Anna Isabella (usually shortened to Annabella) Milbanke. They married on the morning of Monday, 2 January 1815 after a courtship in which Byron often seemed to lose interest for several months at a time and then suddenly decide that he wanted to marry her after all. He was already famous throughout Britain, Europe and beyond as a poet of great skill and expressive genius.

Byron was undoubtedly at one level a selfish scoundrel, but he was also a poet of prodigious talent and astonishing energy, and it's difficult for even the most prolific professional writer to contemplate his life's work (which fills a 900-page volume of closely printed words, despite his early death at the age of 36) without feeling a sense of hopelessness at the prospect of even remotely emulating such a great writer. Yet a better, wiser and nobler response would be to be grateful that humankind was blessed with such a wonderful poet at all.

Giving an idea of what kind of poet Byron was by choosing one of the poems from the vast collection that is his life's work is far from easy and naturally involves much subjectivity. The one I've selected, 'The Destruction of Sennacherib', published in 1815, the same year Ada was born, was extremely popular in its day and was regularly taught to English schoolchildren for more than a century after it was written. It is inconceivable that Charles and Ada were not familiar with the poem, which is based on an event from the campaign by the Assyrian King Sennacherib to capture Jerusalem, as described in the Bible (2 Kings 18–19), which itself is founded on the biblical account of the historical Assyrian besieging of Jerusalem in 701 BC.

Byron brilliantly, and perhaps even unconsciously, echoes in the poem's rhythm and well-organised rhymes the sound of the hooves of galloping horses, as the Assyrian attackers ride into battle. The vigour and wonderfully vivid imagery of the poem resonantly depict what was probably the first account in human history of a great host being felled by a plague epidemic:

The Assyrian came down like the wolf on the fold,
And his cohorts were gleaming in purple and gold;
And the sheen of their spears was like stars on the sea,
When the blue wave rolls nightly on deep Galilee.

Like the leaves of the forest when Summer is green,
That host with their banners at sunset were seen:
Like the leaves of the forest when Autumn hath blown,
That host on the morrow lay withered and strown.

For the Angel of Death spread his wings on the blast,
And breathed in the face of the foe as he passed;
And the eyes of the sleepers waxed deadly and chill,
And their hearts but once heaved, and for ever grew still!
And there lay the steed with his nostril all wide,

But through it there rolled not the breath of his pride;
And the foam of his gasping lay white on the turf,
And cold as the spray of the rock-beating surf.

And there lay the rider distorted and pale,
With the dew on his brow, and the rust on his mail:
And the tents were all silent, the banners alone,
The lances unlifted, the trumpet unblown.

And the widows of Ashur are loud in their wail,
And the idols are broke in the temple of Baal;
And the might of the Gentile, unsmote by the sword,
Hath melted like snow in the glance of the Lord!

Unfortunately, though, Byron's enormous poetic talents didn't make him much of a husband or father. When he and Annabella were on their brief honeymoon, Byron, ever the romantic swain, regularly shouted crazy outbursts at his wife, including the charming declaration that she made him feel he was 'in hell'. During the year that they were married, he also made love with his half-sister Augusta and with an actress named Susan Boyle.

Byron never knew his daughter or vice versa. Ada was born in London, at Piccadilly Terrace, on Sunday, 10 December 1815, only about a mile and a half south from where Charles was soon to set up his marital home. When baby Ada was only one month and five days old, Annabella decided she could take no more of her husband; she stole away with Ada from a sleeping Byron in the early morning of Monday, 15 January 1816.

At first, she planned to see Byron again; she seems to have regarded the separation as only temporary. But once she'd told her parents about how he had treated her, they started to hate him even more than they appeared to have done already and soon turned her against him. In any event, Byron, living in those times when photography had not yet been invented, let alone electronic telecommunications, never saw his wife nor his daughter ever again.

Byron left England permanently on Thursday, 25 April 1816, pursued literally to Dover harbour by bailiffs trying to get payment for the £500 carriage which he had bought, never paid for (he never did pay for it) and in which he travelled to the Continent. He managed to board a ship at Dover in his carriage, leaving the bailiffs shaking their fists at him as the ship embarked for Calais in a tempestuous and bubbling sea; they were not legally entitled to pursue him beyond the English coast.

Byron settled on the Continent. In exile from an England he had come to despise, he often wrote to Annabella, via Augusta, enquiring after Ada. Annabella, surprisingly perhaps, usually answered, but generally via Augusta, and on at least one occasion sent Byron a lock of Ada's hair; another time she sent him a painted miniature of Ada, the equivalent of a photograph in the first three decades of the nineteenth century.

During the next eight years Byron wrote some of his best poems, befriended the poet Percy Shelley and the novelist Mary Shelley, had numerous affairs and fathered at least one illegitimate child, Allegra, who unfortunately died at the age of 5 from typhoid while under the care of affectionate and genuinely caring nuns at an Italian convent where Byron had installed her. He hardly ever visited her, not wanting to be troubled with what he regarded as the inconvenient matter of bringing her up.

Byron himself died on 19 April 1824, aged only 36, in Missolonghi in Greece, from marsh fever. As he was dying, he clasped the miniature of Ada to his breast, and lamented that all he had wanted to do was to see her. Ada was 8 at the time; when her mother informed her of her father's death, she burst into tears.

Ada's education had started when she was only 4 years old. She was fortunate – during an epoch when even girls from wealthy families rarely went to school at all – in being given an excellent education under the auspices of her mother, who was, however, difficult to please and was always firing tutors and governesses she recruited when she decided that they were not doing enough to help develop Ada's mind.

For Lady Byron, Ada was, naturally, a constant reminder of her marriage and of its failure. The embittered widow was determined to give Ada a strongly mathematical education to try to suppress the imagination she feared Ada had inherited from her errant aristocratic father. However, this plan didn't work. Ada became a very competent, though not outstanding, mathematician, and she never lost her imagination.

Eventually, she christened her particular way of thinking 'poetical science'. The daughter of the creator of 'The Destruction of Sennacherib' developed within her unique and brilliant mind a remarkable and unprecedented perspective on science which imbued that magisterial discipline with the glories of a wondrous speculation.

Charles Babbage, in his twenties and interested in mathematics and finding a wife, could never have guessed at this time of his life that a little girl in London would eventually turn out to be a gift to him from the gods, bringing him companionship, affection, deep friendship and a collaborator who very possibly had the potential to make his dreams of building machines of the mind come true.

Meanwhile, Charles was enjoying the social opportunities Cambridge offered. He played chess and whist and helped to form societies that looked into matters of interest to their members. One was a Ghost Club, where Charles and his friends earnestly discussed the supernatural. Another was the so-called Extractors Club, which made plans to extract any member from the madhouse should his relatives ever manage to get him sent to one. As Charles recalls:

> At another time we resolved ourselves into a club which we called The Extractors. Its rules were as follows:
>
> 1. Every member shall communicate his address to the Secretary once in six months.
> 2. If this communication is delayed beyond twelve months, it shall be taken for granted that his relatives had shut him up as insane.
> 3. Every effort legal and illegal shall be made to get him out of the madhouse. Hence the name of the club – The Extractors.
> 4. Every candidate for admission as a member shall produce six certificates. Three that he is sane and three others that he is insane.
>
> It has often occurred to me to enquire of my legal friends whether, if the sanity of any member of the club had been questioned in after-life,

he would have adduced the fact of membership of the Club of Extractors as an indication of sanity or of insanity.

Forming an Extractors Club at the time was not as insane a thing to do as it might seem to us today: Charles and many of his Cambridge friends were heirs to often considerable fortunes, and at the time the law stated that if someone had been judged insane, they could not inherit.

Charles also reveals that he was a keen chess player when a student at Cambridge, and was friends with a more serious player called John Brand, who took up the game in a concerted way after leaving university. He wrote:

During the first part of my residence at Cambridge, I played at chess very frequently, often with D'Arblay and with several other good players. There was at that period a fellow-commoner at Trinity named Brande [*sic*], who devoted almost his whole time to the study of chess. I was invited to meet him one evening at the rooms of a common friend for the purpose of trying our strength.

Charles adds:

Brande [*sic*], during his residence at Cambridge, studied chess regularly several hours each day, and read almost every treatise on the subject. After he left college he traveled abroad, took lessons from every celebrated teacher, and played with all the most eminent players on the Continent.

At intervals of three or four years I occasionally met him in London. After the usual greeting he always proposed that we should play a game of chess.

I found on these occasions, that if I played any of the ordinary openings, such as are found in the books, I was sure to be beaten. The only way in which I had a chance of winning, was by making early in the game a move so bad that it had not been mentioned in any treatise.

We note, intriguingly, the punchline, so to speak, of this recollection: it emphasises Charles' love of winning an advantage over a counterparty by ingenious trickery, just as he had tried hard to win such an advantage over his friend Marryat at school.

Here is another example, also from his autobiography, of this same side of his personality; this time there seems something definitely underhand about his winning of an advantage:

> I was very fond of boating, not of the more manual labor of rowing, but the more intellectual art of sailing. I kept a beautiful light, London-built boat, and occasionally took long voyages down the river, beyond Ely into the Fens. To accomplish these trips, it was necessary to have two or three strong fellows to row when the wind failed or was contrary.
>
> The plan of our voyage was thus: I sent my servant to the apothecary for a thing called an *aegrotat*, which I understood, for I never saw one, meant a certificate that I was indisposed, and that it would be injurious to my health to attend chapel or hall or lectures. This was forwarded to the college authorities.
>
> I also directed my servant to order the cook to send me a large well-seasoned meat pie, a couple of fowls, etc. These were packed in a hamper with three or four bottles of wine and one of noyeau [*sic*]. We sailed when the wind was fair, and rowed when there was none. Whittlesea Mere was a very favorite resort for sailing, fishing and shooting. Sometimes we reached Lynn. After various adventures and five or six days of hard exercise in the open air, we returned to our health and more renovated than if the best physician had prescribed for us.

An *aegrotat*, which is the third person singular present indicative of the Latin *aegrotare*, meaning 'to be ill', is, as is clear from the context, a certificate that declares a student too ill to attend classes or other academic duties. *Noyaux* (Charles misspelled the word) is an almond-flavoured cream liqueur made from apricot kernels. The town of 'Lynn' – a seaport and market town in Norfolk, about 100 miles north of London – is usually known today as King's Lynn. Charles was simply using the shorter form of the name.

This passage about the university students enjoying their day out is engaging enough, but it also reveals that Charles, as a student, felt no moral scruples about telling lies to the university authorities regarding his health. He never lost his enjoyment of trying to gain an advantage over a counterparty when he could.

Which was all very well, but one thing Charles was often bad at was working out who was an opposing counterparty, and who was trying to help him.

4

FAMILY MATTERS

The halcyons brood around the foamless isles;
The treacherous Ocean has forsworn its wiles;
The merry mariners are bold and free:
Say, my heart's sister, wilt thou sail with me?
From 'Epipsychidion' by Percy Bysshe Shelley (1821)

At the beginning of the university summer vacation of 1811, Charles headed back to Totnes. He often spent part of the summer at a house his father still kept there: Birdwood House, which still exists today, can be found at the top of the town's steep High Street.

It's not known exactly when Charles met Georgiana Whitmore, his future wife, but he most likely got to know her during this vacation in the seaside town of Teignmouth, which is about 12 miles north-east of Totnes, and where Benjamin Babbage had bought a house.

When Charles first made Georgiana's acquaintance, he was 19 and she a year younger. She had fine, delicate features and beautiful golden-brown hair. All the evidence suggests that Georgiana and Charles took to each other right away. The following summer they became engaged, and for the first time Charles visited her family at Dudmaston Hall, in Shropshire.

Georgiana's father, William Whitmore, was a seaman from Southampton who had inherited a number of properties, giving him the resources to restore and reshape Dudmaston Hall. He spent large sums on repairs and on refurnishing that stunning and beautiful stately home, which also still exists (Britain is, after all, at one level a treasure trove of history that survives) and, owned by the National Trust, is a popular attraction for day-trippers and tourists.

Charles and Georgiana were married on Saturday, 2 July 1814, shortly after Charles came down from Cambridge. Charles' father Benjamin had been resolutely opposed to the marriage, adamant that his son ought not to get married until he, Charles, had progressed in his career. One can see Benjamin's point: after all, Charles did not even have a job. Yet the marriage took place and Benjamin appears to have relented, or at least reluctantly suppressed his reservations. On Monday, 1 August 1814, Charles wrote to Herschel from a pretty village called Chudleigh, which is a few miles inland from Teignmouth; the newlyweds were evidently having a long honeymoon in Chudleigh.

How fortunate they were to have been born into wealthy families. But, of course, just because one comes from a wealthy family does not mean life is always easy, and Charles was devastated by his father's opposition to the marriage. He wrote as follows to Herschel in the letter of 1 August; one has the clear impression that while somehow Benjamin must have consented to the marriage (it seems extremely unlikely that Charles would have married against the wishes of his father and risk being disinherited), the old man still went on complaining about the marriage even after it had taken place:

To be a little serious however I will tell you the events of the last few days. I am married and have quarrelled with my father. He has no rational reason whatever; he has not one objection to my wife in any respect. But he hates the abstract idea of marriage and is uncommonly fond of money.

I cannot go into the Church for this will not accord sufficient propriety (for a curacy is all I should get). I am therefore thinking of getting some situation connected with the mines where though I might get but a very little at first I might have opportunities of turning my chemical knowledge to advantage. However I should be glad to get any employment where I should have some future prospects though it might not produce much at first. If you hear of anything in any way that you think likely to suit me I should be glad to hear of it. I do not much care what it is only that it should not require very much bodily exertion as I was never well able to bear much of that. I believe I sent you what I have done relative to functions. I have added the following theorems …

On 7 August 1814, Herschel, evidently astonished by his friend's ability to move easily between intense emotion and mathematical matters, replied: 'I am married and have quarrelled with my father – Good God Babbage – how is it possible for a man calmly to sit down and pen those two sentences – add a few more which look like self-justification – and pass off to functional equations?'

How indeed? But evidently Charles could manage it. All his life, he found consolation from emotional stress in intellectual focus, just as he did when, as a boy, he discovered that mental absorption could cure his headache. Under the pressure of his closest friend's inquisitorial pressure, though, the often emotionally reticent young Charles for once let his pen flow, expressing his feelings in an amazing letter, one of the most self-revelatory letters of his that has survived:

August 10 1814

Dear Herschel

Your letter of 7th August has reached me but the other to which you allude has not yet arrived.

My opinions concerning Cambridge are in many respects similar to your own, but there are two reasons for which I shall always value a university education – the means it supplied of procuring access to books – and the still more valuable opportunities it affords of acquiring friends. In this latter point of view I have been singularly fortunate. The friendships I have formed while there I shall ever value; nor do I consider my acquaintance with yourself as one of the least advantages.

You must indeed have been surprised with my letter. I did not mention many circumstances because as we had rarely talked on such subjects, I thought they might be uninteresting. Now however I shall lay aside all reserve and give you an account of my present situation …

You seem to have a great horror at my having quarrelled with my father; were he such a man as from the slight knowledge I possess I conceive yours to be; it would indeed be to me a subject of the deepest regret; but the case is different and you must know a little of his character before you judge.

My father is not much more than sixty, very infirm, tottering perhaps on the brink of the grave. The greater part of his property he has acquired himself during years of industry; but with it he has acquired the most rooted habits of suspicion. It is scarcely too much to asset that he *believes* nothing he *hears*, and only half of what he sees. He is stern, inflexible and reserved, perfectly just, sometimes liberal, never generous, is uncultivated except perhaps by an acquaintance with English Literature and History. But whatever may be his good qualities they are more than counterbalanced by an accompaniment for which not wealth nor talents nor the most exalted intellectual faculties can compensate – a temper the most horrible which can be conceived.

Seeking the happiness of no earthly being he lives without a friend. A tyrant in his family, his presence occasions silence and gloom; and should his casual absence afford opportunity for the entrance of any of the more pleasing sensations they are invariably banished at his return. Tormenting himself and all connected with him he deserves to be miserable. Can such a man be loved? It is *impossible*.

[…]

I will now say something of my wife as it certainly is no secret. She was a Miss Whitmore the youngest of eight sisters of a very good family in Shropshire. She has some fortune and will have more about five thousand in all. My father has no objection to her, or her fortune or her family, this he has said. Why then you will ask have we quarrelled? This I cannot tell. I know as little as yourself what reasons he assigns. Everybody blames him. He allows me £300 during my life simply because he promised it to me. So that I now have about £450 a year which I can live very comfortably for the present; but as I do not expect a shilling more from my Father I am looking for some employment where I may be able ultimately to make some money.

The £450 that Benjamin Babbage provided his son with annually would be worth about £45,000 today: enough at the time, and indeed today, for a married couple to live comfortably.

After their marriage, Charles and Georgiana rented a house at 5 Devonshire Street, Portland Place, London. Perhaps the Babbages liked the idea of living on a street named after the beautiful West of England county where they had met and from which both their families originated.

In any event, Charles wasted no time in making his mark on the mathematical and scientific scene. During 1815 – which was, as we've seen, the year Ada was born on 10 December – Charles gave a series of lectures on astronomy to the Royal Institution. In the spring of 1816 he was elected a member of the Royal Society, a learned assembly of all the great scientists of the land. For the next few years Charles' work was mainly mathematical. He published more than a dozen mathematical papers, all of which were regarded as highly competent, though not of enormous importance.

On 6 August 1816, Georgiana gave birth to a son, Benjamin Herschel, the first of what would be eight children, of whom only two survived to maturity. There is a Babbage line of descent via Benjamin Herschel Babbage that is still extant today; the teacher and writer Lisa Noel Babbage, of Suwanee, Georgia, is a direct descendant of Charles.

By 1816, the Babbages were well established in London. Georgiana and Charles led a pleasant, varied social life, with visits to friends in the country and holding soirées to which influential people were invited. In due course the Babbages' soirées ranked among London's most famous and glittering social occasions.

During the years between his marriage and the end of the second decade of the nineteenth century, Charles continued to do his best to gain paid employment to supplement his limited income. For example, early in 1816 the Professorship of Mathematics became vacant at the East India College at Hailey in Hertfordshire. This college trained young men who would eventually work for the East India Company, an

English joint-stock company founded to develop English trade interests abroad, particularly in the East.

Charles applied for the professorship in a hopeful frame of mind, but he was rejected. He had asked one of the directors how to maximise his chances of winning the position and the director was very frank: 'If you have interest you will get it; if not you will not succeed,' meaning that if Charles knew someone who could speak for him he might have a chance. Charles didn't get that appointment, so he evidently didn't know the right people.

A few years later, in 1819, Charles applied for a Chair of Mathematics in Edinburgh but failed to get that too, very likely because he was not a Scotsman. Whether or not Charles would have enjoyed living in Edinburgh rather than his beloved London, where he generally seemed to flourish, is not clear.

In any event, Charles continued to fail to find any paid occupation to supplement the free money provided by his father. There is no doubt that Benjamin wasn't pleased. However, it is possible that Charles was handicapped by being a Liberal at a time when many senior academic posts were in the hands of Tory patronage. Some things don't change much.

Georgiana's father died in the late summer of 1816, which eventually made more funds available for the couple. Moreover, a slow decline in prices during the second decade of the nineteenth century meant that the money they did have went further.

Charles' family life has received relatively little attention to date, but in fact he was a most devoted family man. One significant glimpse of the Babbages' married life comes from his correspondence with Helen D'Arcy Stewart, of Kinneil House, where he stayed when he was an unsuccessful candidate for the Chair of Mathematics at Edinburgh University. Helen was the wife of Dugald Stewart, former Professor of Moral Philosophy at Edinburgh, friend of Scott, sympathiser with the French Revolution and tutor of Palmerston, Russell and Lansdowne.

Charles wrote to Helen from Torquay, dated 22 September 1819. Charles said that his wife and eldest boy were in good health, and the child was highly delighted with some peacock feathers which Helen had evidently given him, but, as Charles wrote, 'Mamma insisted on two of them being put by until the young philosopher can appreciate the value which the donor's name confers upon them.'

Helen replied on 4 December:

> You make me vain of the admiration the peacock feathers met with, and I assure you when we are walking in the avenue and the pea fowls following us, we often begin to talk of you, without remembering why, and always end with wishing that you and all your family were fairly settled in Edinburgh.

On 6 January 1820, Helen sent her sincere congratulations on Georgiana's recovery from the birth of another son (on 15 December 1819), to be named Edward Stewart Babbage, after the mathematician Sir Edward Bromhead and Dugald Stewart. Helen said that her husband felt most flattered, but lamented that his little godson should not receive a prettier name from him, but thought Edward made amends for that. She begged a description of the little boy and hoped that Georgiana would send her a lock of his hair. She concluded: 'With best respects to Mrs. Babbage and best wishes to all your Pets' – presumably meaning Babbage's children rather than any pet animals.

In April 1821, Charles introduced his young family by name in a letter to a friend whose name is not recorded:

> First I will speak of little Stewart whom you mention so kindly, he is the finest and largest of them all. Although he is fifteen months old he does not walk yet, not from any want of ability but from having a decided opinion that locomotion is much more safely performed by crawling on the carpet at which he is very expert. My eldest boy is named Benjamin Herschel after my father and one of my earliest and most intimate friends. The second, Charles Whitmore, has his mother's name, and my little Georgiana with her Mother's name promises to have her Mother's excellence. I shall find it very difficult not to spoil her. I do not observe that my children are more clever than others of their age, nor should I rejoice if they were so at their period of life. I endeavour to give them habits of observing everything that passes before their eyes and in my elder ones I am very contented with their progress.

When Charles wrote this lovely account, another baby was on the way, Francis Moore, born on 1 June 1821. Francis was soon followed by Dugald Bromhead, born 13 March 1823, and Henry Prevost, born 16 September 1824. The Babbages' only daughter, Georgiana Whitmore, had been born on 17 July 1818. Naturally, the birth of more children made Charles feel even more acutely the responsibilities of fatherhood. He kept on looking for work, but always without success. Here is an example of one of many letters Charles wrote in search of employment:

Honorable Sirs,

Understanding that a vacancy will shortly occur in the Professorship of Mathematics in the East India College of Hereford, I take the liberty of offering myself as a candidate for that situation, and should you on enquiry consider me worthy of the honour to which I aspire you will render it my duty as well as my inclination to promote the improvement of a science to which I have ever been most ardently attached.

Allow me to state for your consideration that I have had an university education; and that my mathematical enquiries have not been confined to the research of others but that I have myself made new discoveries in the science; some of these the Royal Society have thought worthy of a place in the last number of their transactions.

In the course of these pursuits I have successfully had the honor of becoming acquainted with Mr Herschel, with his father Dr Herschel with Dr Hutton and with Professor Ivory; and with two of these gentlemen I am constantly in the habit of corresponding on mathematical subjects.

With Mr Herschel whose talents for these sciences are well known, I am proud of having enjoyed a friendship which has contributed much to the success of my enquiries.

I have had the honor of being known to Dr Hutton for some time and he has very kindly allowed me to refer to him for a testimony of my mathematical abilities ...

Should the honorable directors consider me as qualified for this office I hope to meet with their approbation and I trust no one will be found more anxious to promote the objects or extend the fame of the establishment to which I shall be attached.

I shall take an early opportunity of waiting on each of the Honorable Directors personally, in order to give any farther references and explanations which may be deemed requisite.

With the greatest respects Honorable Sirs.
Your most Obedient and Humble Servant
C B
5 Devonshire Street
Portland Place
March 11 1816

Understandably enough, Charles enlisted his friends to maximise the chance of his application being successful. Here is an extract from a testimonial sent by his friend, the mathematician James Ivory:

My Dear Sir

I take the liberty of recommending to you my friend Mr Babbage. He is a young man who has lately left Cambridge, and is possessed of eminent talents in mathematical learning, in the cultivation of which he had made great advances. The Philosophical Transactions of last year contain a paper of his, which you may have noticed, and another paper of real merit which I have seen, is at present under their consideration.

In 'The Memoirs of the Analytical Society'; a work published at Cambridge, the first paper is of Mr Babbage's writing, as well as the Preface to the work, which shows very extensive reading on mathematical subjects. I have repeatedly seen Mr Babbage in London, and have corresponded with him on mathematical subjects, and I assure you I have formed a high expectation of his future attainment in Science. He is at present a candidate for a Professorship of Mathematics at the East India College at Hertford and I hope, from what I have said, you will be induced to favor his pursuit. Any recommendation you may think proper to give him will be of real consequence, and will contribute to the encouragement of a young man of merit.

I beg you will have the goodness to show this letter to Professor Leslie, and I hope you will solicit him to concur with your recommending Mr Babbage.

I am yours sincerely
James Ivory

Another ally brought into the service of Charles' career plans was Professor John Playfair, who was a Scottish scientist and mathematician, and a professor of natural philosophy at the University of Edinburgh in Scotland:

Edinburgh, 7th April 1816

Though I have not the pleasure to be personally acquainted with Mr Babbage, I have had an opportunity of perusing some of his writings, which have given me a very high opinion of his genius for the Mathematics, and of his acquirements in the most profound and most difficult parts of that science. I have been assured, too, that some of his papers, not yet published, argue no less a degree of knowledge and invention than those which I have perused.

For these reasons, and knowing also that Mr Babbage is a candidate for a situation in which Mathematical knowledge is a requisite, I have taken the liberty of expressing an opinion that is not entitled to any weight, but that of coming from one who has devoted the greater part of his life to the study of the Mathematical sciences, and is zealous to promote the interest of all institutions intended for their advancement, and of all individuals whose exertions are likely to contribute to the same end.

(Signed)   JOHN PLAYFAIR,
Prof. of Nat. Phil. In the University
Of Edinburgh

The intense focus which Charles was in due course to place on his cogwheel computers, his machines of the mind, has tended to overshadow the fact that he did, in fact, carry out some important mathematical work, especially early in his life during these years of married happiness and when he was living the life of a gentleman mathematician in London. In particular, between 1815 and 1820, his mathematical work was extensive and included work on algebra, papers on the theory of functions and other areas of pure mathematics. Yet through all this period, it's hard not to feel that Charles is basically something of a dilettante, writing papers he feels like writing, carrying out other work in the field of mathematics that he enjoys, looking for jobs without any success, and perhaps without any real drive, and generally not being driven by any sheer commercial imperative to earn a living.

On 20 July 1819, Professor Playfair died, at the age of 71 – a ripe old age indeed in the second decade of the nineteenth century. This created a shuffling of career appointments in the scientific world. The following letter, which Herschel wrote to Charles only a week after Playfair died, is self-explanatory:

Dear Babbage,

I understand it is your intention to offer yourself as a candidate for the Professorial Chair, vacated by the succession of Mr Leslie to that of the admirable and lamented Playfair.

I hope I need not assure you of my warmest wishes for your success, convinced as I am from what I know of your acquirements and intellectual energy, that it is a situation you are perfectly calculated to fill with reputation.

Those who, like myself, have read and admired your papers in the Philosophical Transactions, will readily admit your claim to originality of inventive genius, as well as familiarity with the profounder resources of Mathematical science, but those only who are fortunate enough to know you intimately can appreciate your devotion to scientific pursuits, or value as it deserves the blameless tenor of your private life.

I am well aware, that, under ordinary circumstances, you would shrink from such praises, though you know them sincere; but it strikes me, that, in the course of your canvass, you may possibly meet with individuals with whom I may have some slight acquaintance, or literary intercourse; and, as opinions influence one another, if you think mine will be of the least use to you, you have it.

My father begs you to be assured of his best wishes for your success, which he knows, as well as I do, is yours, if merit will ensure it. He would have told you so himself, but for some difficulty he now experiences in the act of writing.

Believe me,

Dear Babbage,

Very sincerely, yours,

(Signed)   J.F.W. HERSCHEL.

Slough, July 27 1819

Charles and Herschel were friends all their lives, and during the second decade of the nineteenth century their friendship developed into a close intellectual companionship. To give an idea of the things they got up to, here is an extract from a letter written by Herschel on 2 September 1816 to a friend, describing a visit he made to Charles in Torquay:

> I went the other day to Torquay and spent a day or two with Babbage who was well and occupied with his functions [presumably meaning mathematics]. I like his enthusiasm on that subject and as we rambled through the noble and romantic scenes which that neighbourhood affords – climbing the rocks with boyish eagerness, and talking of analytics all the while, my brain became once more warmed with the speculations which used to give me such delight, and I swore to return again to those sources of enjoyment I'd allowed myself too long to lose sight of.

'Climbing the rocks with boyish eagerness': despite his moods when he did not enjoy physical exertion, Babbage sometimes had other moods when he delighted in it.

In 1819, Charles travelled to Paris, with Herschel his travelling companion. It was probably the first time Charles had left Britain. It's not known exactly when they left for France, although logically they would most likely have departed in the warmer months – the late spring or summer – rather than in the colder ones.

When they reached the city of Abbeville, situated about 60 miles south down the French coast from the port of Calais, where they most likely made landfall in France, Charles and Herschel wanted breakfast and Charles undertook to order it. He spoke French, but evidently not very well at this stage in his life. He says blithely in his autobiography that he and Herschel usually required a couple of eggs and that he preferred having his moderately boiled but that Herschel liked his eggs boiled quite hard. Charles relates that he explained this to the waiter and also explained to the waiter that 'Each of us required two eggs thus cooked, concluding my order with the words, *pour chacun deux*', which of course means 'two eggs each'. However, the waiter misunderstood this message, presumably because of Charles' poor French pronunciation. As Charles relates:

> The garcon ran along the passage half way towards the kitchen, and then called out in loudest tone – 'Il faut faire bouillir cinquante-deux oeufs pour Messieurs les Anglais.' I burst into such a fit of uncontrollable laughter at this absurd misunderstanding of chacun deux, for cinquante-deux, that it was some time before I could explain it to Herschel, and but for his running into the kitchen to countermand it, the half hundred of eggs would have assuredly been simmering over the fire. A few days after our arrival in Paris, we dined with Laplace, where we met a large party, most of whom were members of the Institut. The story had already arrived at Paris, having rapidly passed through several editions.

It isn't actually all that funny a recollection, but we can imagine Charles and Herschel greatly enjoying it.

Certainly, if you are a fan of puns, you're living in the wrong century: the nineteenth century was your epoch, and you ought to have cultivated Charles' friendship. He also recalls:

> To my great amusement, one of the party told the company that, a few days before, two young Englishmen being at Abbeville, had ordered

fifty-two eggs to be boiled for their breakfast, and that they ate up every one of them, as well as a large pie which was put before them.

My next neighbour at dinner asked me if I thought it probable. I replied, that there was no absurdity a young Englishman would not occasionally commit.

It's not known for certain how long Charles and Herschel stayed in France, but in those days people, if they went abroad at all, did not do so for a weekend, or even for only a week. It is likely they would have spent a month or two on their travels.

During this trip to the Continent Charles and Herschel met many eminent French scientific men, several of whom stayed close friends with Charles and Herschel for the rest of their lives. One of the most significant scientific personages they met was Dominique Francois Jean Arago, who was both a man of science and a political figure.

Born in 1786, Arago had had many adventures of a non-scientific kind, including spending periods of imprisonment at the hands of Spanish corsairs and travelling through northern Africa overland, guided only, reportedly, by a Muslim holy man. Arago had completed several important scientific surveys both in France and abroad, and as a reward for his work in the cause of science he was elected a member of the French Academy of Sciences at the remarkably early age of 23; before the end of 1809 he was chosen by the council of the Ecole Polytechnique to the Chair of Analytical Geometry.

Charles and Arago got on very well from the beginning and Arago played an important role in Charles' life when Charles became interested in the French inventor Joseph-Marie Jacquard – he of the punched-card foot-weaving loom, the Jacquard loom. Charles asked Arago to procure a marvellously complex image, woven on a Jacquard loom, of Jacquard himself sitting in his workshop. Arago was unable to obtain this, but Charles ultimately procured one by his own efforts.

It's not clear what language they spoke in. Charles could write French fluently (there are numerous letters by him in his archive at the British Library written in French) but Charles and Arago tended to write to each other in their own language, so it's not possible to be sure in which language they conversed.

I will discuss the Jacquard loom in more detail later. For the moment, it's perhaps enough to point out that Jacquard had perfected his remarkable loom in the first few years of the nineteenth century. The machine automated the process of weaving complex and beautiful images into silk by using a chain of punched cards that, pressed against the proper part of the machine, governed which rods controlling the raising and lowering of the warp threads in a loom had to move for each pulse of the shuttle.

When Charles was travelling in France he first saw the famous, even fabled, numerical tables of Gaspard Francois de Prony, France's leading civil engineer. Despite being a baron, de Prony had survived the revolutionary period thanks to the protection of the eminent French politician Lazare Cornot, whom the French revolutionaries praised as the 'organiser of the victory'. De Prony had been commissioned during the Republican period to prepare a set of logarithmic and trigonometric tables appropriate for the new metric system that had been implemented. As Anthony Hyman puts it in *Charles Babbage, Pioneer of the Computer* (1982): 'These tables were to leave nothing to be desired in precision and were to form the most monumental work of calculation ever carried out or even conceived.'

Logarithms greatly aid mathematical calculation because they enable complex multiplications to be carried out simply by adding the logarithm of each number together.

For example, the base 10 logarithm of 100 is 2, as 10 to the power of 2 is 100. Similarly, the base 10 logarithm of 1,000 is 3, as 10 to the power of 3 is 1,000. What logarithmic tables do, which was once quite rightly seen as enormously useful, is to give the logarithm of numbers that are not attained simply by raising 10 to the power of a straightforward integer. For example, the logarithm of 1,237 is 3.09234, that is, to five decimal places. In fact, logarithms of numbers that cannot be attained just by raising 10 to the power of a simple integer are always complex, lengthy numbers and do not have a precise and finite quantity, it is a question of how many decimal places you want the logarithm to be calculated to. They were extremely important in Charles' day, and tables of logarithms were regarded as essential for any complex mathematical calculation.

What de Prony had done was to chance on a copy of an edition of Adam Smith's famous economic treatise *The Wealth of Nations* (1776). De Prony had opened the book at random and discovered a chapter on the division of labour. He decided to oversee and manage the enormous job of compiling the new, ideally super-accurate logarithmic tables for the revolutionary government by employing a division of labour system which divided the people doing the calculations into three sections. The task of the first section was to plan the overall strategy of the project. In this section were half a dozen of the best mathematicians in France. They didn't do much of the actual numerical work, but they were the senior managers.

The second section consisted of seven or eight competent mathematicians whose job it was to convert the formulae used to calculate the logarithms into sets of actual numbers. This was, as can readily be imagined, an extremely laborious task. This group then distributed the numbers among the members of the third group, receiving from them in due course the actual computed calculations.

The third section comprised between sixty and eighty people, the vast majority of whom knew no mathematics beyond simple additions and fractions, which were the only two operations they were required to carry out. It was, in fact, the case that these people often produced results that were more correct than those who had a more extensive knowledge of mathematics.

In other words, de Prony had found a way of compiling the extremely demanding and complex logarithmic tables by using a division of labour which at the bottom end of the pyramid relied purely on addition and subtraction – which are the only functions needed if the higher elements of the calculation are handled by other people. The tables occupied seventeen large folio volumes. Charles was enormously impressed, and these tables, compiled by human calculation using a systematic method, were to give him the inspiration to design the first of his two great machines of the mind.

5

THE EPIPHANY THAT CHANGED CHARLES' AND ADA'S LIVES

A fiery chariot floats on nimble wings
Down to me and I feel myself unbuoyed
To blaze a new trail through the upper air
Into new spheres of energy unalloyed.
Oh this high life, this heavenly rapture! …
Nor tremble at that dark pit in which our fancy
Condemns itself to torments of its own framing,
But struggle on and upwards to that passage
At the narrow mouth of which all hell is flaming.
Be calm and take that step, though you should fall
Beyond it into nothing – nothing at all.

From *Faust* by Johann Wolfgang von Goethe
trans. Louis MacNeice (1949)

One summer day in 1821 – the exact date is unfortunately unknown – Charles and Herschel were at Charles' home at 5 Devonshire Street, carrying out some work for the London offices of the Astronomical Society of London. The Society had first met on 12 January 1820. Its object was to support astronomical research, which was at the time mainly carried out by gentleman astronomers. Most of the prominent men of science of the day were, in fact, talented amateurs rather than professionals, partly because there were few jobs for scientific or mathematical people.

Like many of the august societies of nineteenth-century London, the Royal Astronomical Society is still alive and well today, a wonderful institution to be found in Piccadilly, in the heart of London, inside the west wing of the massive and hugely imposing Burlington House, a Palladian mansion that was once a private residence and which traces its origins to about 1664. Back in 1821, the Society occupied rented rooms at the Medical and Chirurgical Society at Lincoln's Inn Fields in London.

That summer Charles and Herschel had joined a committee responsible for furnishing the society with calculations used for compiling mathematical tables. Trigonometrical and logarithmic tables were essential for plotting lunar and planetary trajectories, and for working out other important astronomical information. The tables were also vital for calculations needed for many other practical purposes. They were busy that day at Charles' home checking over calculations that already been made manually by clerks who were known, at the time, as 'computers'.

The process of checking the working of manual calculations was, as can readily be imagined, ultra-laborious and dull. A particular problem was that, when Charles and Herschel found an error, they had no way of knowing whether they might have made a mistake themselves, or if the computers had. As Charles later recalled:

Mr Herschel and myself having been appointed by the Astronomical Society on a committee for the purpose of procuring certain calculations, we first agreed on the proper formulae, and then employing two independent computers to reduce them to numbers, ourselves comparing the manuscript results. On the first of these occasions my friend brought with him the calculations of both computers, and we commenced the tedious process of verification. After a time many discrepancies occurred, and at one point these discordancies were so numerous that I exclaimed, 'I wish to God these calculations had been executed by steam!'

For Charles, his sudden moment of realisation that it might, in fact, be possible to build a machine that used steam power to carry out calculations was the greatest epiphany of his life. Its consequences were to occupy him – and indeed haunt him – for the next fifty years.

Charles himself is so expressive and detailed in his autobiography about the early history of the Difference Engine that it would hardly be respectful towards him not to quote some salient material from this. As he writes in his autobiography:

> Calculating machines comprise various pieces of mechanism for assist-
> ing the human mind in executing the operations of arithmetic. Some
> few of these perform the whole operation without any mental atten-
> tion when once the given numbers have been put into the machine.
>
> Others require a moderate portion of mental attention: these latter
> are generally of much simpler construction than the former, and it
> may also be added, are less useful.
>
> The simplest way of deciding to which of these two classes any cal-
> culating machine belongs is to ask its maker – Whether, when the
> numbers on which it is to operate are placed in the instrument, it
> is capable of arriving at its result by the mere motion of a spring, a
> descending weight, or any other constant force? If the answer be in
> the affirmative, the machine is really automatic; if otherwise, it is not
> self-acting.
>
> Of the various machines I have had occasion to examine, many of
> those for addition and subtraction have been found to be automatic.
> Of machines for multiplication and division, which have fully come
> under my examination, I cannot at present recall one to my memory
> as absolutely fulfilling this condition.

Charles also recalls, in *Passages from the Life of a Philosopher*, his early work on trying to make a cogwheel calculating machine:

> I considered that a machine to execute the mere isolated operations of
> arithmetic, would be comparatively of little value, unless it were very
> easily set to do its work, and unless it executed not only accurately, but
> with great rapidity, whatever it was required to do.
>
> On the other hand, the method of differences supplied a general
> principle by which *all* tables might be computed through limited
> intervals, by one uniform process. Again, the method of differences
> required the use of mechanism for addition only. In order, however, to

ensure accuracy in the printed tables, it was necessary that the machine which computed tables should also set them up in type, or else supply a mould in which stereotype plates of those tables could be cast.

I now began to sketch out arrangements for accomplishing the several partial processes which were required. The arithmetical part must consist of two distinct processes – the power of adding one digit to another, and also of carrying the tens to the next digit, if it should be necessary.

The first idea was, naturally, to add each digit successively. This, however, would occupy much time if the numbers added together consisted of many places of figures.

The next step was to add all the digits of the two numbers each to each at the same instant, but reserving a certain mechanical memorandum, wherever a carriage became due. These carriages were then to be executed successively.

Having made various drawings, I now began to make models of some portions of the machine, to see how they would act. Each number was to be expressed upon wheels placed upon an axis; there being one wheel for each figure in the number operated upon.

Having arrived at a certain point in my progress, it became necessary to have teeth of a peculiar form cut upon these wheels. As my own lathe was not fit for this job, I took the wheels to a wheel-cutter at Lambeth, to whom I carefully conveyed my instructions, leaving with him a drawing as to his guide.

In the early nineteenth century, this lack of an absolutely reliable means of carrying out mathematical calculations was an extremely serious problem, and the more extensive and profound the role technology played in society, the more serious the problem became. As Britain's Industrial Revolution gathered momentum, the difficulty of performing complex calculations accurately became a grave limiting factor to the changes this revolution was bringing to Britain's industry and economy.

Even worse, there was no way of knowing exactly where an inaccuracy in the mathematical tables might lie. This fact created a disturbing climate of psychological insecurity among scientists, astronomers and mathematicians. Under the circumstances, it was hardly surprising that

John Herschel, writing in 1842 to the Chancellor of the Exchequer Henry Goulburn, bitterly observed: 'An undetected error in a logarithmic table is like a sunken rock at sea yet undiscovered, upon which it is impossible to say what wrecks may have taken place.'

Today – with inexpensive electronic calculators readily at our disposal on our mobile phones and watches, and with every desktop computer featuring a powerful calculator function that provides completely reliable results in the time than it takes to click a mouse – we may find it difficult to imagine not having access to all this calculating power. We have to make an even greater effort of the imagination to empathise with the fact that early nineteenth-century scientists could not trust the mathematical tables they were using. Errors could literally appear anywhere, and there might be a terrible mistake in the middle of an otherwise perfect column or row.

Consider the unfortunate English mathematician William Shanks. Shanks is renowned for his calculation of π to 707 places, accomplished in 1873. Unfortunately, his calculation was only correct up to the first 527 places, which meant that many years of work by Shanks were wasted.

Shanks earned his living by owning a boarding school, which left him enough time to spend on his hobby of calculating mathematical constants. He would reportedly calculate new digits all morning, and then would spend all afternoon checking his morning's work. His schedule being what it was, it isn't clear when his pupils got taught; presumably Shanks did little teaching himself.

Despite the error, Shanks' approximation was the longest expansion of π until the advent of the electronic digital computer.

Mercifully, when Shanks died in 1882, at the age of 70, he was still oblivious to the error, which was not pointed out until 1944 by a mathematician called D.F. Ferguson, using a mechanical desk calculator.

Charles was not, in fact, the first inventor to try to build a machine for facilitating calculation. In 1642, the French scientist and philosopher Blaise Pascal had constructed an adding machine to aid him in computations for his father's business accounts. The German mathematician Gottfried Wilhelm Leibniz saw Pascal's machine while on a visit to Paris and worked to develop a more advanced version.

But Pascal's and Leibniz's machines differed in one vitally important respect from the one Charles planned. Theirs were manual devices, but Charles insisted from the outset that his own calculation machine would be automatic. Unlike Pascal's and Leibniz's apparatus, which needed to be operated by an expert operator, Charles' proposed machine was designed to produce column after column of results itself, with the operator only having to turn the handle that powered the machine. The handle-turning action could even have been mechanised: a small steam engine could have been utilised to do the job, and Charles' dream would have come true.

When Charles started work on trying to build a cogwheel calculator he was able to benefit from the excellent quality of clockmaking in his own day. In fact, the manufacture of luxury mechanical watches and clocks in our own age is still one of the most advanced practical precision mechanical sciences in the world. Ironically, there is still a big market for these luxury mechanical timepieces even though many electronic watches and clocks are nowadays very inexpensive.

Charles designed his Difference Engine to use many thousands of metal cogwheels in order to perform calculations. No clock had ever employed anything like as many cogwheels as this, but Charles was confident in his own scientific and engineering powers, and was sure he had a good chance of success.

The cogwheels Charles planned to make were comparatively large, compared − say − with those found inside small clocks. Modern computer scientists who have studied his work do not believe that his task would have been any easier if the cogwheels had been smaller. As Doron Swade says:

My view is that the difficulties and delays [Charles experienced] did not arise from the fact that the scale on which he built was large but that there was no standardisation (he therefore had to rely on one component supplier) and that there was no method of production available that offered inherent repeatability. The difficulty was how to produce large numbers of near-identical parts economically and quickly. The problem would have been the same whether he used smaller wheels.

Charles named his first calculating machine the 'Difference Engine' because it used a mathematical concept called the Method of Differences. This is a technique to calculate mathematical tables by repeated regular additions of the 'differences' between successive items in a mathematical series. A mathematical series is a set of terms in ordered succession, the value of each being determined by a specific relation to adjacent terms. Mathematical series can be generated by a mathematical formula.

The great advantage of using the Method of Differences is that it replaces the process of calculating a long and complex mathematical series with numerous straightforward but monotonous additions. But of course, if a machine is carrying them out, their monotony does not matter. Interestingly, Charles' approach to calculating mathematical tables was basically the same as that chosen by Gaspard de Prony. The Frenchman also made use of the Method of Differences and hired unemployed hairdressers (the Revolution had reduced the demand for elaborate hairdressing as well as the number of heads on which to practise the art) to complete the simple but numerous calculations necessary. Charles was essentially mechanising this process.

Charles' brilliantly ingenious mechanisation was based on the idea that teeth on individual cogwheels (described as 'figure wheels' by Charles) would stand for numbers, and that the machine's operation would be based around meshing independently moving figure wheels arranged in vertical columns with each other. This meshing process would carry out an arithmetical calculation.

Charles elected to use the familiar, everyday counting system for his machine that is based around the fact that most of us have ten fingers and ten toes. The figure wheel at the bottom of a vertical column would represent the units, the one second from the bottom the tens, the one third from the bottom the hundreds, and so on. For example, the setting of a four-digit number such as 7,258 would require the bottom figure wheel to be turned eight teeth to represent '8' – the number of *single units*; the second from the bottom to be turned five teeth to represent '5' – the number of *tens*; the third from the bottom to be turned two teeth to represent '2' – the number of *hundreds*; and the fourth from the bottom to be turned seven teeth to represent '7' – the number of *thousands*. On this occasion all the figure wheels above the fourth wheel would be set to zero, as they were not required. So any number could be set in the machine in a vertical stack of cogwheels as long as there were enough wheels in the vertical stack to cover the tens, thousands, tens of thousands, hundreds of thousands, millions, etc. that were required.

Charles spent a good deal of his time, during the years after having had his epiphany in the company of Herschel, trying to build a working version of the Difference Engine to calculate mathematical tables reliably. While his work on this project was apparently fairly concerted, reading through his papers in the British Library one has the sense that there were times when he was extremely enthusiastic about the project and other times when he did other things and almost forgot about it. But when he did focus on the Difference Engine, he designed wonderfully brilliant and original components for the machine: components which when we look at them now seem almost like the creation by some alien species.

It's impossible not to be astounded by the ingenuity and originality of the components Charles designed for the Difference Engine, a machine that, after all, at the start, existed substantially in his imagination.

He hired a highly talent engineer, Joseph Clement, to help him, but the two men never got on very well; partly because Clement had an annoying habit of sending in bills to Charles for amounts that hadn't been agreed, but also because Charles, in one of the many instances throughout his life of what was at best social clumsiness and at worst actual rudeness, insisted always on treating Clement as an employee rather than as a colleague and Clement, not unreasonably, gradually got fed up with this.

Charles also spent a great deal of time trying to get more money from the government to fund the building of the Difference Engine. By 1832, he had been granted a total of £17,000. It was ironic, in many ways, that the supposedly old-fashioned aristocratic government which was swept away by the famous and even fabled 1832 Reform Bill was the government that advanced Charles an enormous sum of money to help him with his visionary project, while the government that came to power after the Reform Bill was passed never granted him another penny. Perhaps aristocrats are not always as obtuse and devoid of perception as people who aren't aristocrats often like to think.

By December 1832, Charles and his team had succeeded in completing not an entire Difference Engine but a one-seventh version of it. This portion of the Difference Engine still exists, and can be seen in the London Science Museum.

As Doron Swade explains in *The Cogwheel Brain*:

> The demonstration piece was delivered to Babbage's house in Dorset Street in December 1832 and was placed on display in his drawing-room. It stood about two and a half feet high, two feet wide and two feet deep – a weighty bronze and steel embodiment of solidity and precision. It consisted of three columns, each with six engraved figure wheels, representing about one-seventh of the complete calculating section. It incorporated the essential calculating mechanism which was repeated time and time again in the full design, though no printing section was made for it.

The demonstration piece is wonderful, beautiful and fantastically ingenious. With nothing but the mechanical engineering of his own age to provide him with the tools he needed, Charles was obliged to imagine and improvise from scratch the components he needed for his revolutionary machine. To take just one example, the levers for the carry mechanism in the Difference Engine alone were of such complexity that a modern fully dimensioned piece-part drawing of one of them can only be readily understood by specialist mechanical engineers. Charles designed these and numerous other components without any certain knowledge that they would work, his only touchstone being the strength of his own conception.

To make the components, Charles was obliged to pioneer many advances in machine tools and machining techniques. The components of the Difference Engine had to be made one at a time. Unfortunately, the lack of standardisation in the component manufacture at the time meant that no component could be precisely identical with the previous one, which would of course have been the ideal.

It was true that by meticulous comparisons being made of dimensions, parts could be manufactured nearly identically by finishing them with hand tools or by additional machining, and could subsequently be made to fit in the machine by additional filing and tweaking. But this process was labour intensive, time consuming and expensive. As Arthur C. Clarke reasonably points out in his *Profiles of the Future* (1962), Charles could have benefited enormously from the existence of a precision metal industry, but there wasn't one in his day.

As so often in Charles' life and career, he was forced to make do.

6

1827: CHARLES' YEAR OF DISASTER

The golden ripple on the wall came back again, and nothing else stirred in the room. The old, old fashion! The fashion that came in with our first garments, and will last unchanged until our race has run its course, and the wide firmament is rolled up like a scroll. The old, old fashion – Death!

Oh thank GOD, all who see it, for that older fashion yet, of Immortality! And look upon us, angels of young children, with regards not quite estranged, when the swift river bears us to the ocean!

From *Dombey and Son* (1848) by Charles Dickens

But we are jumping ahead of ourselves a little; that successful completion of the one-seventh portion of the Difference Engine took place five years after the most calamitous year in Charles' life.

It began with a bereavement that did not, shall we say, bring him unalloyed grief. On Tuesday, 27 February 1827, Benjamin Babbage, who had suffered from ill health for some time and who was in his seventy-fourth year, died in Teignmouth in Devonshire.

Benjamin had always thought Charles impractical, uncommercial, intellectually self-indulgent and at heart something of a loser. Nor is there any record of the father having ever ascribed any positive qualities to his son to counterbalance these negatives ones. Now Benjamin was dead, the only way Charles could have hoped to redeem himself in his father's eyes would have been through necromancy or a séance, and ever since leaving Cambridge and the Ghost Club, Charles had shown no significant interest in communing with spirits.

As for Georgiana, probably no daughter-in-law was ever less mournful of the death of her father-in-law than she was. The comments about Benjamin's death which she made in the following letter may seem unfeeling and crass, but as she herself says, there is very little point pretending to have an emotion one doesn't possess. As Georgiana wrote to Herschel (the emphases are hers):

Mr Babbage died the *Tuesday* following the same day Charles left Town … To feign sorrow in such a happy release would in *me* be hypocracy [*sic*]. Of the affairs I as yet know but little, but I do not imagine the event will make any material difference to us, during Mrs B's life, and no great a session at *any period*. But I do not speak with any certainty and I've always felt an indifference on the subject than with *my family* almost astonishes myself. It does not proceed from carelessness but the little difficulty I find in accommodating my wants and wishes to my circumstances. Naturally active I am an excellent wife to a poor man but never should have been sufficiently fond of stile [*sic*] or company to make a proper wife to a rich man.

Yours affectly

G Babbage

[Royal Society library]

Georgiana's inaccurate spelling of the word 'hypocrisy' and 'style' should not be taken as indicating that she was semi-illiterate, and/or simply couldn't spell. By the end of the eighteenth century there was a widely accepted standard for the spelling of printed English, partly triggered by Dr Samuel Johnson's magisterial dictionary which was published in 1755. But the influence of the spelling standard applies more at this stage in history to printed documents; people continued to use often idiosyncratic spelling until about the middle of the nineteenth century, when it began to be widely accepted even in personal correspondence that spelling should follow the standard.

When Georgiana writes 'of the affairs I as yet know but little', she is presumably referring to the financial situation after Benjamin's death. Very few letters Georgiana wrote are extant and her style is rather charming and shows considerable self-insight. Judging from this letter,

Benjamin had made Charles and Georgiana's life something or much of a misery, because of his frequent complaints that Charles did not have a proper occupation.

In another, rather curious, letter Georgiana wrote to Herschel after Benjamin's death – Herschel had written to ask whether Charles wished to be a candidate for the Savilian Chair of Mathematics at Oxford University – she implies that Charles recognised that Benjamin's death was likely to make an enormous change to their financial situation that would allow Charles to forgo the need to work if he wished to. The fact that Georgiana knew this even before the will was proved suggests that Benjamin had told Charles that he would inherit most of the estate. Replying to Herschel's enquiry, Georgiana wrote:

> It is seldom that I cannot say a priori what Charles *would* like or would not, but with regard to this professorship I cannot judge. Before his father's death he would have taken it had it been offered or at least a certainty that if he declared himself a candidate he would have it, but when this event will make him *more* or *less* desirous of obtaining it without more knowledge of our affairs I cannot say. One great inducement in endeavouring to procure an addition to his income was his father's always *despairing* his abilities (if I may use the term) and saying C's abilities would never procure him anything. This made dear C feel more keenly the fruitlessness of his endeavours. This trial is now past.

It's not clear why Herschel wrote to Georgiana to enquire about her husband's intentions. Perhaps, in the aftermath of Benjamin's demise, Charles was preoccupied with attending to family matters.

Georgiana's letter confirms what Benjamin was like towards Charles, and it's surely not difficult to imagine Charles' sense of despair at the constant pressure his father put on him to get some kind of job and do something with his life that Benjamin considered worthwhile, which he certainly did not consider the Difference Engine to be. In the event, the appointment of the Savilian Chair did not go to Charles.

Benjamin had made Charles his prime beneficiary. That is a fact, and while we will never know precisely what Benjamin thought of his son,

Benjamin at least retained enough love for him to be willing to leave Charles sufficient money to be free of the need to work at any remunerative activity for the rest of his life.

Apart from a number of small bequests, Benjamin had split his property between his wife, Betty Plumleigh, and Charles, who was also the sole executor. Betty received £9,000 of stock for her absolute use and the interest on a further £10,000. On her death, according to the instructions in the will, the £10,000 was to be divided among Charles' children. Betty also gained in the will the lease on the house in Teignmouth, all Benjamin's silver, china, glass, household goods and furniture, liquors, coal and other goods about the house, and his piano. She had the use for life of a diamond necklace, a king-pin and locket, all probably heirlooms which after Betty's death under the terms of the will were to go to Charles. Benjamin's small bequests included 19 guineas to the Totnes Bluecoat School.

Benjamin's 'plate' meant his gold and silver dishes, which would possibly have been used in the house at formal and important dinners. Whether Benjamin ever hosted any of those events is not known; let's remember that Charles wrote to Herschel that Benjamin had no friends. It seems most likely that Benjamin would have kept his plate securely locked in the house in a room where they could be shown to visitors looking at them through glass cabinets and realise how rich Benjamin was.

Benjamin also left Charles the contents of his library, and, more significantly, the rest of the property, which altogether was worth about £100,000. It included a farm at Dainton and Castle Meadow, a field just outside Totnes that is nowadays a much-loved public path. Following the proving of the will, Charles became a man not only of means, but of enormous wealth: the legacy was worth about £10 million at modern prices.

One mystery about the will is the apparent lack of provision for Charles' younger sister Mary Ann. By now she was married to a Henry Hollier, whom she'd married in December 1823 at St Marylebone Church in London. He had been born at Hagley Hall, Worcester in 1755; his ancestors were from the extensive Hollier family of the town of Barton-under-Needwood in the county of Staffordshire.

Hollier's father worked in India, but ill health forced his return to England in 1784; he married in around 1785 and moved to Cardiff where his two children, Fanny and Henry, were born. Henry Hollier forged a career in public service after being steward to the 1st Marquess of Bute, who was notable for restoring Cardiff Castle from ruins. Hollier proceeded to hold a number of public posts in Cardiff in addition to looking after the marquess's affairs.

Henry and Mary Ann had six children. Two became solicitors, while Thomas Henry was rector at Priston, Somerset from 1863 to 1899.

The only reasonable conclusion is surely that by the time of Benjamin's death, Mary was well set up with Hollier, who was a man of means, and as Benjamin would have known this, he saw no need to make any extensive provision for Mary in his will.

Benjamin Babbage's will no longer survives, but a record was kept of the bequests he made. However, there is no record of whether Mary Anne Hollier was left any money, but it seems that she was either left nothing at all or very little; in any event, not enough to make any dent in the residue of £100,000 left to Charles. By the time Benjamin died, Charles was in the process of taking on a paid position as a director of a newly formed assurance company in 1824 called 'The Protector' for £1,000 a year. Georgiana believed that he took this position only to gain his father's approval as he was still haunted by Benjamin's conviction that he, Charles, was fundamentally incapable of making any money by his own efforts.

In fact, what happened was that the life assurance company which had the name of 'The Protector' had promised to pay Charles £1,500 a year, with limited practice, as an independent actuary, and apartments over the establishment. One of Charles' friends, Francis Bailey FRS – an astronomer whose name has survived in 'Bailey's beads', the sharp points of sunlight around the moon as a solar eclipse is ending – who had practised as an actuary, told Charles that he himself could probably expect to make another £1,000 per annum from freelance actuarial work.

But, in fact, the project never gave Charles any significant income because it was abandoned at an early stage and all Charles received was 100 guineas, which more or less covered his expenses. He did use this experience to write a short book called *A Comparative View of the Various Institutions for the Assurance of Lives* (1826). It was an analysis of the life assurance offices in London available at that time and also a kind of guide for customers.

The truth about what provision was made for Charles' sister by Benjamin may never be fully known. What is certain is that later in her life she wrote on at least one occasion to try to borrow money from her brother, in order to raise some capital so that one of her sons could be made an apprentice. It's not known whether Charles said yes to this proposal. What seems to have happened as far as Mary Anne is concerned was that when she got married some settlement was made for her, and very likely at this point Benjamin had given her some money which he regarded, in effect, as her legacy.

Once the news of Benjamin's death reached Charles in London – the telegraph had not yet been invented, and the fastest way for news to be conveyed was at the pace of a horse's gallop – he at once booked a stagecoach for the approximately five-day journey to return to Teignmouth to be with his mother Betty.

The church where Benjamin was buried was St Michael the Archangel at Teignmouth, where he had been a churchwarden. Once Benjamin was safely buried, the prospects for the young married couple Charles and Georgiana and their family seemed excellent. After all, Charles' relationship with his father was so bad that Benjamin's death was, as Georgiana had said, a happy release.

Unfortunately, destiny had other plans.

When Benjamin died, Georgiana was about two months pregnant. In the summer of 1827, their young son Charles died at the age of 10; there is no record of the cause of death. In the absence of any documentary evidence of what Charles and Georgiana felt about the death of poor little Charles, we can only assume, reasonably enough, that it was a disastrous blow for them and that Georgiana's reaction to it was very different from their reaction to the death of Benjamin.

Soon after young Charles died, Georgiana herself became very ill. She was by now about seven months pregnant. Childbirth was extremely hazardous before the advent of modern medicine, and of course can still be hazardous today. At this time, if a pregnancy ran into problems such as the baby being in the wrong position or the mother being ill in labour, or some obstruction in the woman's body, the results could be utterly catastrophic, with the woman suffering the most appalling pain that could not be relieved by anaesthetics, as they didn't exist, and with doctors and nurses being able to do very little to help either mother or baby.

On 4 August 1827, by which point Georgiana was extremely ill, Charles took her and her children to Boughton, a village in Worcestershire, 2 miles from Worcester, to the house of her sister, Harriet, who had married one Elias Isaac. And there Georgiana and her baby died – nominally the Babbages' eighth child – on Saturday, 1 September, almost certainly during childbirth.

Nothing is known about the baby, or even whether it was a boy or a girl. There is a rumour on the Internet that the baby was named Alexander, but I have not found any primary source evidence for that, and my enquiries among the current descendants of Charles Babbage through Benjamin Herschel have unfortunately proved fruitless.

In *Charles Babbage: Pioneer of the Computer*, Anthony Hyman remarks:

In his [Charles'] public controversies, there is a new note of bitterness of which there was no trace while Georgiana was alive. Far more than the difficulties over the Calculating Engines, far more than any public battles and disappointments, the loss of Georgiana left Babbage a changed man.

Georgiana's death, in what should have been the heyday and prime of the Babbages' married life, not only came close to destroying Charles emotionally but also literally destroyed the family. Charles became a different person. Although eventually his wit and charm recovered, his inner core of happiness – and the secret, private and wonderful world that love brings to a person, providing a refuge from all the cruelties, indifferences, and iniquities of the world – was gone and there was, at least for the time being, nothing in its place except emptiness.

7

ADA DREAMS OF A FLYING MACHINE

In dreams begin responsibility.

Old Play (quoted at the start of W.B. Yeats'
1914 volumes of poems, *Responsibilities*)

Ada adored science even as a young child. She had a distinctly inventive cast of mind, and it was practical, rather than abstruse, science that she loved; one possibility she especially liked was the notion of building a flying machine. She didn't dream of this in a childish way without making any practical plans to do it, but devoted much time to drawing a pair of wings that might, she hoped, carry her up into the heavens. On Wednesday, 2 April 1828, while staying at a large country house, Bifrons, near Canterbury in Kent, Ada wrote to her mother, who was on a rest cure elsewhere, about these ideas she'd been having. Ada was 12 years old at the time, and living at Bifrons with her governess, a Miss Stamp, and Ada's cat Puff, on whom Ada doted:

> Since last night I have been thinking more about the flying, & I can find no difficulty in the motion or distension of the wings, I have already thought of a way of fixing them onto the shoulders and I think they might perhaps be made of oil-silk. If that does not answer I must try what I can with feathers.

She continues:

> I know you will laugh at what I'm going to say but I'm going to take
> the exact patterns of a bird's wing in proportion to the size of its body
> and then I'm immediately going to set about making a pair of paper
> wings of exactly the same size as the bird in proportion to my size …
>
> I ought not to forget to tell you that in my new flying plan, if it
> answers, I shall be able to guide myself in the air by a method I have
> lately thought of. I have now a great favour to ask of you which is
> to try and procure me some book which will make me thoroughly
> understand the anatomy of a bird, and if you can get one with plates
> to illustrate the description I should be very glad because I have no
> inclination whatever to dissect even a bird. I do not think that without
> plates I could be made thoroughly to understand the anatomy of a bird.

Five days after this, Ada wrote another letter to her mother about her plans.
By now her speculations had progressed to the dream of powered flight:

> As soon as I have got flying to perfection, I have got a scheme about
> a … steamengine which, if ever I effect it, will be more wonderful
> than either steampackets or steamcarriages. It is to make a thing in
> the form of a horse with a steamengine in the inside so contrived as
> to move an immense pair of wings, fixed on the outside of the horse,
> in such a manner as to carry it up into the air while a person sits on
> its back. This last scheme probably has infinitely more difficulties and
> obstacles in its way than my scheme for flying, but still I should think
> that it is possible.

Sadly, Ada didn't grasp that powered flight would have to wait until the
invention of an engine that had a far superior power-to-weight ratio
than a steam engine, which is much too heavy in relation to its power
output to be satisfactory for propelling a plane through the sky. This is
why airports smell of aviation fuel rather than coal, and why planes don't
take off with steam billowing out of their engines. Still, you must admit
the idea of a flying steam horse is a lovely notion, especially from a girl
who in modern terms wasn't even a teenager.

What is especially inspiring and remarkable about Ada's thoughts about flying is, surely, that Ada didn't just fantasise about it but actually planned how she would do it, just as, about six years earlier, Charles didn't just dream of building a cogwheel machine that would allow mathematical tables to be calculated by the Method of Differences but set out specific plans for how it could be achieved.

Lady Byron, predictably enough (for someone who had actively sought Byron out and persuaded him to marry her, she was thoroughly hopeless at dealing with geniuses), didn't approve of Ada's flying plans. Perhaps she even feared that at some point her daughter might fly away – either literally or figuratively – to some remote, decadent place where maternal influence could not reach her. There is a letter from Ada to her mother which Ada wrote on Tuesday, 8 April 1828, which begins:

> My dearest Mammy. I received your letter this morning & really do not think that I often think of the wings when I ought to think of other things, but it was very kind of you to make the remark to me …
>
> I have now decided on making much smaller wings than I before intended and they will be perfectly well proportioned in every respect, exactly on the same plan and of the same shape as a bird. Though they will not be nearly enough to try and fly with, yet they will be quite enough so, to enable one to explain perfectly to anyone my project for flying, and will serve as a model for my future real wings.

There is a suddenly subdued note to this letter. Ada had obviously received a ticking-off from her mother, who believes she should be thinking of things other than the great art of flying, which humankind was to start to master within a century after Ada wrote this letter. Again, we see Ada's astonishing prescience. Gradually, under her mother's baleful influence, she abandoned her flying ambitions.

It wasn't the first time Ada and Lady Byron would disagree over the nature and direction of Ada's interests, and it certainly wouldn't be the last. Reading letters from mother to daughter and vice versa, one sees a definite love there which at any moment is likely to break out into antagonism and quarrels. While her mother's disapproval eventually quenched Ada's enthusiasm for flying, in the meantime she continued to devise ways to pursue her aviation ambitions. For example, on Wednesday, 9 April 1828 she wrote to her mother that she (Ada) had had 'great pleasure today in looking at the wing of a dead crow and I still think that I shall manage to fly and I have thought of three different ways of flying that all strike me as likely to answer'.

Not long afterwards, Lady Byron hired a tutor at £300 a year to teach Ada mathematics. This equates to around £30,000 today and was a substantial salary. Clearly Lady Byron thought her daughter merited such an expensive education, and she wrote to the tutor with careful instructions: 'Her greatest defect is want of order, which mathematics will remedy. She has taught herself part of Paisley's Geometry [presumably Batty Langley's *Practical Geometry* 1726, dedicated to Lord Paisley], which she liked particularly.'

Remarkably – or not – the estranged Lady and Lord Byron, despite existing in a state of mutual remote animosity, were in complete agreement that their daughter should not be allowed to give her fancy too much rein. When Byron had asked for a description of his daughter's character from Lady Byron via Augusta, just before his death, he had said: 'I hope the Gods have made her anything save poetical – it is enough to have one such fool in the family.'

Four years later, when Ada was a young woman of about 16, she had a brief love affair with one of her male tutors, possibly a teacher of shorthand, though neither his subject nor his name is known. The affair did not proceed to full intercourse, or 'connection', as Ada termed it when she related to one of her confidants what had happened. Lady Byron found out about the fling and instantly fired the tutor. She regarded Ada's lapse into independent emotional self-expression as confirmation that Ada must be kept well checked lest she in any way start to emulate her father.

This episode of Ada trying to assert her progression into adulthood through that most powerful and enjoyable of all means of self-assertion, sexuality, made Lady Byron more determined than ever to pursue her master plan as far as Ada's education was concerned. Lady Byron resolved that it was absolutely necessary to load Ada's brain with mathematics until all of what she regarded as Ada's petulance, wilfulness and tendency to become preoccupied by absurd notions, such as aviation, were squashed out of her.

8

THE SOLITARY WIDOWER

He had much industry at setting out,
Much boisterous courage; before loneliness
Had driven him crazed;
For meditations upon unknown thought
Make human intercourse grow less and less;

'All Souls Night', from *The Tower* (1928) by W.B. Yeats

Charles was utterly distraught at Georgiana's death, and especially by the nature of her passing: death in childbirth in this age before anaesthetics could be agonising and unspeakably dreadful. The devastated man felt he had no alternative but to accept his mother Betty's offer that the children come and live with her. Charles found living in London at Devonshire Place (the very word 'Devonshire' may have painfully reminded him of happier times), in the old familiar streets where he and Georgiana had made their married life, emotionally impossible, and his distress was so great that he contemplated suicide.

That this was so is provable by a letter which, to my knowledge, has never previously been published. He wrote it on 1 March 1829, about eighteen months after Georgiana's death, referring to his beloved wife's death making him want to consider suicide, which he describes in his letter as the 'long sleep'. He also reveals how much he relied on his mental activities to bring emotional solace, or, one could perhaps rather say, mental anaesthesia, following the terrible loss of his wife and their new child. We recall Charles noting that mental preoccupation could even cure him of a headache; the poor man now had to confront a far more serious problem than a headache and indeed his sole resource to try to cure it was mental diversions.

I have not been able to identify his correspondent here, Medley, nor even to ascertain the gentleman's Christian name. It is, however, clear from the context that Medley was a correspondent who had sent Charles some work from a third party for Charles' consideration:

My dear Medley

I have looked over the work you sent and from a very cursory ex n [examination] I should say it tends to neither excess. It is not original but can history be so? It is not profound but I should imagine its author might do several articles not of the highest class. With respect to furthering him or any other person in communication with me it is useless. I have suffered so severely in health that however much I desire to be active all my friends and more especially my medical ones urge me to lay aside my pursuits and to set my mind at rest or asleep. The alternative in case of refusal seems to be the *long sleep*.

Charles heavily underscored the words 'long sleep' in the letter. He continues:

The intense occupation which I have used as a remedy has had its effect. I have lived through two years and I may live two or twenty more but the medicine has produced a [illegible] and if I am to finish the machine I must cure the new complaint. I have therefore decided on giving up everything but that.

We can very reasonably conclude from this letter that Charles found his ambition to build his Difference Engine pretty much his sole consolation in his loneliness and misery. It isn't possible to know to what extent he found his other children also to be a consolation; no doubt to some extent he did, but not enough to feel that now Georgiana was dead, his own life was to some extent also over.

Edward Tenceley, a friend of Charles, wrote to him about seven weeks after Georgiana's passing to try and offer him some consolation:

Dulwich October xxviii 1827
My dear Babbage

Before I commence on the business part of your kind letter, let me say how sincerely glad I am, on your own account, that you have determined to travel …

Time – and time alone – is our certain Physician under mental suffering – as this advances your sorrow will lose its intensity and oppressiveness without any diminution (and who would wish there diminution) – of its sincerity and enduringness. I shall cordially rejoice to hear that you have embarked?

If writing is not annoying you let me hear how you are and when you go. I would come to you, but that I know my present helplessness must be troublesome and distressing.

Edward Tenceley

Evidently the most helpful friend of all to Charles at this time of terrible crisis was Herschel, who tried his best to give plenty of careful and sympathetic support and advice. Indeed, Herschel not only recommended to Charles that he travel in Europe but, in fact, offered to accompany him. However, for some reason that is not clear the two friends did not travel together this time. But Charles did go to stay with the Herschels at their home in Slough, where Herschel tried to reassure Betty Babbage that her son would soon start to feel better, but she found this impossible to believe. As she wrote to Herschel on 8 September 1827: 'You give me great comfort in respect of my son's bodily health. I cannot expect the mind's composure will make hasty advance. His love was too strong and the dear object of it too deserving.'

Before Georgiana died, she and Charles had been planning a visit to Ireland, although presumably this would only have happened after their baby was born and was at least some months old. Herschel and Charles now made a short trip there, visiting their friend Thomas Colby and also Trinity College, Dublin. Possibly the trip to Ireland had at least made Charles feel slightly less hopeless than he did before. At any rate, he decided that his only chance of recovering some kind of mental equilibrium – he seems for the moment to have abandoned any chance of personal happiness – was to take a long tour of Europe.

At first the grieving widower planned to travel alone, but his mother urged him to go with a friend or a servant. In the end, Charles decided to go with one of his workmen, Richard Wright, who was subsequently to rise to be one of his chief workmen. Presumably during the trip Wright became Charles' *de facto* servant.

Charles' eldest son, Benjamin Herschel, was by now staying with Charles' mother Betty during the school holidays. His daughter Georgiana stayed with Betty too, while the two younger boys, Dugald and Henry, went to live with their aunt and uncle, Harriet and Elias Isaac, at Boughton. Edward Stewart and Francis were unfortunately dead by now, they had both died very young. Herschel offered to supervise the work on the Difference Engine that was being done by Joseph Clement while Charles was away. It's not clear how much Herschel did or was able to do, but it would certainly have been a comfort to Charles that his closest friend was providing assistance during his time away.

Now is perhaps a good time to talk about the other Georgiana in Charles' life, his only daughter, who, as we've seen, was born on 17 July 1818. One of the most frustrating aspects of my research into Charles' life is that I have been unable to find out anything whatsoever about his daughter, other than when she was born and when she died. I wish there was a surviving portrait of her or even just one surviving letter, but there isn't, at least not to my knowledge. I've often wondered whether Georgiana might have ever met Ada Lovelace, who was only about two and a half years her senior, and there is no logical reason why they wouldn't have ever met. On the other hand, Ada wrote quite extensively about her life in her letters to her mother and to her friends, and none of the extant letters say anything about Ada having ever met Charles' daughter Georgiana.

Charles made many careful preparations for his foreign trip. He had decided to stay away for about a year, which may seem heartless for him to be away from his children, who had lost their mother, but they were being well looked after. It was usual in those days (and, indeed, into the twentieth century) for wealthy men who lost their wives – as many did, due to hazards of childbirth – to make an extensive trip abroad. Presumably Babbage thought such a length of time might give him a chance to get over the death of his wife to some extent, and he took with him many materials and artefacts which he thought he could show to the learned gentlemen he thought he would meet on his travels.

For example, he took with him parts of an instrument which could be used to pump someone's stomach (the stomach pump had been invented recently) or a syringe for drawing blood. He also took diffraction gratings. These ingenious optical devices split light up into its primary colours and make attractive gifts. In addition, he took a steel die and large and small gold buttons and other curiosities that interested him. Surely it says much about Charles that, lost in his deep, even overwhelming, grief as he was, he took meticulous care to take different devices with him to provide entertainment and interest to people he might meet on his tour of Europe.

Just before setting off, Charles paid a visit, accompanied by his son Benjamin, to the Thames tunnel which was being built by Brunel. During that visit Brunel only narrowly managed to staunch a flow of liquid mud. Soon afterwards the tunnel was flooded and six men were drowned, and Brunel himself only escaped with his life by swimming to safety.

Studying documentation about Charles' year abroad to try to cope with his desperate grief, it's hard to escape the conclusion that his travels *did* eventually blunt it a little, did give him back some sense of himself as a coherent human being who found the practical applications of science endlessly, and often mischievously, fascinating. He was a man with a purpose: to transform humankind's ability to make reliable calculations.

Charles' year abroad brought him into contact with eminent people throughout Europe. He crossed to the Low Countries and visited Louvain, where he met the university's rector. He also visited Liege and Maastricht, and then went to Aachen on the German border before moving on to Frankfurt and Munich. A Russian whom Charles met on the journey begged him to accompany him to Moscow, but Charles apologised and said he couldn't go there as he was keen to press on through Italy to Turkey and to the East.

In the Bavarian capital of Munich, the stomach pump which Charles had brought with him aroused interest and a Dr Weisbrod, the physician to the king of Bavaria, had an exact copy made by the chief surgical instrument maker. From Munich, Charles and Wright travelled through Innsbruck, Verona, and Padua to Venice.

In Venice, Charles toured the factories and visited one where the famous Venetian gold chains were made. He wanted to buy samples of a few inches of each type of chain but was told that they were only sold in longer lengths. He then produced one of his diffraction gratings, which allowed light to be refracted into its primary colours when a lamp was shone on to it in a darkened room. His hosts were extremely impressed by this and they decided to reward Charles by allowing him to purchase short pieces of all the types of gold chain he wanted to buy.

This is yet one more example of Charles using charm and ingenuity to get his own way, by no means an unpraiseworthy characteristic, of course. After he returned to London he measured the pieces of gold chain he'd bought and used them to produce data that illustrated the relative contributions of the cost of raw material and the amount of labour employed in making the commodities. He wrote this up in his book *The Economy of Machinery and Manufactures* (1832), which is the subject of the next chapter. Subsequently, he was interested to hear that the factory in Venice which he visited had taken up his idea and was selling short lengths of gold chain mounted on black velvet as souvenirs.

Charles had hoped to travel to the Far East from Venice, but he learned there that the route was closed. The decision by the Sultan of the Ottoman Empire to close the Dardanelles to Russian ships had sparked the Russo-Turkish War of 1828–29, and the Ottoman Empire was also at the time blocking land travel to the Far East via Constantinople (known today as Istanbul). Charles would presumably have planned to travel via Constantinople as it's difficult to believe that he would seriously have been planning to travel by sea; it would have been an extremely long and hazardous journey.

In any event, disappointed of his eastward travelling ambitions, Charles visited Parma, Reggio and then Bologna, where he spent several weeks at the university. He continued his journey through Florence, where he met the Grand Duke of Tuscany. By March 1828, about six months after Georgiana's death, he was in Rome for the first time.

In April or May, Charles and Richard Wright reached Naples. Charles was keen to see Vesuvius, a volcano whose notoriety in history is sufficiently known – especially to the erstwhile inhabitants of Pompeii and Herculaneum. Fortunately for Charles, Vesuvius wasn't spoiling the fun by doing anything as boring or uncooperative as being dormant; it was, rather, in a state of moderate activity. Charles took apartments that were close enough for him to watch the eruptions through a telescope while lying on his bed.

But seeing the eruptions through a telescope wasn't enough for Charles; he wanted to descend into the fearsome innards of the combusting mountain. Perhaps he wanted to experience a literal hell, as a way of taking further steps to forget the hell of Georgiana's dreadful death and his permanent separation from her this side of the grave. He wanted to descend into the crater itself and persuaded a guide to take him there – although this guide, having more sense than his eminent customer, prudently declined to enter the crater.

Assisted by a rope, Charles and an unnamed companion – it might have been Wright; this is not known for certain, though it's difficult to imagine anyone else descending into Vesuvius with Charles without being heavily bribed – did descend into the crater.

They must have climbed down slowly and used the rope as a security measure. Charles carried a heavy barometer strapped to his back so he could measure air pressure when he was down there. He then proceeded to make a tour and survey of the fiery crater. This was criss-crossed with fissures, which glowed red hot. The exploration must have taken quite a lot of nerve, as a sudden major eruption would have converted our hero to a mass of bloody Babbagean vapour. He even found a way of approaching on a projecting rock and looking into the sea of molten lava. He watched the lava bubbling slowly until his watch told him that a minor eruption was almost due, whereupon he and his travelling companion ascended from the imminent Hades and returned hastily to Naples. The thick boots he'd been wearing fell to pieces on his return, destroyed by the heat. Charles was lucky he wasn't.

When he'd cooled down, Charles travelled to Venice after visiting Florence and he also visited Graz, which was then the capital of Styria, now part of modern Austria. Next he proceeded to Vienna, where he designed his own carriage after having first been given a lesson in the art from the son of the Tsar of Russia's coach maker. In those days, if you were rich, rather like today, you mingled with all sorts of eminent and prominent people; the tour Charles made would have been completely beyond the means, or indeed imagination, of pretty much anyone living in Victorian London who was not as well off as he was.

Charles subsequently visited Berlin, where he met Alexander von Humboldt, who had been born in 1769 in the Prussia of Frederick the Great. Von Humboldt was one of the great liberal intellectuals of nineteenth-century Europe.

On 18 September 1828, a major congress opened in Berlin dedicated to the sciences. Charles attended this congress and was deeply impressed by it. It seemed to him then, and he never forgot this, that science was accorded far more respect in Europe than it ever was in Britain.

Charles left Berlin determined to take steps towards encouraging Britain to generate more enthusiasm for science. Yes, Britain was the cradle of the Industrial Revolution and was more advanced in terms of industrial technology than any country in Europe, but that didn't mean Britain had a deep respect for the more abstruse and abstract pursuit of science, which may or may not have immediately had beneficial practical consequences but which was the seedbed for the future evolution of technology.

Charles returned to England later in 1828, probably in the late autumn. Not even he would have wanted to trudge round an icebound snowy Europe: winters in Continental Europe in the early nineteenth century were usually extremely cold. His response to being in Berlin at the congress inspired him to write a polemical book, *Reflections on the Decline of Science in England* (1830), and he pioneered a scientific reform movement.

After his return from his tour of Europe, Charles also took an interest in politics, organising several election campaigns for Liberal candidates and later in his life stood twice for election to the newly reformed parliament, but he failed on both occasions to win a seat. It is difficult to imagine Charles being very happy or effective in the House of Commons and probably his failure to get there can only be described as a blessing for himself and British politics. He still pursued his interest in the Difference Engine, but gradually progress on the machine slowed, though the one-seventh demonstration piece was eventually completed. The problem was that Charles did not see how he could continue his work on the machine without further government money.

But that was in the future. In the meantime, Charles had to live somewhere. His mother Betty and sister-in-law Harriet looked after his children, though doubtless they visited him at his new home. He had decided to buy a house, 1 Dorset Street, near Manchester Square, London. Perhaps it wasn't just that Charles wanted a new home and a new life without memories of his family life with Georgiana in his house on Devonshire Street; perhaps, indeed, even the very word 'Devonshire' brought on an unbearable nostalgia for the time he had spent in that beautiful south-west of England with his beloved wife.

After returning from his tour of Europe, Charles – very likely because he wasn't just alone but lonely – started holding Saturday evening soirées at his house on Dorset Street. At first they were quiet affairs for friends and family, with his now elderly mother Betty, his eldest son Benjamin and his much-beloved daughter Georgiana – while almost nothing is known about her, what *is* known is that Babbage was absolutely devastated when she died – there to enjoy the company of eminent people Charles knew. The number of people he invited was initially small, but gradually the parties became famous, and invitations were much sought after and they became a major feature of the London season.

George Ticknor, an eminent man of letters from Boston, Massachusetts, who was in 1849 to publish a major and magisterial three-volume history of Spanish literature, describes a visit to one of Charles' parties on 26 May 1838:

About eleven o'clock we got away from Lord Fitzwilliam's and went to Mr Babbage's. It was very crowded tonight, and very brilliant; for among the people there were Hallam, Milman and his pretty wife; the Bishop of Norwich, Stanley, the Bishop of Hereford, Musgrave, both the Hellenists; Rogers, Sir J. Herschel and his beautiful wife,

Sedgwick, Mrs Somerville and her daughters, Senior, the Taylors, Sir F. Chantrey, Jane Porter, Lady Morgan, and I know not how many others. We seemed really to know as many people as we should in a party at home, which is a rare thing in a strange capital, and rarest of all in this vast overgrown London. Notwithstanding, therefore, our fatiguing day, we enjoyed it very much.

Ticknor's account is wonderfully energetic and, incidentally, a corrective to the idea that nineteenth-century people went to sleep at sundown. Poorer ones may often have done, but wealthier nineteenth-century people who could afford ample supplies of candles, chandeliers and oil lamps loved to stay up late having fun.

By the early 1830s, the completed one-seventh portion of the Difference Engine was a permanent fixture at Charles' home on Dorset Street. It was much admired by visitors to the soirées, although most likely very few of them knew what it was actually designed to do other than in very general terms. Charles used his base at Dorset Street to conduct what eventually became a busy and energetic London social and intellectual life, often using the services of the horse-drawn cabs that were to be found at a rank close by. Charles, at heart, remained alone in his soul, but he did his utmost to have a social life which meant he could, most of the time, avoid solitary dismal evenings with nothing but his attempts to build his cogwheel calculators, and memories of his now-distant life as a loving and loved husband to keep him company.

Today, you can visit the quiet, beautiful Dorset Street and readily gain a sense of the environment in which Charles lived in the 1830s, and indeed for the rest of his life. Dorset Street is about 200 yards from the bustling Marylebone High Street, but is itself not bustling. It's a beautiful and elegant eighteenth-century terrace which is in a kind of L-shape, with the site of Charles' home at the corner of the L and the long stave of the letter reaching down to Manchester Square.

However, Charles' home is the only one on the entire terrace that is no longer there. His house was demolished in the late 1930s for reasons I have not been able to ascertain. The house on the site now is modern and is in a very different design to the others. The street is relatively quiet, and as you stand there, looking at where Charles' house would have been, you can, if you listen hard, hear in your imagination the echoes of the busy life that he conducted in this charming and romantic corner of Dorset Street when he first came to live here almost two centuries ago.

Biographers have to avoid being sentimental or letting their imaginations too loose on their subject matter. But I do feel that there are three places on the planet where you will feel closest to Charles. One is in the manuscript room of the British Library, when you handle his papers and see the letters that friends and supplicants wrote to him. The second place is the Babbage exhibition at the Science Museum in London, where you can see the one-seventh portion of the Difference Engine and learn about Charles' life in science, and Ada's contribution to the thinking behind mechanical computation. And the third is here, by the site of his house on Dorset Street in London.

Apart from the astonishing 'long sleep' letter quoted earlier in this chapter, Charles is usually discreet about how Georgiana's death affected him. There is no doubt that he tried to anaesthetise himself to emotional pain and deep loneliness by focusing on his work, his social life and abstract (and indeed abstruse) thought. We can readily guess this from circumstantial evidence. However, in the Babbage Archive in the British Library, buried deep in one of the thick, dark-brown manuscript albums, each one of which contains about 500 folios, there is a highly revelatory letter. In it, Charles, writing to his friend the Irish physician and amateur geologist William Henry Fitton on 5 September 1852 – just over a quarter of a century after Georgiana's death – freely admits how the disaster of her loss compelled him to seek an 'intellectual taskmaster' that would let him to some extent forget his grief.

Fitton himself had sustained a major loss (I have not been able to ascertain what this was) and Charles wrote to console him. Charles' reference in this letter, incidentally, to the twenty-fifth anniversary of Georgiana's death *may* mean that he had forgotten the precise date of her death (1 September 1827). Perhaps he found it too painful to remember:

My dear Fitton

I have heard with much grief the severe calamity you have sustained a few days since. The anniversary of my own loss a quarter of a century ago recalled with more than usual force that never unforgotten event which changed the whole course of my existence.

I sought intense occupation as a recourse against the memory of the past and conjured up an intellectual taskmaster of which I am now the slave.

You are in some respects less unfortunate for you have pursuits which you can follow with moderation and you have daughters who will relieve you from the desolation of a solitary house.

God help you my dear Fitton.

Charles then goes on to the discuss scientific matters in the letter; it is the start of it, though, that most interests us here. Ultimately, of course, we can't really ever know what really went on in Charles' mind emotionally after Georgiana's death. We're all aware, from our own personal relationships, how difficult it is to feel that we truly 'know' someone we've known for years, and very possibly it is in fact impossible ever to know anybody completely anyway, even if we think what knowing somebody completely really means.

Did Charles ever contemplate soothing his loneliness by marrying again? That is indeed a perfectly reasonable question. The Charles of the photographs of the 1860s looks by no means very prepossessing, but let's remember that when his beloved Georgiana died, he had not yet had his thirty-sixth birthday. Charles, in his thirties and forties, was by no means unattractive. He had a high forehead, a thoughtful face and a slim figure. That he could be charming, if unpredictable, in company we've already seen. As for his habitual gruffness, sometimes coupled with a tendency towards irascibility, if these were due to loneliness, the love of a good woman might have cured him of both.

There was one inconclusive episode, a few years after Georgiana's death, which might have been a half-hearted attempt by the lonely widower to try to find a fresh marital solace. Charles had evidently asked a friend, the Reverend Francis Lunn, who lived in Somerset, to meet a clergyman's daughter in that county, whom Charles may have wanted to consider as a prospect for remarriage. Lunn did meet the lady, whose name is not recorded, and reported back to Charles that she didn't seem to be suitable, though he gave no reason.

This letter is undated, but the envelope in which it was sent also survives and the postmark is dated 8 September 1830:

Chez Fellowes
En passant

Dear Babbage

I think a short letter in haste will be more acceptable to you than a more studied one but delayed. Of property I could hear nothing.

I shall speak in plain English as to the other point in the matter between us.

Could it be shown that any of the family in line of blood was *jury* mad it might form a very unfortunate affair, but I could not hear that such was the case – mind my words are 'I could not hear of such a thing' – the parties were not known formerly but were spoken of as very clever and not handsome. – I should think you had better make more enquiries, for the more safely you proceed the more will you secure yourself from any future vexation.

Certainly nothing that I could learn seems a sufficient obstacle for you for you. Know our creed on the subject of talent and oddity is not that for all the world. – So goodbye but mind you do not fall in love – propose and then enquire particulars afterwards.

I found poor [illegible] dangerously ill. Tomorrow I go to Hatleigh where I hope to hear from you.

Ever yours most sincerely
F. Lunn

Mind you are booked for Zummerzet after Malvern

The phrase 'jury mad' is presumably a reference to someone being found to be mad by a court deciding on such matters; people could indeed be certified insane by a court in those days – relatives often had a financial interest in this happening, as insane persons could not, as we've seen, inherit.

Lunn's letter is rather creepy, despite its comic postscript. 'Zummerzet' is a deliberately jovial misspelling of Somerset, and might refer to Lunn anticipating a visit from Charles. Country yokels in Britain, especially those from counties in the West of England, such as Somerset, are often portrayed as pronouncing an 's' as a 'z', and this idea has a long tradition, going back at least as far as Edgar pretending to be rustic in Shakespeare's *King Lear.*

The whole Lunn episode does indeed have a half-hearted feel to it, and there never seems to have been any prospect of an engagement ring resulting from it. The letter doesn't even make clear to what extent Charles wanted Lunn to make his enquiries.

It is impossible to know whether Charles saw his machines as his great consolation after the tragic death of his wife, or as a demanding distraction that took energy from him that he might otherwise have devoted to a new marriage and married happiness.

Very possibly the truth is that both of these were true in different moods. In the 'long sleep' letter already quoted, Charles made clear that after Georgiana's death his work was his great consolation when he wrote, 'the intense occupation which I have used as a remedy has had its effect'. He also apparently said – I put this in its context later in this book – 'Fond as I am of domestic life, I should have married again if it had not been for my machine.' The latter remark is, in fact, as I shall show, only hearsay evidence rather than the direct evidence of a letter, but all the same, the hearsay remark does sound like something Charles, in a different mood, might have said.

Charles, meanwhile, was lovelorn and professionally unsuccessful too. So to console himself further, early in 1832 he wrote a remarkable and wonderful book.

9

ON THE ECONOMY OF MACHINERY AND MANUFACTURES

'To invent, you need a good imagination and a pile of junk.'
                                        Thomas Edison (attributed)

As Charles' friend Charles Dickens writes near the start of Chapter Five of his novel *Hard Times* (1854), 'Let us strike the key-note […] before pursuing our tune.'

Charles was a great but comprehensively misunderstood genius. He was also a grieving widower whose wife Georgiana, the love of his life, had died five years earlier in 1827, the same year that he also lost his beloved little son Charles. Since then, apart from a year travelling in Europe, the widower toiled under stressful and difficult conditions to work with talented (but not especially sympathetic) engineers, in particular Joseph Clement, to try to build a Difference Engine. One-seventh of the machine had been built in 1832, but the work then stalled.

One of the signs of geniuses, surely, is that they continue to produce great work no matter what adversity confronts them. This is certainly true of Charles. His book *On the Economy of Machinery and Manufactures* (1832) is a largely forgotten gem, a masterpiece even, that absolutely deserves to be reprinted in an illustrated user-friendly version. It is available on the Internet on a print-on-demand basis, but that edition, the one on which I'm basing this chapter, has very small type and cries out to feature some period illustrations that add to the energy, fascination and clarity of Charles' expositions. There are fortunately several gratis electronic versions of the book available online.

Charles had a wonderfully eclectic mind and this is shown to great advantage in *On the Economy of Machinery and Manufactures*, a book it is almost impossible not to enjoy. It is written in a racy, inspired, consistently interesting and frequently deeply engrossing style. It's replete – that's the right word – with beautifully expressed accounts of the machinery and industry of Europe at this thrilling time of technological history, before the birth of hi-tech but when wonderful ingenuity was being applied to engineer machinery and ingenious manufacturing processes.

It's all very well for Dickens, two decades later, to lambast the social and human consequences of the 'hard fact' manufacturing world, and yes, at one level they needed lambasting, but the ingenuity that went into creating those processes is surely unarguable: it was, however, unfortunate that, in that pre-hi-tech epoch, the only way those processes could be made profitable was if millions of people were set to work doing boring, monotonous and poorly paid labour in carrying them out.

Charles' book is so absorbing and so packed with interesting information that really any attempt to summarise it, as in this chapter, cannot possibly do it justice; on the other hand, a summary is better than nothing. The book is one of the great scientific works of the nineteenth century and, as in so much of his work, Charles' brilliant analysis is well ahead of its time.

Charles had by now in his life travelled widely and had extensive personal experience of watching many of the industrial processes which he chronicles in the book. Moreover, there is a clear link between *On the Economy of Machinery and Manufacturing* and Charles' attempts to build at least one machine of the mind, for, as he explains in the very first paragraph of the preface:

> The present volume may be considered as one of the consequences that have resulted from the calculating engine, the construction of which I have been so long superintending. Having been induced, during the last ten years, to visit a considerable number of workshops and factories, both in England and on the Continent, for the

purpose of endeavouring to make myself acquainted with the various resources of mechanical art, I was insensibly led to apply to them those principles of generalization to which my other pursuits had naturally given rise.

Charles, like many geniuses, is often at his most revealing of himself in his throwaway remarks, and when I say throwaway, I'm not only referring to his boots post-Vesuvius. On the same first page of that same preface, we find:

> Those who possess rank in a manufacturing country, can scarcely be excused if they are entirely ignorant of principles, whose development has produced its greatness. The possessors of wealth can scarcely be indifferent to processes which, nearly or remotely have been the fertile source of their possessions. Those who enjoy leisure can scarcely find a more interesting and instructive pursuit than the examination of the workshops of their own country, which contain within them a rich mine of knowledge, too generally neglected by the wealthier classes.

The point here is that at the time Charles was writing, it certainly *wasn't* the case that most wealthy people were deeply interested in factories and industrial processes, not unless they were ironmasters, anyway. In fact, the landed gentry would in general have been about as eager to visit a factory as they would have been to descend into the crater of Vesuvius. In Charles' great book, he shows an enthusiasm for industrial and practical scientific processes that are in a curious way reminiscent of a schoolboy, yet expressed and analysed with the mind of a man.

He has an enormous gift for writing in an entertaining and engaging way about technical matters, rather as Sir David Attenborough today has an enormous gift for writing attractively and engagingly about animals. That's not an inappropriate comparison, either, for it's clear from *On the Economy of Machinery and Manufactures* that Charles saw machinery as a kind of living entity, something utterly remarkable which humans use to make their life on the planet easier and, more subtly, to show their dominance of the fundamentally hostile world in which they find themselves. There really is no substitute for reading this book; it's not very long, the print-to-order edition I'm using here is only 136 pages in length and Charles conveniently, though slightly nerdishly, numbers the individual topics up to number 467.

A little later in the preface he explains, with typical Babbagean desire for transparency and an intent concern for the reader: 'It has been my endeavour, as much as possible, to avoid all technical terms, and to describe, in concise language, the arts I have had occasion to discuss.' He achieves this vital aim in *On the Economy of Machinery and Manufacturing,* even if he does not achieve it in all his writing.

Considering that Charles was by now in his life well known both as the inventor of the Difference Engine and also as something of an eccentric who would provide entertainment arising substantially from the obscure way in which he routinely saw otherwise familiar things, it is commendable in this book how clear and articulate his language is. In Chapter One, summarising his admiration of British inventiveness – the book is by no means a hymn to British ingenuity, covering as it does inventions from several European countries, although he does praise the British particularly – Charles says:

> There exists, perhaps, no single circumstance which distinguishes our country more remarkably from all others, than the vast extent and perfection to which we have carried the contrivance of tools and machines performing those conveniences at which so large a quantity is consumed by almost every class of the community.
>
> The amount of patient thought, and repeated experiment, and happy exertion of genius, are which our manufactures look around the rooms we inhabit, or through those storehouses of every convenience, of every luxury that man can desire, which deck the crowded streets of our larger cities, we shall find in the history of each article, of every fabric, a series of failures which have led the way to excellence; and we shall notice, in the art of making even the most insignificant of them, processes calculated to excite our admiration by their simplicity, or to rivet out attention by their unlooked for results.

Another indication of genius, surely, is a deep and effectively automatic knack for generating defamiliarisation: that is, an ability to see and present, in what to most people seems ordinary, the innate wonder of an otherwise familiar process or activity. What Charles is saying here applies not just to Britain but to pretty much any country in the world that has displayed particular inventiveness.

His words also apply very fundamentally to our species; the reason why we are no longer hiding in caves against the predations of leopards and scavenging the leftovers of large predators is because our brains have enabled us to create a world beyond the imagination of anyone, except perhaps God.

Charles is alive to this, and when one reads this remarkable book from the perspective of the twenty-first century, one is forced continually to remind oneself that Charles is writing about a period from the past, whose technology, compared with our own age, is pretty much rudimentary.

All this said, we should never make the mistake of condescending towards the technology of the past, because it is in itself remarkable and, in fact, by the 1830s the science of heavy machinery and of using coal and steel to produce motive force and energy was far advanced. One of the major technological resources Charles' age was missing compared with ours was, of course, information technology, and as we've seen, Charles was trying to do something about that.

While the numbered paragraph technique Charles uses is clearly designed to give a sense of order to his book, in fact he tends to adopt a fairly eclectic approach to his subject matter and to discuss such inventions and manufacturing processes that occur to him even if there is not a great deal of connection between other paragraphs in the vicinity.

What is especially loveable about Charles' book is the sophisticated yet often schoolboyish gusto with which Charles looks at inventions. Here, for example, is an account of a technology that has long been superseded by telecommunications – speaking tubes – which are still occasionally used in ships but otherwise are obsolete:

> The simple contrivance of tin tubes speaking through, communicating between different departments, by which the directions of the superintendent are instantly conveyed to the remotest parts of

an establishment, produces a considerable economy of time. It is employed in the shops and manufactors in London, and might with advantage be used in domestic establishments, particularly in large houses, in conveying orders from the nursery to the kitchen, or from the house to the stables.

Its convenience arises not merely from saving the servant or workman useless journeys to receive directions, but from relieving the master himself from that indisposition to give trouble, which frequently induces him to forgo a trifling want, when he knows that his attendant must mount several flights of stairs to ascertain his wishes, and, after descending, must mount again to supply him. The distance to which such a mode of communication can be extended, does not appear to have been ascertained, and would be an interesting subject for enquiry. Admitting it to be possible between London and Liverpool, about seventeen minutes would elapse before the words spoken at one end would reach the other extremity of the pipe.

This is a classic Babbagean paragraph, starting with reality and then fantasising about how that reality might be extended into fantasy. In fact, as Charles would surely have known, a London-to-Liverpool speaking tube would never have worked, as the sound would have been dissipated against the walls of the tube. In practice, speaking tubes only work for up to about 300 feet.

But Charles clearly *wanted* to be able to speak to someone in Liverpool (or anywhere else far afield) when he was in London. The technology to do just that would become available, but not just yet; the telephone was first invented by Alexander Graham Bell in 1876, five years after Charles died. It's a great shame he never lived to see the invention; he'd have surely loved to have made a telephone call.

Charles was also always fascinated by the uses to which materials could be put. He especially enjoyed obscure uses of materials that on the face of it might be regarded as pretty much worthless and useless. For example, in paragraph nine of *On the Economy of Machinery and Manufactures*, he notes:

The skins used by the goldbeater are produced from the offal of animals. The hoofs of horses and cattle, and other horny refuse, are employed in the production of the prussiate of potash, that beautiful, yellow, crystallised salt, which is exhibited in the shops of some of our chemists.

The worn-out saucepans of our kitchens, when beyond the reach of the tinker's art, are not utterly worthless. We sometimes meet carts loaded with old tin kettles and worn-out iron coal-skuttles [*sic*] traversing our streets. These have not yet completed their useful course; the less eroded parts are cut into strips, punched with small holes, and varnished with a coarse black varnish for the use of the trunk-maker, who protects the edges and angles of his boxes with them; the remainder are conveyed to the manufacturing chemists in the outskirts of the town, who employ them in combination with pyroligneous acid, in making a black dye for the use of calico printers.

Generally, *On the Economy of Machinery and Manufactures* is rather a personal work, and indeed many parts of it read rather like a fairly informal letter which Charles has written to a friend whom he knows to be interested in industrial processes. Sometimes Charles states what are on the face of it obvious points with a degree of interesting analysis that makes one reflect on the process or activity involved, and admire not only how he expressed it but also the ingenuity and remarkableness of human beings. The following paragraph is particularly relevant today, with the worldwide concern about the level of carbon dioxide in the atmosphere:

17. The force of vapour is another fertile source of moving power; but even in this case it cannot be maintained that power is created. Water is converted into elastic vapour by the combustion of a fuel.

The chemical changes which thus take place are constantly increasing the atmosphere by large quantities of carbolic acid [this was how Charles described carbon dioxide] and other bases noxious to animal life. The means by which nature decomposes these elements, or reconverts them into a solid form, are not sufficiently known: but if the end could be accomplished by mechanical force, it is almost certain that the power necessary to produce it would at least equal that which was generated by the original combustion.

Man, therefore, does not create power; but, availing himself of his knowledge nature's mysteries, he applies his talent to diverting a small and limited portion of her energy to his own wants: and whether he employs his regulated action of steam, or the more rapid and tremendous effects of gunpowder, he is only producing on a small scale compositioned and decompositioned which nature is incessantly at work in reversing, for the restoration of that equilibrium which we cannot doubt is constantly maintained throughout even the remotest limits of our system. The operations of man participate in the character of their author; they are diminutive, but energetic during the short period of their existence: whilst those of nature, acting over vast spaces, and unlimited by time, are ever pursuing their silent resistless career.

That's an especially lovely paragraph, particularly with its reference to God (i.e. 'their author') and his hinting at his belief that the laws of nature found on Earth apply throughout the universe, even though of course in Charles' day, knowledge of the universe was considerably less than it is today. It's part of Charles' genius to be able to speculate about relatively ordinary things and remarkable and profound things in the same sentence.

In paragraphs 241 to 251, Charles gives a detailed appreciation of logarithmic tables that were, as we've noted, the inspiration for him to design his Difference Engine, which was designed to print mathematical tables accurately by using the method of differences.

Charles offers particular attention to how the work undertaken by de Prony was broken down among teams of people with different specialisations, including the first section who investigated 'amongst the various analytical expressions which could be found for the same function, that which was most readily adapted to simple numerical calculation by many individuals employed at the same time', and then the second section. As he says:

This section consisted of seven or eight persons of considerable acquaintance with mathematics: and their duty was to convert into numbers the formulae put into their hands by the first section, an operation of great labour; and then to deliver out these formulae to the members of the third section, and receive from them the finished calculations.

As for the third section, Charles notes that 'the members of this section, whose number varied from sixty to eighty, received certain numbers from the second section, and, using nothing more than simple addition and subtraction, they returned to that section the tables in a finished state'. He continues: 'It is remarkable that nine-tenths of this class had no knowledge of arithmetic beyond the two first rules which they were thus called upon to exercise, and that these persons were usually found more correct in their calculations, than those who possessed the more extensive knowledge of the subject.'

Charles loved analysing processes and activities into their constituent elements: he clearly writes with great relish of these three orders of mental workers in de Prony's undertaking. It is a fair point about him that he preferred analysing systems that were capable of being analysed by being broken down into their constituent elements over systems which didn't yield to analysis in this way. Modern science frequently considers processes – an obvious example is the living human body – which by definition cannot be dissected and analysed without being destroyed.

This is perhaps a flaw not only in Charles' scientific thinking but in his emotional life too. After Georgiana's death he seemed to view emotional matters with a certain amount of forensic analysis, as if to protect himself against getting hurt or to prevent his grief over his beloved wife's death from rising to the surface of his soul, by believing that feelings could be analysed in this particular way. This may explain many things about Charles, and in particular why he found it difficult, if not close to impossible, to form intimate relationships after Georgiana died. This aspect of his personality was something which Ada spotted and commented on, as we shall see.

To take another example, Charles marvelled at the slide of Alpnach, which was was an enormous wooden slide, 9 miles long, built in Switzerland to enable timber to be cut down at or close to the mountaintop and be sent to the foot of the mountain easily. Charles does not mention the number of pine trees used to construct the slide; it was between 25,000 and 30,000, and the harvested trees that were plunged on to it descended into the lake at the foot of the mountain in about six minutes, although larger trees reportedly sped down in half that time. Watching the slide in action must have been great fun, a sort of arboreal Olympic downhill ski race. As Charles writes:

> Amongst the forests which flank many of the lofty mountains of Switzerland, some of the finest timber is found in positions almost inaccessible. The expense of roads, even if it were possible to make them in such situations, would prevent the inhabitants from deriving any advantages from these almost inexhaustible supplies. Placed by nature at a considerable elevation above the spot at which they can be made use of, they are precisely in fit circumstance for the application of machinery to their removal; and the inhabitants avail themselves of the force of gravity to relieve them from some portion of this labor. The inclined plains which they have established in various forests, by which the timber has been sent down to the water courses, have excited the admiration of every traveller.

In many ways the *leitmotif* both of *On the Economy of Machinery and Manufactures* and this book is a sentence which starts Chapter Eight, paragraph 329: 'The first object of machinery, the chief cause of its extensive utility, is the perfection and the cheap production of the articles which it is intended to make.' A fairly obvious observation, perhaps, but one that is usefully made here and which brings an immediate insight into Charles' lifelong effort to build a cogwheel brain. He knew that the effort of making them would be easily requited by the endless amount of utility they would afford. As he observes:

> Whenever it is required to produce a great multitude of things, all of exactly the same kind, the proper time has arrived for the construction of tools or machines by which they may be manufactured. If only a few pairs of cotton stockings should be required, it would be an absurd waste of time, and of capital, to construct a stocking-frame to weave them, when, for a few pence, four steel wires could be procured by which they may be knit. If, on

the other hand, many thousand pairs were wanted, time employed, and the expense incurred in constructing a stocking-frame, would be more than repaid by the saving of time in making that large number of stockings.

Charles, of course, wasn't in the business of making stockings (though clearly this business interested him) but in the business of enacting calculations. No one could possibly doubt his enthusiasm and commitment (even given that a tendency to being an occasional dilettante was indeed part of his nature) but, in 1832, eleven years since he'd had his epiphany and conceived a desire to build a calculator that would calculate by using steam, he was clearly no significantly closer to achieving his goal.

Charles wrote numerous books and articles in his life; Anthony Hyman's biography of him contains a comprehensive bibliography of his works in an appendix. It's reasonable to say that *On the Economy of Machinery and Manufactures* is the book of Charles' that speaks most eloquently and grippingly to the modern reader. So now, with that book having been published, Charles just keeps on working at his Difference Engine. Already the idea for another, even more remarkable, cogwheel calculating machine was forming in the recesses of his mind.

What he needed now was an ally. Fortunately for him, fate was, at least in this respect, on his side.

10

CHARLES AND ADA MEET

Is thy face like thy mother's, my fair child!
ADA! sole daughter of my house and heart?
When last I saw thy young blue eyes they smiled,
And then we parted, – not as now we part,
But with a hope. –
Awaking with a start,
The waters heave around me; and on high
The winds lift up their voices: I depart,
Whither I know not; but the hour's gone by,
When Albion's lessening shores could grieve or glad mine eye.

From 'Childe Harolde's Pilgrimage', Canto III,
stanza 1, Lord Byron, 1816

Charles loved his social life. It allowed him to forget how lonely he was, and he genuinely enjoyed meeting new people and attempting to charm them with his hit-or-miss puns and his eclectic conversation. He was certainly popular with hostesses and hosts, who liked to be able to tell their friends that 'Mr Babbage is coming to dinner'. Generally, one gets the impression that while Charles liked to throw himself into his social life with his customary gusto, he was never completely at home with social life and often took part in it to cheer himself up.

On Wednesday evening, 5 June 1833, Charles and Ada Byron met. It was a meeting that changed both their lives forever.

We only know about Charles' very first meeting with Ada, who in due course became Ada Lovelace, because of a letter which her mother, Lady Byron, wrote to a Dr William King on Friday, 7 June 1833, two days later. Charles himself did not write anything about the meeting, at least not unless it has not yet been unearthed after meticulous investigation by Babbage scholars. Dr King, who was born in 1786 and was one of Lady Byron's closest friends, was a British physician, philanthropist, lunatic asylum manager and devout evangelical Christian (the two professions often went hand in hand in the nineteenth century).

Lady Byron said this when she wrote to King:

Ada was more pleased with the party she was at on Wednesday than with any of the assemblage in the *grand monde*. She met there a few scientific people – amongst them Babbage with whom she was delighted. I think her power of enjoying such society is in a great measure owing to your kindness in conversing with and reading with her on philosophical subjects.

As Lady Byron also wrote: 'Babbage was full of animation and talked of his wonderful machine (which he is to shew [show] us) as a child does of its plaything.'

Unfortunately, it isn't known at whose party Charles and Ada met, nor indeed where the party was, except that it was in London. Even less do we know anything specific about what Charles and Ada talked about when they met, except for Lady Byron's remarks to Dr King that he talked about his machine. This must have been the Difference Engine, because the Analytical Engine, while undoubtedly at this point an idea in Charles' mind, was not yet realised even in any sketchy notes or plans.

But even if we don't know specifically what Ada and Charles talked about when they met, it's not hard to imagine Charles going into a voluble soliloquy about his Difference Engine and some of the problems he had with getting it built, and telling Ada that he had at least finished a one-seventh portion of it. As for what Ada said to him, knowing that would be no less wonderful than knowing what he said to her. Her wonder and excitement about science must surely have manifested itself in the questions she asked him.

We do know that, as we've seen, she was delighted to have met Charles and from that moment on their friendship – which would, to put it mildly, have its shared ups and downs – lasted until the end of Ada's life, which, tragically, only had another nineteen years and a few months to run, even though when she met Charles she was only 17, twenty-four years younger than him. They were, incidentally, both December babies – Ada was born on the 10th and Charles on the 26th – which is why we need to be careful not to overstate their age at any moment in their life; they may well not have had their birthday for that year yet.

Whatever the precise details of the conversation between Charles and Ada when they met, they certainly got on well enough for him to invite her and her mother, either there and then at the party or by some subsequent letter that has now been lost, to visit him at his home at 1 Dorset Street, on Monday, 17 June 1833, only twelve days after they first met. Charles was excited to have the opportunity to show Lord Byron's relict and only legitimate daughter the completed one-seventh portion of the Difference Engine.

Again, while we don't know much about the actual meeting on 17 June, we do have some details from a letter which Lady Byron wrote, again to King, four days after the visit. As she explained: 'We both went to see the thinking machine (for such it seems) last Monday. It raised several Nos. to the 2nd and three powers, and extracted the root of a quadratic equation. I had but faint glimpses of the principles by which it worked.'

The beautifully synchronised cogwheels of the demonstration piece of the machine captivated Ada and captured her imagination. Seeing the cogwheels operating convinced her that this astonishing device, incomplete as it was, brought mathematics to life in an exciting, elegant and – as far as Ada's imagination was concerned – revolutionary way.

Doron Swade, who headed the modern project to build Babbage's Difference Engine No. 2. (Sarah Sceats)

Charles Babbage's Difference Engine No. 2, designed 1847–49, completed 2002. It consists of 8,000 parts and weighs 5 tonnes. (Doron Swade)

Charles Babbage Esqr Lucasian Professor of Mathematicks, Cambridge, by John Linnell (1792–1882). (Llyfrgell Genedlaethol Cymru – The National Library of Wales)

Charles Babbage as an old man. (Public domain)

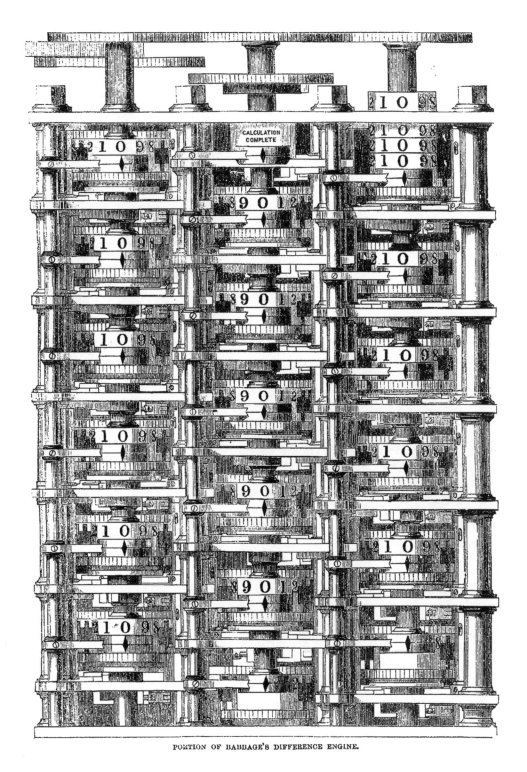

CALCULATION
COMPLETE

PORTION OF BABBAGE'S DIFFERENCE ENGINE.

A woodcut print of a portion of Babbage's Difference Engine No. 1 (1832). (*Harper's New Monthly Magazine*, Vol. 30, Issue 175/Harvard University)

Ada Lovelace in 1835. (Carl H.
Pforzheimer Collection/New York
Public Library)

Ada Lovelace. (© Crown copyright: UK
Government Art Collection)

Lord Byron. (Library of Congress)

Benjamin Babbage, Charles Babbage's imperious father, who caused his son and daughter-in-law such distress but left his son a wealthy man. He seems to be smiling slightly here – perhaps he was thinking about his own money. (Totnes Museum)

Modern Totnes, looking down the steep High Street, with the East Gate Arch in the middle of the photograph. The Babbages would have been very familiar with the East Gate Arch, which was once the medieval gateway to the town. The current East Gate Arch has been faithfully reconstructed following a fire in 1990. Downhill beyond the arch, the High Street becomes Fore Street. (Kate Jewell)

Charles Dickens. (Library of Congress)

The Jacquard loom. (Wellcome Collection)

Joseph Marie Jacquard. (Metropolitan Museum of Art)

Trinity College, Cambridge, with the Great Gate and Great Court in the foreground and Nevile's Court and Wren Library in the background. (Cantabrigia Illustrata, Cambridge, 1690)

11

THE REMARKABLE ADA BYRON

Let the mad poets say whate'er they please
Of the sweets of Fairies, Peris, Goddesses,
There is not such a treat among them all,
Haunters of cavern, lake, and waterfall,
As a real woman …

From 'Lamia', John Keats (1819)

Between Monday, 17 June 1833, when Charles showed Ada and Lady Byron the portion of the Difference Engine he'd managed to complete, and another Monday, about eighteen months later, 19 December 1834, there is little documentary evidence of any contact between Charles and his new friend Ada Byron, but it is clear from at least one letter that they did meet socially in that period, and probably frequently.

The relative lack of evidence forces us to use conjecture regarding how their friendship developed, yet we should not be afraid of concluding that Charles and Ada probably did meet quite often, because when two people are fond of each other and are not constrained by geographical distance or finance – and Charles and Ada weren't – they tend to do so. However, as Ada only had her eighteenth birthday on 10 December 1833, it is difficult to believe that Charles would have met her, at least in these early days, without Lady Byron accompanying them.

Did Charles ever think of Ada as a potential wife to himself, a lonely widower? Very likely he did. His wife Georgiana had died, after all, almost six years before Charles and Ada met, and Charles had to some extent recovered his spirits. Moreover, all of us are likely to run through a gamut of emotional moods in one day, or indeed in one hour. Very likely there *were* times when Charles felt deeply emotionally loyal to Georgiana and absolutely opposed to any notion of remarrying. But surely he had moods when he felt completely differently. And besides, how we feel about the notion of falling in love tends to be intimately linked (in every way) with whom we meet.

The simple truth is that we don't know for certain what Charles felt about the idea of Ada as a prospective new wife. Ada was fascinated by Charles, by his one-seventh portion of the Difference Engine and by his ideas. There's no unequivocal evidence, from the very beginning of their friendship, that Ada had any definite romantic interest in Charles, although, as we shall see, there many hints of this sprinkled through their acquaintanceship. For a rich man of 41 to marry a charming young woman of 17, who herself came from what was now a wealthy family – Lady Byron had inherited substantial sums of money since her impoverished days with Byron and was now one of the wealthiest landowners in Britain – was far from uncommon in the nineteenth century and is hardly unknown today.

What is unquestionable is that the friendship Charles Babbage and Ada Lovelace enjoyed is one of the most interesting, passionate collaborations in the history of science. It is possible to trace the friendship in considerable detail by means of the extant correspondence between them; it covers the years from 10 June 1835 to 12 August 1852, which was when Ada wrote her last (known) letter to Charles.

The surviving correspondence between them consists of eighty-five letters from Ada to Charles and twenty-five letters from him to her. There are often references in the correspondence to other letters that have apparently not survived.

In 1853, Charles wrote a letter to Lady Byron's solicitor in which he referred to an 'extensive correspondence' he had carried on with Ada 'for years'. He is surely referring to a larger correspondence than what survives. Indeed, in 2000, a small cache of letters from Ada to Charles turned up in the storeroom of the Northumberland County Archive in the north of England, and it is possible that more may yet materialise.

Most of the letters that do survive date from 1843, the year Ada was at her most productive as a scientist.

It is known that after Ada's death in November 1852, her mother Lady Byron arranged for most of the letters in her deceased daughter's collection to be burnt by servants in a bonfire. This terrible conflagration immolated hundreds of letters that would today be priceless artefacts, doubtless including many from Charles.

It is also known that there is at least one letter from him to her which has not survived, as it is referred to in a surviving letter. Yet common sense tells us that as Charles and Ada knew each other for nineteen years from their meeting on that fateful 5 June 1833 to her death on 27 November 1852, and as Charles loved writing letters, there are very likely many that haven't survived.

This said – and this is an important corrective – Charles was in the habit of handwriting copies of letters he regarded as important, so several of his letters to Ada survive not only in her collection but also as copies in his own. This doesn't, of course, mean that we can be certain he made copies of every letter he sent to Ada, and in fact he didn't, but it may mean that the number of letters from Charles to Ada that didn't survive are more likely to rank in the dozens than in the hundreds.

So why did *any* of Charles' letters to Ada survive the bonfire? Ultimately, it is impossible to know. Some may simply have been overlooked by the servants carrying out their mistress's iron will, or perhaps the servants were not as thorough as they might have been. My own theory, however, is that Lady Byron caused to be spared from the flames certain letters from Charles to her daughter that were especially revealing of Charles' high opinion of Ada's talents, or of the closeness of their friendship.

Lady Byron never warmed to Charles; she found his fondness for puns annoying and disliked his tendency towards pomposity. But when all is said and done, by the time Ada passed away, Charles was one of the most eminent men of science in Britain. Lady Byron, being an aristocrat (by marriage) and something of a snob (by nature) would hardly have been impervious to Charles' high opinion of her daughter.

It may have been that even Lady Byron could not bring herself to destroy those letters from Charles to Ada that she, Lady Byron, regarded as especially important. The fact that by far the greater part of the surviving letters from Charles to Ada were written in 1843, when Charles and Ada worked most closely together, surely lends support to this otherwise unprovable theory. Lady Byron would have known, of course, about how intently her daughter and Charles worked together that year, and was perhaps reluctant to discard his letters to Ada from that period. But again, this is conjecture, and the truth of the matter will probably never been known.

As for Ada's letters to Charles, many of those may not have survived due to the general fragility of physical letters to time. It is difficult to believe that Charles would ever have deliberately destroyed any letter Ada wrote to him, and we have him to thank for the survival of the longest and unquestionably the most important letter she ever wrote to him, of which more anon.

Whatever else is unclear, Ada was greatly impressed by Charles. She regarded him with what she once described in a letter to her mother as a 'fondness ... by no means inconsiderable'. Ada and her mother kept in contact with Charles and it seems certain Ada saw him on several other occasions as her mother's search for a suitable husband continued.

In the summer of 1834, Ada and Lady Byron embarked on their tour of the industrial north of England, visiting many factories and seeing with their own eyes the immense potential of machinery. They saw a Jacquard loom in action, and Lady Byron even drew a picture of a punched card used to control the loom's operation.

In the spring of that same year, Ada and Lady Byron's friendship with the wonderfully talented mathematician Mary Somerville had begun to blossom. It was an exciting friendship for Ada, because by now Mary Somerville was one of the best-known mathematicians in Britain, unlike the well-meaning Dr King whom she prodded for a proper study programme in mathematics. Somerville College at Oxford University (which was originally known as Somerville Hall when it was founded in 1879) was named after Mary Somerville.

On Thursday, 19 March 1834, Ada wrote a brief letter to Mary saying that she hoped to meet her on Saturday evening at 'Mr Babbage's'. This appears to be a reference to Charles' Saturday evening soirées, which had started in the 1820s for his family but by the 1830s had become events for other guests. As we shall see, the soirées had their heyday in the 1840s but evidently they were already an important part of Charles' social life at this stage.

Ada having turned 19 on 10 December 1834, Lady Byron was determined that the time had come for her daughter to find a husband. It appears that Charles hovered on the radar in this respect, and Ada may even have discussed the possibility with Lady Byron.

If Charles ever thought that Ada might have made an excellent new wife, that would hardly have been surprising. In fact, immediately after Ada married someone else, Lady Byron wrote to her to ask 'has Babbage cut you since your marriage?' By the time she finally dumped Byron, Lady Byron had become pretty acute when it came to understanding male motivation, and so very possibly it's true that Charles had entertained some warm marital hopes in connection with Ada. But if he had, there is also no doubt that Lady Byron quenched them. She didn't much like Charles, and certainly didn't want him as a son-in-law; and besides, she was determined that Ada would marry an aristocrat, which Charles wasn't.

What Lady Byron didn't, and indeed couldn't, quench was the strong and genuinely affectionate, even romantic, friendship that developed between Charles and Ada into a close friendship. What is certain is that the catalyst for the later development of the friendship was not, in fact, the Difference Engine at all, but a completely new machine of the mind, which Charles began working on concertedly in 1834, though it had most likely been gradually growing in significance in his thinking for several years before it emerged into the foreground.

Up until that year, 1834, the machine was the most ingenious device that had been invented since the dawn of humanity, and indeed it would remain so for the remainder of the nineteenth century and some years into the twentieth. Even today, in our science fiction modern world, the machine astounds the reason as much as the imagination.

He called this new machine the Analytical Engine.

12

A FRESH TRAGEDY;
THE ANALYTICAL ENGINE;
AND ADA'S MARRIAGE

BABBAGE
What an amazing idea, a computer!
A machine that's mechanically cuter
Than any device I intended.
I didn't know what I'd invented!

ADA
Sometimes we don't know what we're doing
When some cunning invention we're stewing,
We think we're just being evolutionary
When in fact we're totally revolutionary.

From *Ada Lovelace: The Musical*
Libretto and lyrics by J. Essinger

Malign fate had not yet finished with Charles. The year 1834 saw him having to face a fresh personal disaster, and perhaps in some ways the worst one of all. His beloved daughter Georgiana, who had turned 16 on 17 July 1834, tragically never saw her seventeenth birthday. One of Charles' sons, Henry Prevost Babbage, writes in his 1910 book *Memoirs and Correspondence*, 'My sister died in the autumn of 1834.'

The exact date of young Georgiana's death isn't found in Anthony Hyman's biography of Charles; Hyman just gives the year 1834. But there is a reference to the event in the London newspaper *The Standard* for Tuesday, 30 September 1834. Admittedly, Hyman did not have the advantage of access to online newspaper achives.

There are three deaths listed in *The Standard* of 30 September. I have retained below the details of the other two passings, as they unconsciously accentuate how young Georgiana was.

She died at Boughton House, just like her mother did, which suggests that Georgiana (the daughter) became ill either when she was already there, or became ill in London and was sent to Boughton to get better, though, as the journey from London to Worcestershire in 1834 would hardly have been a comfortable one, the former case seems the more likely. In fact, Georgiana was even younger than the age given erroneously in the newspaper, she was only 16.

DEATHS
Sept. 25, Napthali Hart, Esq., of South-Street, Finsbury-square, aged 75.
Sept. 26, at Boughton-house, Worcestershire, aged 17, Georgiana, the only daughter of Charles Babbage Esq., of Dorset-street, Manchester-square.
Sept. 29, at his residence in Albion-road, Stoke Newington, John Mill Esq. aged 84.

What was the cause of Georgiana's death? Like almost everything else about her, this isn't known for certain. There was a serious epidemic of scarlet fever – a disease that can fatally weaken the heart; it was the cause of the premature death of Wolfgang Amadeus Mozart, for example, during the autumn of 1834 and the winter of 1834–5, but I have found no definite evidence that Georgiana died from it.

Young life was, tragically, always precarious in this era before modern medicine gave humankind some approximate mastery over the slings and arrows of outrageous medical fortune. When anyone began to suffer from a fever of any kind, all doctors could do was wait for what was known as the 'crisis': the worst moment of the illness when the patient either triumphed over the fever and started to get better, or succumbed. Having a child seriously ill in the days before the discovery of effective antibiotics must have been a complete nightmare; nowadays, a ten-day course of antibiotics is an effective treatment for scarlet fever.

John Herschel, certainly, had no doubt how terrible this new blow was for his great friend. Writing to Charles on 20 January 1835 (Herschel was travelling in the Cape of Good Hope in southern Africa, and the awful news would have taken some months to reach him, and likewise his reply would have taken time to get back to Charles) Herschel said:

My Dear Babbage

My last [letter] had not been gone a week when to my inexpressible surprise and grief, the news of your great and distressing calamity caught our Eye in the English Paper. I hardly know that even I experienced such a shock or one that brought back more & more painful recollections. It is the first occasion which has reminded me painfully of our distance from home – Had I been near you I think I should have had it in my power if not to afford you comfort & Consolation, at least to have helped you to distract your thoughts from brooding over such a misfortune.

As it is I must content myself with telling you how very deeply both my wife & myself feel for your Situation and that of your mother, whose acute sensibility must I fear have caused this blow to fall very heavily on her. Pray offer her our warmest sympathy, and if you can, soon after the receipt of this, let us know how she bears the loss, which to her must be even greater than to you …

Farewell & believe me
Dear B
Yours truly

JFW Herschel

John Herschel was, we see, aware just what a calamity Georgiana's death would be for Charles. Yet, even such a good friend as Herschel did not perhaps realise the full extent of Charles' grief.

Charles plunged himself back into his work, as he always did, and it would be wrong to suggest that he never had any more fun, because he certainly did. After his daughter Georgiana died, he tended to take for granted that the enjoyment he would have of life would derive from his intellectual pursuits, his travels and his friendships; he ceased expecting enjoyment from the day-to-day pleasures of family life. Yes, he still had his sons, but sons didn't stay with you, they drifted away, and indeed one of his sons, Henry Prevost Babbage, did made his career far from London, in India.

An intriguing adjunct to this very sad story of Georgiana's death is highlighted by Doron Swade. He recalls that a mathematician, Jim Roberts, who spent a lot of time in the 1980s and 1990s locating archival sources about Charles, was able to show that around the time when Georgiana died, Charles was successful at solving a problem with his designs relating to what he called the 'anticipating carriage' mechanism. This is a particularly ingenious and inventive part of his plans, where his cogwheel engines were able to anticipate a future carriage that exceeded ten because Charles designed a special arm that received information about the carriage from a previous stack of cogwheels.

This interesting discovery by Jim Roberts suggests that our probable instinct about Charles – that he tried to console himself from personal tragedy by delving deep into trying to solve an engineering problem connected with his inventions – is right.

And if Georgiana had not died, but lived? Well, even if Ada never did have the chance to meet her before September 1834, I'm sure she would have done so if Georgiana had survived into adulthood. A living Georgiana would have been a helpmate for her father, and who knows what influence she might have had on him to accept that, for all his genius, he needed some external assistance if he was going to make his dreams of cogwheel computation come to fruition? Perhaps Georgiana would have persuaded him, at a crucial time in his life, that he needed Ada's help. In that case, maybe everything might have been different.

But back to business.

Charles' Difference Engine was, as we've seen, to be an automatic cogwheel-based machine designed to calculate mathematical tables. Completely revolutionary in concept, it still fell far short of the fully automated and versatile general mathematical machine – in effect a Victorian computer made from cogwheels – that Charles eventually glimpsed on the most distant regions of his own intellectual horizon.

The precise link between Joseph-Marie Jacquard's work and his own did not strike Charles until the mid-1830s, when he conceived of a much more ambitious and complex device than the Difference Engine. He christened this new machine the Analytical Engine. It was the world's first digital computer. Charles was thrilled about the extraordinary new horizon that had opened up in his mind. He was like an explorer who glimpses a new continent, or an undiscovered ocean, from a mountaintop.

We can get a good idea of just how excited he was from a journal entry made late on the evening of Monday, 15 December 1834 by Lady Byron, who had spent the evening in Charles' company with Ada, who had turned 19 just five days earlier. Mary Somerville, that excellent friend of Lady Byron, Ada and Charles himself, was also there. How one wishes for a hiss-free recording of the conversation of that evening! But as we don't have that and presumably never will, we need to rely on what Lady Byron subsequently wrote in a journal entry about the events of the evening.

Generally, Lady Byron only tolerated Charles because of her daughter's liking for him and because of the social opportunities Charles opened for both mother and daughter. Most of Lady Byron's letters that mention Charles do so in a more or less disparaging way. Interestingly, in this particular journal entry, she reports on the evening with surprising neutrality, perhaps because she herself was rather caught up in his excitement.

According to Lady Byron, on this Monday evening, Charles didn't reveal to his guests precisely *what* it was he had discovered, nor exactly *when* he had made his breakthrough. His excitement and enthusiasm, however, suggest he may have had his great intellectual breakthrough not long before, even though he had surely brooded on it for many months. He apparently spoke about his discovery in metaphorical terms rather than seeking to explain it in precise detail. Why did he choose to use metaphors at all? He cannot have feared that the three women would have been incapable of understanding what he was saying – they all knew his work well anyway, and Mary Somerville, as we've seen, numbered among the leading mathematicians in Britain. We're entitled to guess that most likely what Charles really feared was revealing too much of his discovery prematurely.

He told Lady Byron, Ada and Mary that his first glimpse of his discovery had aroused in his mind a sensation that was something like 'throwing a bridge from the known to the unknown world'. According to Lady Byron's journal, Charles also said that the breakthrough made him feel that he was standing on a mountain peak and watching mist in a valley below start to disperse, revealing a glimpse of a river whose course he could not follow, but which he knew would be bound to leave the valley somewhere.

The closest the women got to knowing exactly what it was that Charles had discovered was a comment he uttered that his stroke of insight lay 'in the highest department of mathematics'. Writing in her journal, Lady Byron later noted in her sober and pedantic way, 'I understand it to include means of solving equations that hitherto had been considered unsolvable.'

The origins of the Analytical Engine date back to a paper on the Difference Engine that Charles read to the Astronomical Society of London on 13 December 1822. In this paper, he explained that, as useful as the Difference Engine was, it would always have the disadvantage that it would need to be reset for each new set of calculations.

At the start of a Difference Engine calculation, the values that would govern it had to be entered by setting the figure wheels by hand. Once the Engine was properly set up, the handle could be turned so that the machine calculated automatically. The Difference Engine would (had it been completed) carry out calculations without further intervention by whoever was operating it. However, where some calculations were concerned, the longer the calculations went on, the more inaccurate the results that were output would become. This, Charles explained, wasn't in fact the fault of the machine but was due to the evaluation process that the Difference Engine would use being based on a mathematical formula, which would be exactly precise for every result.

Eventually, Charles found a way to design a machine that would not feature this continual slight reduction in accuracy; a machine which could do much more than only calculate mathematical tables. He named this machine the Analytical Engine.

Why did he call it that? This is not known. Possibly it was because the machine was designed to *analyse* all kinds of practical mathematical problems and find solutions to them. Charles' entire way of seeing the world was, in a sense, analytical: that is, he tended to solve problems by reducing them to their constituent elements and analysing those elements. In this he was in many respects typical of nineteenth-century men of science; the difference was that Charles took analysis much further than anyone else, especially in the area of calculation.

Charles pursued the notion of the Analytical Engine relentlessly during the months that followed his evening with the three women. Unfortunately, little is known precisely about how his work progressed. In fact, Charles never published a comprehensive account of the Analytical Engine, let alone details of when he made all his discoveries. He made many drawings and diagrams for the Analytical Engine, and completed some small working cogwheel components designed to be used in its mechanism. But modern computer scientists who have spent months or even years examining his plans in detail have concluded that it would almost certainly be impossible to build a complete working Analytical Engine from the plans without considerable additional work, and by making certain assumptions about his intentions without having any way of knowing that those assumptions were correct.

None of this is to belittle the incredible achievement of intellect and imagination that the Analytical Engine represents. Even though a completed Analytical Engine was never built, though perhaps one may yet be built in our century, Charles' plans for the machine make clear beyond any doubt at all that the Analytical Engine would indeed have been nothing less than a massive Victorian computer, made out of cogwheels.

How massive? The machine Charles designed would have been about at the size of a small steam locomotive in his day or a large lorry today. It would have used about 20,000 cogwheels as well as thousands of gearshafts, camshafts and power transmission rods. A completed Analytical Engine would have been mind-boggling in size, concept and in the functions it carried out.

One especially fascinating point is that the Analytical Engine's operation would have been controlled by punched cards like those Jacquard used in his loom. In Volume II of Charles' notebooks – his handwritten journals that are at the Science Museum in London, which he called his 'Scribbling Books' – there is an entry for 30 June 1836: 'Suggested Jacard's [*sic*] loom as a substitute for the drums.' It was the first time Charles misspelled Jacquard's surname. It wouldn't be the last.

I've already mentioned Joseph-Marie Jacquard and his loom. It's now useful to look at his work in greater detail. Jacquard had been born in Lyons on 7 July 1752, and had died in Oullins – then a French town, today a suburb of Lyons – on 7 August 1834. Jacquard was one of the greatest inventors in history and certainly one of the most important French inventors; moreover, it is possible to trace a technological connection between his work to build the world's first automatic loom and – via the punched-card tabulators of the American Herman Hollerith, whose organisation became part of International Business Machines (subsequently IBM) when it was founded in 1924 – to the modern computer. I tell this story in my book *Jacquard's Web.*

Jacquard understood that the problem with the drawloom – that is, the old-fashioned loom used in his home town of Lyons in France, and elsewhere, to weave images into silk by the fantastically cumbersome process of having a second weaver (known as the draw-boy) sitting on top of the loom and manipulating the individual string that controlled the desired raising or lowering of the warp threads – was that it did not really solve in any constructive sense the problem of how to rapidly raise and lower the warp threads to form the shed when a decorated fabric was being woven. The drawloom was really nothing more than an *aid* to the weaving process, just as an abacus is a helpful manual aid to calculation but not in any sense a calculating machine.

By the time Jacquard began applying himself to solving the problem, the world of machinery had advanced considerably even compared with fifty years earlier. The time was ripe for a mechanical solution to the problem that had, in a sense, bedevilled the Lyons weaving industry since its foundation.

What made the solution possible were the punched cards. Jacquard does not appear to have been the first loom inventor in Lyons to think of using punched cards, but he was the one who brought the automatic punched-card loom to perfection. In fact, Jacquard's brilliant loom had a competitor in Lyons, Jacques de Vaucanson, who lived from 1709 to 1782, and who invented a loom that used a revolving studded drum. But de Vaucanson's loom was much less practical than Jacquard's, for the revolving studded drums needed to be changed regularly for a long piece of fabric, and also, as one might imagine, the drums were more expensive and difficult to produce than the punched cards.

Perhaps the most amazing piece of fabric ever woven by the Jacquard loom was a monochrome portrait of Jacquard himself, sitting in his workshop. These portraits were first produced in 1839, and numerous examples were made (it isn't known how many, but as several survive even today, it's reasonable to suppose that several dozen were produced); they required a total of 24,000 punched cards to be used in the weaving process. As we've seen, Charles tried to obtain one via his friend Arago.

The woven picture of Jacquard was an exceptionally complex image. It was not designed to be a consumer product but a special production designed to show (or indeed to show off to) major customers how remarkable Jacquard's loom really was. The usual total of cards required for even the most sophisticated commercial woven fabric on a Jacquard loom was generally in the vicinity of 4,000.

The Jacquard loom enabled decorated fabric to be woven about twenty-four times more quickly than the drawloom. Before Jacquard invented his loom even the most skilled weaver and draw-boy duo could only manage two rows (or 'picks') of woven fabric every minute; a skilled lone weaver using the Jacquard loom could manage to fit in an average of about forty-eight picks per minute of working time.

This was a prodigious gain in speed for the technology of the time. We can more readily appreciate the impact of the speed increase when we consider that today a supersonic jet aircraft flies at up to about twenty-four times the average speed of a motor car. The increase in speed was as remarkable as that: a skilled weaver using the Jacquard loom could produce 2 feet of stunningly beautiful decorated silk fabric every day compared with the 1 inch that was the best that could be managed with the drawloom.

❖

Returning now to London in 1836 from Lyons at the start of the nineteenth century, what exactly did Charles' entry – 'Suggested Jacard's [*sic*] loom as a substitute for the drums' – actually mean?

It means that before having the brilliant realisation that the Jacquard cards were ideal for operating his Analytical Engine, Charles toyed with the idea of programming his new machine by using a revolving drum featuring little raised studs as a mechanical means of inputting data and operating the machine. This type of drum was, as we have seen, the basis for the control system of Jacques de Vaucanson's loom.

The notebook entry of 30 June 1836 marks the decisive moment when Charles abandoned that plan in favour of the Jacquard punched-card system. It was as though the evolution of the best method for controlling an automatic silk-weaving loom had been re-enacted in Charles' mind. And, just as had happened in the silk-weaving industry itself, the Jacquard cards had won a resounding victory over the de Vaucanson revolving studded drum in Charles' inventive imagination.

Certainly, it made very good sense for Charles to plump for the Jacquard cards. For one thing, producing punched cards is easier and cheaper than manufacturing metal drums. Yet, more importantly, the Jacquard control system offered the possibility of a potentially *limitless* programming system, whereas a revolving drum will, by definition, start to repeat itself before long.

It's not possible to be sure when Charles first heard of the Jacquard loom, but he was so interested in science and inventions that I absolutely can't believe he went through his Cambridge days without being aware of it. What we can be certain about is that by 1836 he was entirely familiar with the machine and with the details of how it operated. By the mid

1830s there were several hundred Jacquard looms in Britain, with many of the weavers who worked on them plying their trade in London's Spitalfields district, where a silk-weaving industry had sprung up that offered far from merely token competition to the silk industry in Lyons itself. Charles would have been well aware of this industry.

In all fairness to Charles, he liked to give credit where credit was due. Writing in his 1864 autobiography, he makes explicit the enormous influence and importance of the Jacquard loom:

> It is known as a fact that the Jacquard loom is capable of weaving any design which the imagination of man may conceive. It is also the constant practice for skilled artists to be employed by manufacturers in designing patterns. These patterns are then sent to a peculiar artist, who, by means of a certain machine, punches holes in a set of pasteboard cards in such a manner that when the cards are placed in a Jacquard loom, it will then weave upon its produce the exact pattern designed by the artist.
>
> Now the manufacturer may use, for the warp and weft of his work, threads which are all of the same color; let us suppose them to be unbleached or white threads. In this case the cloth will be woven all of one color; but there will be a damask pattern upon it such as the artist designed.
>
> But the manufacturer might use the same cards, and put into the warp threads of any other color. Every thread might even be of a different color, or of a different shade of color; but in all these case the *form* of the pattern will be exactly the same – the colors only will differ.

The day when Charles decided to make use of the Jacquard cards in his design for his Analytical Engine is one of the most momentous in the story of his work and in the prehistory of the computer. It is, literally, the day when the bridge between the weaving industry and the embryonic information technology industry was created. Charles' decision was the most explicit confirmation, that in essence a computer is merely a special kind of Jacquard loom.

Charles recognised that Jacquard's *automatic* use of the punched card as the means to control the raising and lowering of the warp threads on the loom for weaving brocade was a development of great importance. After all, Charles was basically trying to build a computer program a century before the word 'program' acquired this meaning, and at a time when 'computers' were – as we have seen – people, not machines. He found what he was looking for in Jacquard's cards. The moment he did, the global information revolution that is such a major part of our lives today took its first substantial step towards incarnation.

Bruce Collier, in his study of Charles' work *The Little Engines that Could've*, makes the important comment:

> The introduction of punched cards into the new engine was important not only as a more convenient form of control than the drums, or because programs could now be of unlimited extent, and could be stored and repeated without the danger of introducing errors in setting the machine by hand: it was important also because it served to crystallise Babbage's feelings that he had invented something really new, something much more than a sophisticated calculating machine.

The Jacquard card can be said to constitute the invention of the binary digit or 'bit'. A rod went through a hole in the card when a hole was there, and not when one wasn't. The hole determined whether a rod lifted up a thread or didn't. This fundamental on/off configuration of switch is at the heart of any digital computer; modern computers simply carry out the process billions of times a second and use a variety of operating systems and computer languages to enable those billions of switches to carry out work that is useful to us.

Writing in his autobiography, Charles explains how the Analytical Engine would operate. He states that the machine would consist of two parts. These are, firstly, the *store* containing 'all the variables to be operated upon'; and, secondly, the *mill* 'into which the quantities about to be operated upon are always brought'. In his autobiography Charles writes 'qualities' rather than 'quantities', but this appears to be a misprint. Charles' use of the terms 'store' and 'mill' are far-sighted anticipations of the modern computer features of computer memory and computer processor, respectively.

In choosing the terms he did, Charles was also alluding, very likely unconsciously, to the cloth industry of Totnes. As we've seen, the first new machines of the Industrial Revolution were invented for that same textile industry, which was so important in Totnes in the eighteenth century and vital in the development of Benjamin Babbage's banking business and so also Charles' inheritance, which funded his work on his machines of the mind. The links between the Jacquard loom and the Analytical Engine were, consequently, cultural as well as technical.

In his autobiography, Charles points out that every formula the Analytical Engine may be required to compute consists of certain algebraic operations to be performed upon given letters, and of other modifications depending on the numerical value assigned to those letters. By 'letters' Charles is referring to letters in algebraic formulae such as $3x = 1$; $4x^3 = 32$, etc, although the machine was designed to handle far more complex formulae than this. He adds:

> There are therefore two sets of cards, the first to direct the nature of the operations to be performed – these are called operation cards: the other to direct the particular variables on which those cards are required to operate – these latter are called variable cards.

Strictly speaking, Charles was specifying *three* types of cards, because in practice there were also cards that contained the values to load into the machine. Some (the operation cards) were to be used, as the name suggests, to control the Analytical Engine's operations, whereas the variable cards specify where in store the number that was to be operated on was to be retrieved. There were also number cards that, as the name suggests, were to indicate the numbers on which the Analytical Engine was designed to operate.

Essentially, a modern computer program works just like this, except that it uses electrons rather than cogwheels to make the switches, which consequently operate almost infinitely faster than a cogwheel-based computer ever could. Yet all the same, the fundamental idea of Charles' brilliant invention was still, in all its functions and purposes, a digital computer.

Charles never used the words 'programming' or 'program'; these terms would not enter the language until about seventy years after his death. He was therefore obliged to resort to expressions that to us today will seem quite obscure. For example, he describes the Analytical Engine as being made 'special' for the mathematical formula in question. In precisely the same way, we could visualise a Jacquard loom that was programmed to weave a lily as being made 'special' for the task of lily weaving.

Almost as far-sighted as Charles' entire concept of the Analytical Engine was his perception of it as having, in effect, a mind of its own. In a fascinating anticipation of the tendency of our own age to invest computers with a will and personality of their own ('I can't seem to do this; the computer doesn't like it'), Charles consistently writes about the Analytical Engine as if it were a separate, reasoning entity. For example, in the chapter in his autobiography about the Analytical Engine he observes at one point:

> Thus the Analytical Engine first computes and punches on cards its own tabular numbers. These are brought to it by its attendant when demanded. But the engine itself takes care that the *right* card is brought to it by verifying the *number* of that card by the number of the card which it demanded. The engine will always reject a wrong card by continually ringing a loud bell and stopping itself until supplied with the precise intellectual food it demands.

Charles comprehensively borrowed from – and readily acknowledged the borrowing – Jacquard's plan of creating what Charles describes as a 'library' of cards that carry out different functions, with the Analytical Engine's operator being able to take cards from the library as required and input them into the machine in order to make it special for the task.

The enormous advantage of the Jacquard loom was, of course, precisely that it was able to weave any picture or pattern for which a chain of cards had been made. Weavers would keep these chains of cards in a storeroom whose function was very much the same as that of the library – or we might even say software library – which Charles was proposing to create.

Charles planned the Number Cards to express numbers in length up to $10^{50} - 1$: that is, 9 followed by forty-nine 9s. In principle, each number would be represented by columns, with as many holes punched in each column as were necessary to represent the units, tens, hundreds, thousands and so on.

Charles, who always did his utmost to maximise the practical usefulness of the Engines, envisaged a variety of methods in order to simplify how the machine would handle large numbers. These methods involved the Analytical Engine incorporating a variety of card-counting operations, with special holes being used in some cards to indicate that a number exceeded a particular quantity, or that the number itself was negative. The machine was designed to 'read' the cards much as the Jacquard loom did. Metal rods in the Analytical Engine mechanism would press against the cards, and a particular hole would only register if the rod could poke through it.

Another inspired aspect of Charles' punched-card system was that it provided a permanent record of the machine's read-out. Furthermore, if the operator was certain that the correct series of punched cards had been installed in the machine at the start of the calculation, the operator could be confident that the entire calculation would be done without error.

Charles also developed his own methods for reducing the number of operations needed to perform a particular calculation – some of these are so complex that even today they are not fully understood. In addition, he designed systems by which the Analytical Engine would be self-correcting in the event that anything went wrong with it. In particular, his plans included measures that would render the machine unable to act on instructions from, say, a card that had inadvertently slipped out of place.

These techniques used a system of locking devices that immobilised certain wheels during a calculating cycle, so that they would not be at risk of accidental movement. Charles also designed mechanisms to ensure that a wheel could only be moved by an input from a legitimate source. He stated specifically in his plans that when the machine was working properly, it would be impossible for an operator to take any action that would produce false results.

As 1834 became 1835, the Analytical Engine was far from the only thing on Ada's mind. She had celebrated her nineteenth birthday on 10 December and Lady Byron had decided that the time had come for her to find, or be found, a husband. Was Charles a possible candidate? Maybe he thought he might have been, but Lady Byron didn't. While some of her best friends were middle class, she was decidedly orthodox about blue blood, and she wanted Ada's husband to have a title that was at least a century old. Mary Somerville's son Woronzow Greig writes (a long time after the marriage was contracted), 'During the spring of 1835 I suggested to my friend Lord Lovelace, then Lord King, that she would suit him as a wife. He and I had been at college together [Trinity Cambridge, Byron's and Charles' college] and have continued through life on the most intimate terms.' Whether Greig was involved or not, in the spring of 1835, Ada was introduced to William, Lord King, who was 30 years old, on a visit to the Warwickshire home of a Sir John Philips.

William was a sort of Mr Darcy of his day: rich and potent and looking for a mate. Even Lady Byron could hardly wish for much more. He came from an influential political, social, intellectual and religious background. With a title created in 1725, his was just on the right side of Lady Byron's hundred-year watershed. And he came with a number of substantial properties, including Ockham Park, Surrey, the Jacobean family seat (he was Lord King, Baron of Ockham) and Ashley Combe in Somerset. He had also just bought 12 St James's Square two years earlier, whose facade he demolished a year after the marriage to be rebuilt by Cubitt in the style he had seen on his own Grand Tour: opulent, Italianate, with a glamorous staircase and enfilade of rooms that set it quite apart from its severe seventeenth-century original.

Nor was Ada indifferent to William. On 28 June 1835, less than a fortnight before their marriage, she wrote to him: 'What a happiness it is to feel towards any one what I do towards you, & to feel too that it is reciprocal!' And Ada went on:

I do not think there can be any earthly pleasure equal to that of repos-
ing perfect trust & confidence in another, more especially when that
other is to be one's husband.

I hope, my dear William, that I shall make you a very affectionate
and very conscientious wife, & shall fulfil all my duties towards you &
towards your family in such a manner as to make you the only return
I can make for all I owe you, & of which I am so sure that I shall never
be reminded by you, that I must take care to keep the remembrance of
it in my head.

The marriage took place on 8 July 1835 at Fordhook, after which Ada
and William had a honeymoon at their stately home, Ashley Combe in
Porlock, near Minehead in Somerset, that William had set about reno-
vating in a Romantic style. In one letter to William, on Friday evening,
9 October 1835, when they were temporarily apart, she describes her
pregnancy as 'the commencement of the hatching', and refers to herself
as a 'hatch bird'. She adds, 'I want my Cock to keep me warm' – William's
nickname, chosen by Ada, was 'Cock' – signing off, 'My dearest mate,
yours most affectionately.'

In short succession Ada did what was expected: a son and heir, Byron,
was born on 12 May 1836; a daughter, Annabella, on 22 September 1837;
and a second son, Ralph (the 'spare'), on 2 July 1839. It helped no doubt
that loveable, malleable William seems almost from the outset to have
accepted that his wife was more intelligent than he was and to have been
willing to adopt a fairly subservient position in the relationship. Later in
their marriage he would say, 'what a General you would make!'

However, once their sexual passion had worn off a little, it didn't
take Ada too long to realise that William was a somewhat purposeless
fellow. He spent a great deal of time and money designing and order-
ing the construction of tunnels at their country houses. The precise
purpose of all these tunnels was never clear and it is perfectly possible
that there was none other than to provide William with something to
do with his time.

When Princess Victoria became Queen in 1837, William was elevated
in the peerage from Baron to Viscount of Ockham, and to the Earldom
of Lovelace, an extinct title from Lady Byron's family the Noels (upon

the death of her uncle Lord Wentworth, she and her father had inserted 'Noel' before 'Milbanke'). But rather than rewards for any particular achievements of William's, they appear to have been political pleasantries from the new monarch prompted by one of her ministers. Ada herself would henceforth sign her name 'Ada Lovelace', using her own family name. Paradoxically, Lady Byron never dropped her husband's name, even when she eventually inherited her uncle's title and became Baroness of Wentworth.

After a few years of what appears to be genuine happiness, Ada began to find her husband's lack of overall purpose intensely irritating. This was evidently a problem throughout their marriage; one of the letters discovered in the north of England and written by Ada on Christmas Day 1846 amounts to a ticking-off of Charles for, as she saw it, obstructing the procurement of a possible appointment for William. '*You* can have no conception of what my husband is, when his home *alone* occupies his irritable energies,' she writes. She craved a husband who would do great things, be great, stride to fame and illustriousness with her by his side and understand her own pressing needs for an intellectual life. But William was not that man.

Would Charles have been? At one level it is an academic question, as Lady Byron would not have heard of it, but it's a reasonable question and in the absence of any further evidence coming to light, all we can really say is that very likely Charles did think of Ada as a possible wife, but must have known early on that Lady Byron wanted Ada's husband to be an aristocrat, which Charles, for all his wealth, was not. Subsequently, he often visited the married couple, frequently staying for several days. How did he feel about living under the same roof as a married couple? Again, we simply don't know. Did Charles have a closeness with Ada that William didn't know about? We don't know that either.

In 1840, Charles again went travelling in Europe. He had been working on the Analytical Engine concertedly since 1834, but it was still only a succession of plans and notes, with a few small trial components having been made. Nonetheless, the very idea was a work of prodigious genius.

With no actual full-size completed version of a Difference Engine or Analytical Engine to show the world, he was obliged to seek what seemed the next best thing: the society of those who seemed to understand what he was trying to do. The fact that he was prepared to travel all the way to Italy – a far from easy journey in 1840, even for a man of Charles' financial resources and energy – suggests how cut off from empathy and support at home he perceived himself to be.

Very likely his decision to travel to Turin was influenced by his knowledge that Lyons was on the way to Turin, and Charles wanted to visit Lyons to find out more about Joseph-Marie Jacquard. The Lyons silk industry had sprung up there partly because of the city's proximity to Italy, and now Charles was exploiting that very fact to combine his excursion to Turin with a visit to Lyons. Charles left England for Paris in the middle of August 1840; while there, he collected letters of introduction from Arago and other friends to people in Lyons. A few days later he arrived in Jacquard's birthplace. As he relates in *Passages*:

> On my road to Turin I had passed a few days at Lyons, in order to examine the silk manufacture. I was especially anxious to see the loom in which that admirable specimen of fine art, the portrait of Jacquard, was woven. I passed many hours in watching its progress.

What Charles says here is unfortunately ambiguous. Does he mean that he spent the 'many hours' just watching a Jacquard loom operating, or that he actually watched the loom weaving a 24,000-card Jacquard portrait?

There is the tantalising implication that the latter is the case, especially as it seems a more plausible scenario for Charles to have done this rather than just watching the loom weaving the kind of standard brocade fabrics it would have woven day to day. On the other hand, he does not specifically mention that he watched a Jacquard portrait being created, and one rather thinks he might have done had this, in fact, been the case.

If Charles had watched the portrait being woven, it would indeed have been an undertaking requiring 'many hours'. Assuming that the weaver was working at the usual Jacquard loom speed of about forty-eight picks per minute (that is, 2,800 per hour), the entire weaving process for the 24,000 picks would mostly have taken more than eight hours per portrait, excluding breaks at the local *bouchon,* the Lyonnais name for a type of restaurant that serves traditional filling local cuisine, such as sausages, duck pâté or roast pork. When Charles was immersed in an intellectual pursuit, the intensity of his concentration was beyond compare. Whether he did, in fact, observe a Jacquard portrait being woven or not, it is surely perfectly possible to imagine him observing the creation of the woven portrait of his hero from the very first pick of the shuttle to the very last.

When we think of Charles leaving for Turin to discuss the Analytical Engine with Giovanni Plana and other leading Italian scientists in the summer of 1840, it is easy to romanticise the situation and assume that Charles was at the pinnacle of his achievements as a scientist and inventor. But that really was not the case at all. The truth is that when Charles left for Italy, his career at home was in shreds. Yes, he had invented what was at this stage a brilliantly thought-invention, the Analytical Engine, but he had no way of building one and no realistic expectation that one ever would be built. In his own day, few people – with the notable exception of his good friend Ada Lovelace – actually understood what a mind-bogglingly brilliant invention the Analytical Engine was.

Yes, among some of Europe's greatest minds, Charles could look forward to receiving the respect and understanding he longed for. Back in Britain, though, negotiations with the government over the provision of funding to continue his work had foundered. This was to a large extent because Charles was finding it increasingly difficult to be taken seriously in his native land. He was a genius, but diplomacy was not his strong point. Back in 1834, he had made the mistake of telling the British government he had abandoned work on the Difference Engine because he had invented another machine which 'superseded' it. The other machine was, of course, the Analytical Engine. But why would he inform the government he had abandoned work on the very machine they had supported with such lavish financial grants?

The confession did not even turn out to be strictly true: he never entirely abandoned his labours on the Difference Engine and was still conducting useful work on it in the 1850s. But Charles was obsessively honest and throughout his life motivated by a sense of justice so pronounced that it often placed his own interests in jeopardy. He felt it was, in effect, only fair to mention the new direction his work was taking. Another likely factor was that he was proud of his new idea and keen to tell people about it. One sentence from his letter to the government about his intentions reveals the strength of his sense of justice; he explained that he was revealing his plans in detail in order that 'you may have fairly before you all the facts of the case'.

His mistake also stemmed from his often almost incredible naïveté in political matters. He largely lacked the politician's essential skill of having a canny understanding of the likely effect of a particular action or statement on an audience. Besides, financial backers want good news, not honest but unpleasant revelations. Under the circumstances, the government could hardly be blamed for putting its own sense of justice to work and concluding that Charles was behaving with utter irresponsibility.

The fact was that the British government had, as we have seen, spent more than £17,000 on the Difference Engine – an enormous sum. Many people in the government responded, understandably, with indignation, suspicion and even fury to the news that work had stopped on the Difference Engine. There had always been those in the corridors of power, and in the scientific world generally, who found it convenient and easy to regard Charles as a troublesome fraud, bent only on cadging money from the Exchequer. Some even put it about that Charles was dishonestly using the money to prop up his own lifestyle.

Charles returned to Britain in September 1840, to some extent cheered by knowing that one of the Italian scientists whom he had recently visited might stick to his promise to write a lengthy and detailed paper on the Analytical Engine. Charles hoped that such a paper would affirm the importance of the invention and give him leverage with the British government. His host in Turin, Giovanni Plana, had said he wasn't in sufficiently good health to undertake the job, but Luigi Federico Menabrea, a talented young mathematician whom Plana had introduced to Charles in Turin, appeared interested in carrying it out. Charles remained in touch with Menabrea and supplied him with comprehensive information about the Analytical Engine.

Eventually, Menabrea wrote a paper about the Analytical Engine, in French (the language of scholarship on Continental Europe in those days), which was published in October 1842, in an obscure Swiss journal, *Bibliothèque Universelle de Genève,* in issue number 82, under the title 'Notions sur la machine analytique'. Charles, who knew that his friend Ada Byron, now Ada Lovelace, spoke and wrote French fluently, was to have a brainwave concerning this article.

In the meantime, though, he decided to try once more to get the British government to give him another chunk of money, this time so he could complete the Analytical Engine. Charles was determined to take this request to the very top, and arrange a meeting with Sir Robert Peel, the prime minister.

13

DABBLING IN POLITICS

BLACKADDER: Well, Mrs Miggins, at last we can return to sanity. The hustings are over, the bunting is down, the mad hysteria is at an end. After the chaos of a General Election, we can return to normal.
MRS MIGGINS: Has there been a General Election then, Mr Blackadder?
BLACKADDER: Indeed there has, Mrs Miggins.
MRS MIGGINS: Well, I never heard about it.
BLACKADDER: Well, of course you didn't; you're not eligible to vote.
MRS MIGGINS: Why not?
BLACKADDER: Because virtually no-one is: women, peasants, chimpanzees, lunatics, lords …

From 'Dish and Dishonesty', *Blackadder the Third*,
set before the Reform Act of 1832,
by Richard Curtis and Ben Elton (1987)

Robert Peel was born in Bury, Lancashire, on 5 February 1788, only two weeks after Lord Byron. Peel was the privileged son of another Sir Robert Peel (1750–1830), a Member of Parliament and a wealthy manufacturer of cotton garments. The son benefited from the unreformed state of the British voting system when he became MP in 1809 for the Irish seat of Cashel City, Co. Tipperary, a borough with only twenty-four voters.

Unlike the satirical depiction of such 'rotten boroughs' (i.e. boroughs that had once been heavily populated and which now had tiny populations but a parliamentary seat, while some towns and even cities had no representation in parliament at all) in the *Blackadder* comedy TV show, there wasn't even a contested election held for the seat Peel 'won'. What *Blackadder* was right about, though, was that the Britain of rotten boroughs was, from the perspective of aspiring to be a democracy, a joke.

Peel first became prime minister on 10 December 1834. His initial stint in the job only lasted until 8 April 1835, when his Tory government, which was ruling with a minority mandate, resigned due to frustrations at being regularly defeated by the opposition. Peel was then leader of the opposition until 30 August 1841, when he became prime minister again.

For at least six years, Charles had been intermittently trying to get a fresh grant from the government to help fund his work on the Analytical Engine. There were, as was usually the case with Charles, times when he was desperate to pursue this initiative, and times when he seemed to lose interest in it. What is pretty certain, though, was that by the start of the 1840s Charles had, according to his own statement, already spent about £20,000 of his personal fortune on the Difference Engine. By the time he went to Turin via Lyons, it is likely he had come to realise that there was in practice no chance of completing a Difference Engine or an Analytical Engine without further financial help from the government.

In all Charles' vexed correspondence with friends about this matter, it never seems to occur to him that common sense would surely have taught anyone that the government was hardly likely to be impressed that it had given him £17,000 to complete the Difference Engine and he had never delivered one. He preferred to focus his thoughts on what he regarded as the injustice of other scientists being given grants by the government, apparently for not doing anything specific, whereas he had used the government's money on trying to build a Difference Engine and had also spent £20,000 of his own money on doing so.

He was strangely naive and impractical about financial matters, doubtless at least partly because he had never had to earn a living. Nor was he at his best when imagining what the agenda of a counterparty was likely to be and finding ways of making the counterparty feel better about the situation and positively inclined to his interests, techniques that are objectively fundamental to anyone running a successful business or managing a large development project.

On Monday, 17 January 1842, Charles embarked on a campaign to try to get some more money from the government by writing to his good friend Lord Ashley. Styled Lord Ashley from 1811 to 1851 and then Lord Shaftesbury following the death of his father, Ashley was an English politician, philanthropist and social reformer, who played a crucial role in improving conditions and working hours for children in factories.

Henry Goulburn, who is mentioned in Charles' letter to Ashley, is an important, though vexing, figure in Charles' life in 1842. Born in March 1784 and so more than seven years older than Charles, Goulburn was an English Conservative statesman and a member of the Peelite faction after 1846. His inheritance included an estate in Jamaica, populated by a number of slaves who worked on sugar plantations in an area of more than 2,000 acres. Goulburn was Chancellor of the Exchequer from 26 January 1828 until 22 November 1830, and from 3 September 1841 to 27 June 1846.

Clearly, here, Lord Ashley was being an influential intermediary between Charles and Peel:

Dear Lord Ashley

In preparing a statement respecting the Calc. Engine for Sir Robert Peel I find the only document I have respecting the terms of the arrangement you so kindly accomplished for me with Mr Goulburn and the Duke of Wellington is a note I made on my return home after I had seen your on that subject. It runs thus.

The decision of the Government was:

1st Although the Government would not pledge themselves to complete the Machine they were willing to declare it their property.
2nd That professional Engineers should be appointed to examine the bills.
3rd That the Government were willing to advance £3000 more than the sum (£6000) already granted.
4th That when the Machine was completed the Government would be willing to extend to any claim of Mr Babbage for

remuneration, either by bringing it before the Treasury or the House of Commons.

The three first propositions had been suggested by myself: they were fully acted upon and I have official documents from the Treasury proving them to be correct. I will not therefore trouble you on that part of the question.

With respect to the fourth it was entirely unexpected upon my part and was proposed as I understand it by the Duke of Wellington. It was not merely gratifying to me at the time: but from the nature of the discussion in which I had been engaged it greatly increased my respect for the character of the Duke.

I am unwilling to state that fourth proposition to Sir Robert Peel in my own memory unless it is confirmed by your recollection.

An early answer to this enquiry will greatly oblige.

My dear Lord Ashley
Yours very sincerely
C B
Dorset S
17 Jan 1842

The following is a copy or draft of the statement for Robert Peel made by Charles, including several crossings-out and interpolations:

Dear Sir
I do myself the honor [this was how Charles usually spelt this word] of sending you a statement respecting the Calculating engine which I have had put into type to save you the inconvenience of MSS.

Of course when I undertook to give that invention to the Government ... there must have been an implied understanding that I should carry it to its termination ...

The better part of my life has now been spent on that machine and no progress whatever having been made since 1834, the understanding may perhaps be considered by the Government as still subsisting.

I am therefore naturally very anxious that this state of uncertainty should be put and end to as soon as possible.

I shall be most ready to give any further information on the subject and will wait on you for that purpose if you should wish it at any time you may find it convenient to see me.

I am my dear Sir, Yours
Charles Babbage

Charles wrote at the end of this letter: 'Sent this with 3rd Revise of Statement 10 o'clock 22 Jan 1842.'

Then, on 4 February 1842, Charles wrote the following letter to his friend Sir George Clerk, who was also acting as an intermediary between Charles and the government.

Charles could have written to Peel himself, and subsequently did, but for the time being he was, clearly, trying to use his influential friends to give his case the maximum chance of being advanced. Sir George Clerk was a Scottish politician who served in his political career as the Conservative MP for the three constituencies Edinburghshire in Scotland, Stamford in Lincolnshire and Dover in Kent:

4 Feb 1842
My dear Sir

Two points are referred to in your letter of the 29th in which I wish to offer some observations. The effect of my letter to Sir R P was to *terminate* an *understanding* which has existed indefinitely during 20 years. I am sure neither Sir R P nor yourself will refuse me that justice. I accompanied that request with some printed pages of the *past history* of the circumstances attending that understanding. At page 37 I stated the question, the decision for which I had during several years requested from the Government namely whether etc.

You will see on attentively examining that statement or the documents in your own office that I have *never* either *offered* or *asked* to make any other machine for the Government.

2nd ly the other point is the probable expense of completing the Difference Engine according to the original plans. You seem to incline to the opinion that about £8000 will complete the old Difference Engine. I presume this view is founded upon an opinion of the R S given in a reply dated 26 March 1831 in which it is conjectured that 8 or 12 thousand would be required to complete the Machine.

The opinion I have formed from the whole experience I have had is that it will cost as least as much to finish it as has already been expended. Whether the sum already spent has been 14 or 17,000 I do not precisely know, because the latter payment has been made direct to Mr C.

Charles adds at the end of the letter:

To Sir George Clerk Bart ['Bart' was a commonly used abbreviation at the time for 'baronet': the lowest level of aristocratic title. The abbreviation is still sometimes used in Britain today.]

9 July 1842 I dined with Sir G Clerk. I then pressed him to get Sir R P to decide and he promised to recall the subject to his attention.

Meanwhile, amid Charles' hopes for favourable consideration by the government for his application for more funds, his busy social life continued. In particular, invitations for the elegant and sophisticated parties he held most Saturday nights at his home on Dorset Street for the great, the good and the intellectually gifted were in great demand. For example, here is a letter Charles received from a would-be attendee; the name at the end of the letter is unfortunately illegible:

Saturday afternoon the 18th June 1842

My dear Sir

When I saw you last, you were kind enough to invite me to your Conversazione for this evening. At least so I understood. I now send as to enquire whether I am right as to the day; and if so, to request that you will allow me to bring my son, a youth of seventeen, particularly fond of science.

I remain
My dear Sir
Yours very faithfully

Yet Charles could not always use his social life to anaesthetise himself against stress, worry and disappointment. Charles had asked the government whether he might now finally have a decision over whether he would be granted any more money.

What he received, however, was a letter from the Secretary to the Treasury, Sir George Clerk, that basically aimed to put him off, telling him of the great pressure of business before the opening of parliament. Charles no more liked being fobbed off than anyone does, and he renewed his application to the government. But no reply was forthcoming, so, near the middle of August, Charles wrote to Sir George Clerk again:

12 August 1842

To Sir George Clerk Bart

My dear Sir

I had hoped from your note just previous to the session that Sir Robt Peel would have entered on the consideration of the Calc Engine within a few weeks at furthest after that event.

I have waited patiently until the close of the session and I hope that I shall not be considered unreasonable in pressing for the immediate decision of a question which has been a source of the most harassing anxiety to me during a suspense of nearly eight years.

I am my dear Sir
Very truly Yours
C B

The above letter, like all those under Charles' name in the archive at the British Library, is a draft or a copy: it is usually impossible to know which of the two it is unless the letter has lots of crossings-out and interpolations, in which case we can safely assume it is a draft. It is worth noting, by the way, that Charles was economical in his use of scrap paper. This draft is on the back of a subscription document for the British Association for the Advancement of Science.

Next, mostly likely on 6 October 1842, Charles wrote to his friend Sir William Follett, another ally who had good contacts at the government, to warn him that he had now written directly to Peel. Sir William was an English lawyer and politician who served as Member of Parliament for Exeter from 1835 to 1845, the year of his death. He served twice as Solicitor General, in 1834–5 and 1841, and as Attorney General in 1844. He was knighted in 1835. He was reputed by some to have been the greatest advocate of the nineteenth century. However, by 1838 his heath had begun to fail, and by now, 1842, his health was precarious. However, the previous year he had been appointed Solicitor General, an extremely important post, to which he surely would not have been appointed if he'd been seriously ill, and indeed if such was the case I don't believe Charles would have troubled him:

Dear Follett

I have just sent a note to Sir R Peel pressing on him the necessity of coming up some decision respecting the Calc Engine.

I do hope that during this temporary repose of political affairs he will be able to take up and terminate an uncertainty which has been to me a source of constant and painful anxiety during nearly eight years. When you have looked at the question I will give you any further information you think necessary.

I am very truly yours
C B

This was the letter which Charles wrote to Peel. It is polite, but only up to the final paragraph, which by any standards is most ill-judged:

8 Oct 1842

Sir

On the 22nd of January last I did myself the honor of transmitting to you a printed statement of the circumstances connected with the Calculating Engine (Difference Engine), the construction of which

I had been superintending for the government since the year 1823. That paper was accompanied by a note requesting the decision of the following question whether it is the intention of the government to call upon me to complete for them that Difference Engine the construction of which has been suspended since 1833 or finally to give up its completion and thus put an end to the understanding which has subsisted since the year 1823.

I received an answer in a note from Sir G Clerk stating that Sir R Peel hopes that as soon as the great pressure of business 'previous to the opening of the session of Parliament is over he may be able to determine the best course to be pursued.'

I waited until the important discussions of the last session and even the session itself had terminated. Nor did I think it right to press upon your time during the continuance of the business in the manufacturing districts nor during the Queen's visit to Scotland.

The decision of that question which I have repeatedly but unfortunately without effect applied for during the last eight years is to me a matter of considerable importance and I now must earnestly request you to examine it and to favor it with the earliest information of the result.

I am Sir

Your very obedient friend

Charles Babbage

The eventual interview between Charles and Peel was not only a complete disaster for Charles but also – more to the point – made it most unlikely that there was ever going to be a British computer revolution in the 1840s unless a miracle occurred.

Even the letter, just quoted, which Charles wrote to Peel, reveals much about Charles' lack of diplomatic skills and indifference to the agenda of a man who was, after all, prime minister of what was in the 1840s the most powerful nation on the planet (though the United States was fast catching up) and who had enormous cares of state weighing upon him.

Charles was doubtless right to think that if only the government would help financially once more this would at least open the way to further concerted work being done on the Difference Engine and the Analytical Engine. Charles also had great foresight – almost uncanny intuition, indeed – in realising that the outcome of the approach he was making to Peel was enormous for posterity.

Robert Peel was a man of great intelligence, though perhaps less foresight, but certainly with a considerable gift for attending to details – he knew all about the history of Charles' relations with the government and the enormous sum of the money the pre-Reform government had granted him. Peel, himself a rich man through inheritance, wished the government had never given any money to Charles at all; he didn't see the function of the government as being to award free money to inventors, eccentric or otherwise, and he had never really understood what Charles was doing anyway.

What Charles didn't know was that on Wednesday, 31 August 1842, Peel had written a confidential and scathing letter about Charles to a friend, the geologist William Buckland. The letter makes only too clear what Peel thought of Charles and 'his calculating Machine'. Peel is clearly unaware that there were, in fact, two Engines:

What shall we do to get rid of Mr Babbage and his calculating Machine? I am perfectly convinced that every thousand pounds we should spend upon it hereafter would be throwing good money after bad. It has cost £17,000, I believe – and I am told would cost £14 or £15,000 more to complete it.

Surely if completed it would be worthless so far as science is concerned?

What do men really competent to judge say of it *in private?*

It will in my opinion be a very costly toy to complete and keep in repair. If it would now calculate the amount and the quantum of benefit to be derived to Science it would render the only service I ever expect from it.

I fear a reference to the Royal Society, and yet I should like to have some authority for treating this Calculating Machine as I should like to treat the Caledonian Canal - and would have treated it but that I was told it would cost £40,000 to unravel the web we have spent so many hundred thousand pounds in weaving.

I will consider any opinion you may give me as to the course which should be pursued strictly confidential.

Pray read the enclosed papers.

Most truly yours
Robert Peel

Viewed from a simple cost perspective, Peel's caustic attitude to Charles was hardly unreasonable. After all, Charles had been given a stupendous sum to deliver a Difference Engine, and hadn't. But it might also be said that prime ministers are elected to be leaders and visionaries rather than accountants. On this account, he might have done well to pay closer attention to Charles' ideas, or at least to have given Charles a proper hearing rather than regarding him as a kind of outlandish eccentric whose ideas did nothing but cost money and didn't earn any.

However, Peel was much too cunning an operator to make public the strength of his contempt for Charles. Like many prime ministers, and indeed like many politicians of all types and political affiliations, Peel was profoundly interested in how the world saw him, and he was only too aware that it often does not do for politicians to make public what they are really feeling.

Peel knew that Charles was one of the leading scientists in England, with influential friends in science, business and politics, many of whom were leading Conservatives. In particular, Peel was aware that Charles was good friends with the Duke of Wellington and Prince Albert. The duke had been the prime mover behind Charles securing funding for the Difference Engine back in the 1820s. And so Peel, as cunning as the foxes he loved to hunt in what spare time he had, placed the burden of the funding decision on someone else's shoulders.

Peel commissioned a report on the Difference Engine from the Astronomer Royal, George Biddell Airy. Airy had been appointed Astronomer Royal in 1835, at the early age of 34. By then he had already made many valuable contributions to science, especially in the field of optics. He was to remain Astronomer Royal until 1881, yet he was never regarded as having distinguished the appointment.

Later in his career, in 1846, Airy was heavily criticised by the public for failing to act on the findings of a young English astronomer, John

Couch Adams. After laborious calculations, Adams concluded that there were certain irregularities in Uranus's orbit, and that these irregularities made it likely that there was a hitherto undiscovered planet affecting it. But Airy, instead of instigating a major telescopic search for the possible new planet, chose not to act on Adams' information. Neptune was discovered in 1846 by the German astronomer Johann Gottfried Galle.

Airy should, in theory, have been the very person to understand how much potential importance there was in Charles' ideas; during the course of his astronomical work, he had to carry out a large number of complex, repetitive arithmetical calculations. But in practice Airy was less a scientist than a bureaucrat, and his dislike of Charles stemmed at least partly from not being able to understand what Charles was trying to achieve.

Charles was working at the very limits of scientific and mathematical possibility, and it could be said that only those with the most fearless and visionary intellects were likely to grasp exactly what he was seeking to do. In any event, Airy took something of a relish in attacking Charles' plans for developing cogwheel calculating machines.

Peel would certainly not have been disappointed with Airy's report; his opinion of the Difference Engine was just the sort of thing Peel was hoping to hear. As Airy himself complacently recalled:

On Sept. 15th [1842] Mr Goulburn, Chancellor of the Exchequer, asked my opinion of the utility of Mr Babbage's calculating machine, and the propriety of expending further sums of money on it. I replied, entering fully into the matter, and giving my opinion that it was worthless.

Evidently Airy, too, was unaware that there were two machines, not one. In any event, most likely on Thursday, 3 November 1842 (at that time letters posted in the morning in London were generally delivered in London on the same day), Charles received a letter from Goulburn:

3 November 1842
Downing Street

My Dear Sir

The Solicitor General has informed me that you are most anxious to have an early and decided answer as to the determination of the Government with respect to the completion of your calculating Engine. I accordingly took the earliest opportunity of communicating with Sir Robert Peel on the subject. We both regret the necessity of abandoning the completion of a machine on which so much scientific ingenuity and labor has been bestowed. But on the other hand the expense which would be necessary in order to render it either satisfactory to yourself or generally useful appears on the lowest calculation so far to exceed what we should be justified in incurring that we consider ourselves as having no other alternative. We trust that by withdrawing all claim on the part of the Government to the machine as at present constructed and by placing it at your entire disposal we may to a degree assist your future exertions in the cause of science.

I have the honour to be

Dear Sir
Yours ever most faithfully
Henry Goulburn

Sir Robert Peel begs me to add that as I have undertaken to express to you our position now on this matter he trusts you will excuse his not separately replying to the letter which you addressed to him on the subject a short time since.

This was, surely, rather like a kind of 'Dear John' letter in which John is dumped by his lady love with her convivial good wishes that he might at some point find someone else to make him happy. Nobody likes to receive a 'Dear John' letter and Charles was certainly not an exception. As Doron Swade succinctly points out in *The Cogwheel Brain*, after twenty years the Treasury was 'axing the project, writing off the massive expense and offering Charles the physical debris of his labors for his own use at no charge'.

Sir William Follett had done his best, but all he'd really done was facilitate the communication of bad news. We can be sure that Charles certainly didn't excuse Peel for not personally replying. On Sunday, 6 November, Charles wrote to Goulburn a hurt, sulky but perhaps not unreasonable response:

To Henry Goulburn

My dear Sir

I beg to acknowledge the receipt of your letter of the 3 Nov containing your own and Sir Robert Peel's decision respecting the Engine for calculating and printing mathematical tables by means of Differences the construction of which has been suspended for about eight years.

You inform me that you both regret the necessity of abandoning the completion of the Engine but ['and' crossed out in pencil in Charles' handwriting and replaced by 'but' also in pencil] that not feeling justified in incurring the large expense which it may probably require you have no other alternative.

You also offer on the part of Government to withdraw all claim on the machine as at present constructed and to place it at my entire disposal with the view of assisting my future exertions in the cause of science.

The drawings and the parts of the machine already executed are as you are aware the absolute property of government and I have no claim whatsoever to them.

While I thank you for the feeling which that offer manifests, I must under all the circumstances beg leave to decline accepting.

I am dear Sir ever yours most faithfully

C B

6 Nov 1842

Charles also wrote to Follett the following day, Monday, 7 November.

Dear Follett

I find by a letter from the Chancellor of the Exchequer that you have also aided me in that quarter in expecting the decision of the Government.

I do feel really gratified with your immediate and active assistance on this occasion.

One question is already decided and I write tonight to Sir Robert Peel to request an interview upon another *which is certainly the more important of the two because so much of the future depends upon it* [author's italics].

I wish very much to have your assistance upon two points. It will be unnecessary that I should enter into every detail and I think if you could spare me ten minutes it would be sufficient.

Independently of the importance of the result to myself I think it may be of some consequence to Sir Robert Peel. But at all events whatever may be the result I do not think myself justified in [illegible; maybe 'omitting'] any effort to help him into what I conceive the right course.

Let me know where and at what hour I can find you and I will be punctual.

Charles also again wrote to Peel himself. It is a strange letter; some of it reads as if Charles were thinking like a rejected suitor (or indeed a stalker), desperately fantasising that his beloved has feelings she doesn't actually have. Charles' assumptions about Peel's stance on the machines was quite erroneous; all Peel really wanted to do was to get rid of Charles. Charles ended the letter by requesting an interview:

6 November 1842

Sir

The Chancellor of the Exchequer has communicated to me your decision respecting the final abandonment of the Engine for calcu-lating and printing tables by means of Differences, the construction of which I commenced superintending for the Government about twenty years ago.

I have to thank you for the offer on the part of government of that portion of the Engine which has been completed although under all the circumstances I am compelled to decline accepting it.

I infer however both from the regret with which you have arrived at the conclusion as well as from the offer itself that you would much more willingly assist if the creation of the Analytical Engine became the official cause of its [presumably Charles means the Difference Engine's] total suppression or possibly of its first appearance in a foreign land.

I also perceive in that communication the expression of feeling that although I have no other than a moral claim for twenty years of exertion accompanied by great pecuniary as well as personal sacrifices, yet that those exertions in the cause of science ought not to remain utterly unrecognised and unresolved by the Government.

These views have rendered the task I had proposed to myself in this letter somewhat [the first half of the word is illegible but 'somewhat' seems the most likely overall reading] less difficult. Its object is to request you to take those claims into consideration.

But as I am convinced that it would be unjust to you as well as to myself to ask for a decision without personally communicating facts and views which ought to be brought before you I should esteem it a favor if you would allow me the honour of an interview.

I have the honour to be Sir, your obedient Charles Babbage.
8 Nov 1842

Not that Charles was at all obedient as far as Peel was concerned.

The following day, Peel wrote back to agree to the interview. On the face of it, his willingness to meet Charles is surprising; we can be quite sure that Peel did not want to meet. But Charles was an influential and famous man, and Peel presumably knew that refusing the request for an interview would have been a mistake. Or maybe Peel wanted the opportunity of telling Charles to his face what he thought of him?

In any event, Peel sent Charles a brief note:

Sir Robert Peel presents his compliments to Mr Babbage and will have the pleasure of seeing him at eleven o'clock tomorrow (Friday) morning.
Whitehall
10 November 1842

Charles prepared carefully for his interview with Peel, making detailed notes that presumably he didn't actually take into the meeting room (I presume the meeting took place at 10 Downing Street, although I haven't been able to find any definite confirmation of this) but tried to commit to memory. He made a fair copy of these notes, but the rough draft, below, seems to me to indicate more clearly the vexed and stressed state of his mind. His notes are full of personal resentment; they aren't very professional and they hardly augur well for the meeting:

Notes for Peel interview
His advisers and zealots
Sheepshanks
Dr Rob
Secretary of [illegible]
Test of their sincerity will carry me publicly
Grounds of claims
Takes up because useful for marine not for me personally
Gave up profession in early life to follow science
hence invented Machine
Gave the government all that sacrifice and undertook at their wish to make it for them
made no [illegible]
The public insist that the money expended has gone into my pocket
Unless the government do [illegible] public act this cannot be disproved if they do anything it will rebut it if they do not the public will continue to say that it is because I have been paid
2 Refused during that period 2000
3 Twelve years of labor advance of money
4 Eight years of anxiety and indecision preventing every other arrangement
Doubt about Engineers [*sic*] life
5 Govt wished me to make it for them
– it was discontinued from causes under which I had no control
– it was abandoned by Govt
Other men of science rewarded
Airy 1300

Buckland 1000
Peacock 1800
Herschel Baronet
Sedgwick 1000
Whewell 2000
[illegible] to all sorts of people
Scarletts [*sic*] compensation

The interview took place on the fateful morning of 11 November 1842.

Charles wrote a detailed account of the interview – including actual verbatim dialogue – in his diary, if 'wrote' is the right word to express the way in which, hot with fury and disappointment, he raced back from his meeting with Peel to scratch out a report on paper, as though this was the only way he might obtain a vestige of relief. Charles' immense upset is evident in the very scrawl he sets down on the page, in marked contrast to his usual neat, orderly compositions. Uncharacteristically, his description of the meeting leaves out much of the punctuation and even some of the words.

The timing of the meeting was certainly unfortunate. Peel had come to power during an economic recession, which had featured a slump in world trade and a budget deficit of £7.5 million run up by the previous Whig government. Britain was full of half-starved families – it must be said that Charles' £17,000 would have fed thousands of them – and there was no indication things would get better in the short term.

The following winter, in November 1843, Charles Dickens would sit down to write his *A Christmas Carol*, a book that seems poignant enough today and which seemed almost unbearably moving at a time when most British working people were undernourished, and children such as Tiny Tim were routinely at risk of dying of malnutrition. As for Peel, so far 1842 had been an exceptionally tough year for him. Shortly before the day when he met Charles, he had written to his wife, Julia, that he was 'fagged to death' with the cares of office. Hunger and rioting were widespread. Peel was in no mood to meet Charles at all, let alone in the mood for a stressful confrontation with a man for whom diplomacy was not, to put things mildly, a strong point.

Here is the full account Charles wrote of his meeting with Peel. To my knowledge, this has never been published before: the circular parentheses are Charles' and the square ones are mine.

Recollections of an interview with
Sir R Peel on Friday November 11 1842 at 11am

I first asked Sir Peel [*sic*] if he had seen Sir Wm Follett within the last two days giving as my reason that if he had it might perhaps save him time as in that case Sir Wm Follett would have anticipated for me some part of what I had to communicate.

I then informed Sir RP that many circumstances had at last forced upon me the conviction which I had long resisted that there existed amongst men of science great jealousy of me. I said that I had been reluctantly forced to this conclusion of which I now had ample evidence, which however I should not state unless he asked me. In reply to some observation of Sir RP in a subsequent part of the conversation I mentioned one circumstance that within a few days the Secretary of one of the foreign embassies in London has incidentally remarked to me that he had long observed a great jealousy of me in certain classes of English Society.

I then said that as he Peel must of course obtain his views both of the Difference and the Analytical engine from others I thought it right without wishing to allude to any individuals nor wishing to know the name of any of his scientific advisers yet for his P's sake as well as my own to mention this conviction.

I turned to the next subject, the importance of the Analytical Engine. I stated my own opinion that in the future scientific history of the present day it would probably form a marked epoch and that much depended upon the result of this interview. I added that the Difference Engine was only capable [of] applications to one limited part of the science (although that part was certainly of great importance and capable of more immediate practical applications than any other) but that the Analytical Engine embraced the whole science.

I stated that it was in fact already invented and that it exceeded all anticipations I had ever entertained respecting the powers of applying machinery to science.

I then mentioned to Sir R P that one of the first mathematicians in Europe Plana had written to me his views respecting it. 'We hitherto' (said Plana) 'have possessed full power over the Legislative department of Analysis in the Executive we have been all feeble – your invention appears to have given us the same controul [the word "control" was often spelt like that in Charles' day] over the executive as we have hitherto had over its legislative.'

I now observed that I came to the point on which I had asked for an interview. I stated that at an early period of life I gave up the prospect of succeeding my father in a lucrative profession (that of a banker in the city) in order that I might devote myself to science. [I have not found any documentary evidence for this claim and Charles may simply have raised it to try to bolster his argument.] That in following out that pursuit I had invented the Difference Engine. That the in 1822 government wished that such a machine should be constructed. That at their desire I had undertaken the construction of it for them. That during twelve years I had amidst many difficulties had [*sic*] devoted my whole time unceasingly to that object.

That circumstances over which I had no control [Charles here spells this word without a 'u'] caused what was then thought a temporary cessation – that during this interval I had been examining other combinations of machinery and had opened out views which seemed likely to have the most important bearings on the machine then constructing.

That when new arrangements had been made and the government wished the work to be resumed I thought it would [be] improper to withhold from them the knowledge I had thus acquired. That I did communicate that knowledge but that no decision was arrived at by the government. That as time advanced those views became gradually more clear and distinct so that ultimately it appeared it would be both a *shorter* and *more economical* course to throw aside all that had been done and to make a new Difference Engine using for it some of the more simple contrivances which I had invented for the Analytical Engine. Finding still that the government after repeated applications came to no decision I confined my subsequent applications to the simple question whether they intended to call on me to complete the old difference engine [Charles does not use initial capitals here for the name of the machine] or to abandon it altogether.

Year after year passed in which I was kept in the most harassing state of uncertainty that now after nine years [Charles wrote 'eight' but crossed it out and replaced it with 'nine'] I had just received notice of the government altogether to abandon the engine that during this time I had myself expended a large sum of money [on] and that the public had constantly accused me of having received that money which [the] government has paid so that on the grounds of the great pecuniary and personal sacrifices which I had made and on that of the expectations I might reasonably have entertained upon the completion of such a machine which had now been by *their decision* abandoned I thought that the services I had rendered ought not to be utterly unrequited and unrewarded.

I then adverted to another circumstance that whilst I had been thus exerting myself in advancing science, many others pursuing the same career had been rewarded by the government for their labors whilst I was made the marked exception.

Sir R P himself immediately adverted to the pensions given to science and literature which amount only to 1200£ each year. I remarked that although I partly alluded to them yet that there were other occasions on which science was rewarded and said I would mention half a dozen names not known to him leaving him to put the amount of income derived by them which he probably knew better than I did.
Airey Astrom. Royal 800 + pension + house 1500
Buckland [illegible word] of Christ Church 1000
Herschel – a baronet -----
Peacock Dean of Ely 1800
Sedgwick Dean of Norwich 1000
Whewell Master of Trinity 2000
I then concluded with stating that on those grounds I thought I had some claim to the consideration of the government.

Sir R. P. denied altogether that either of these claims entitled me to any thing [Charles writes this here as two words]. He observed that I had rendered the Difference Engine useless by inventing a better [machine; Charles leaves this word out but we can infer it].

I remarked that it [Charles clearly means the Difference Engine] would if finished do more than I had promised and that although it was undoubtedly superseded by better machinery yet that I had never stated that it was useless. I said that the general fact of machinery being superseded in several of our great branches of manufacturing was perfectly well known.

In reply to the statement of the anxiety I had suffered and the vexation of finding that the public believed I had profited by the money expended I mentioned that the belief was so [not legible but probably 'prevalent'] that several of my intimate friends had asked if it were not true; and that I had even met with it on the hustings at Finsbury.

Sir B took up the latter remark and said that I was too sensitive to such attacks [and] that men of sense never cared for them.

I looked at him and said, 'You must Sir R Peel in your own experience of public life have frequently observed that the best heads and highest minds are often the most susceptible of annoyance from the injustice of the public.' (He seemed to admit it but I am not sure that the name of Romilly Whitbread and others occurred to him.)

With respect to the other ground of claim that as one of the class of men of science I had been neglected entirely.

He tried, rather artfully, to interpret the statement I had made of the emoluments of the half-dozen men I had quoted as meaning to put myself in competition for the places held by the individuals Airy and Herschel (Peel seeming to think Herschel held some office). I had commenced my statement with denying this expressly and had again repeated at the conclusion though they were all men eminent in science and that not wishing to disparage them in the slightest degree I had yet a right to be considered as belonging to that class.

Sir R Peel's first remark, however, was that most of them were professional rewards. This I at once denied and said that it was perfectly well known that they were *not* given for professional services for that though they were eminent in science they had *not* any of them *ever done* any thing to distinguish them *professionally*. (This of course alluded to the clerical portion of the list)

[There is a short phrase here which I have not been able to decipher fully and which may be some note that Charles wrote to himself.]

Here from [it is not definite that this word is 'from' as the word is illegible but 'from' seems to make the most sense in context] finding Sir R P utterly denying that I had any claim I merely remarked that I considered myself as having been treated with great injustice but that as he was of a different opinion I could not help myself, at which I got up and wished him good morning.

On the other side of the last folio of paper giving an account of the meeting, Charles writes, in a slightly calmer way:

Sir R P seemed excessively angry and annoyed during the whole interview but more particularly when I knocked over with some vivacity his argument about professional service. He then proceeded to attempt humbug, saying that the institutions of the country admitted of certain places being given to certain professions for services not exactly professional.

I listened to all his statements looking him steadfastly in the face. When he got aground, I still retained my view upon him as if expecting at last some argument would be produced. This position of course was not very agreeable and certainly not very dignified for a prime minister.

In *The Cogwheel Brain*, Doron Swade quotes a letter to Charles from Charles' friend Sir James South, in which Sir James 'tried to warn Babbage that Peel was beleaguered and that Babbage should tread warily'. As Sir James writes: 'I write this to *entreat* you in your interview with Peel which we think he will not deny you, not to say anything which *can possibly* irritate him. He is at present in a false or bad position, pray mind *you* do not change places with him.'

But Charles, disastrously, ignored this advice. Swade also says: 'Someone less proud, principled and aggrieved than Babbage might have read the signs and succeeded in prevailing upon Peel who was, publicly at least, well disposed towards science. Not Babbage.'

One imagines Steve Jobs handling this interview infinitely better, and saying things about both Engines to inspire Peel rather than trying to score points off him.

The Peel/Babbage interview is surely one of the most significant events in the history of science, defining as it did what turned out to be the government's final refusal to grant Charles any more funds.

This extraordinary interview is certainly much less well known to history than it deserves to be. For example, there is no mention of it at all in Douglas Hurd's lengthy biography of Peel, *Robert Peel* (2007). In that 436-page volume, Charles does not get a single mention. Nor, for that matter, does Airy.

This document in which Charles transcribes his recollection of the meeting – frequently seeming to use his pen so harshly that he almost scratches the words on to the paper and also leaves many words out, such was his frenzy at wanting to get everything down – sets down with painful precision exactly why he never achieved his dream. How can he possibly have thought that the way he was behaving during the meeting could advance the machines' interests at all?

Sadly, I think the answer to that question is that, in the end, he didn't care as much about the fate of his Engines as about his own ego. Instead of trying to explain to Peel the exact reasons why he, Charles, had abandoned work on the Difference Engine and started working on the Analytical Engine and trying to let Peel see the potentially enormous benefit that both machines would bring to the British Industrial Revolution and to Britain generally, Charles is clearly more interested in scoring points off Peel, and in making his opponent seem small, than in advancing the cause of the cogwheel computers.

In fact, Charles' discussion about his machines during the interview with Peel occupied, by Charles' own account, quite a small portion of the interview. The rest of the time he was bitching about people in the scientific world who he knew had been given grants and high status by the government, and Charles doesn't even baulk from implying that even his close friend Herschel was given unjust preferment by the government, as Herschel seems to be included by implication in the accusation that these scientific people have not done anything to deserve their position. Indeed, the whole interview was a complete shambles and pretty much put paid to an information technology revolution taking place in the nineteenth century.

We see precisely in this reported interview what Charles' weaknesses were. As we've already seen, he liked winning an advantage over other people and presumably gained some perverse satisfaction from being able to criticise Peel and trying to score intellectual points over him, just as he had tried to do so on other occasions in his life, during the incident with Marryat and on other occasions after that.

Charles was unquestionably a hero of the history of computing, but here, in his own report on the meeting, he unconsciously reveals his weaknesses. Besides, not everything that he told Peel was actually true. It simply wasn't the case that over twelve years Charles had devoted his whole time unceasingly to the Engines: he never devoted his whole time to the Engines, for all his lengthy periods of work on them over many decades.

Also, it's intellectually rather dishonest of him to imply, as he did by his own account at the meeting with Peel, that the only reason he, Charles, worked on the Difference Engine at all was because the government wanted it to be completed. The government certainly did – they would hardly have granted Charles £17,000 otherwise – but the truth was that Charles was fascinated and indeed obsessed by the idea of a mechanical calculator, and he himself took the initiative to design the machine as best he could and spent his own money, perhaps about £20,000, on developing it.

You feel in this interview that Charles is more interested in putting pressure on Peel than in having a proper conversation with him about the machine, and the way the meeting apparently ended, with a completely futile argument about the nature of professional service to the government, is indeed embarrassing. Peel clearly didn't like Charles, and it's quite clear that the feeling was mutual. But unfortunately if you want to win over intelligent, influential and powerful people, you don't do so by annoying them. You win over them by showing you care sincerely about their own agenda and own interests, their own time frame and their own feelings.

After the interview, Charles could hardly be blamed for thinking that, when it came to furthering the Difference Engine and in particular the Analytical Engine, he was on his own. On the other hand, even if Peel had assented to Charles' request, can we be certain that, if Peel had granted Charles, say, another £10,000, then the government's bill for underwriting cogwheel calculation would simply have been £27,000 rather than £17,000?

The truth of the matter, surely, is that Charles simply was not able to manage the project to build the Difference Engine or the Analytical Engine satisfactorily and no amount of righteous indignation on his part that he had invested a huge portion of his own fortune in trying to achieve this negates that point.

Nathan Myhrvold, formerly the chief technology officer of Microsoft and the founder of Intellectual Ventures (an organisation which invests in innovative and promising technology), has studied Charles' life in detail and believes firmly that this inability on the part of Charles to manage a large project was the main reason why he did not bring any of his cogwheel machines to fruition.

On the other hand, we should sympathise and empathise with Charles, who was trying single-handedly not only to create a new kind of profession – the profession of computer scientists – but also was seeking to start a new kind of industry, the computer industry, although he did not fully realise that at the time. Yet if he had been more gracious, if he had approached Peel with a humble sense of having not, in fact, delivered a Difference Engine despite the government's enormous grant to him, surely he would have done better. If only Ada had been at the meeting too! Had she been, the early history of the computer could have been, and probably would have been, very different.

But after the disastrous deaths of the two Georgianas in Charles' life, his loving and wonderful wife and his no doubt charming yet sadly unrecorded daughter, Charles was wary of allowing feminine influence into his life again, let alone in a crucial meeting with the chief of Britain and of its global Empire.

14

A STAGE PLAY THAT HELD UP A MIRROR TO CHARLES' HEART

'Could we do something so difficult, something so … huge?' Pook asked. 'You and me?'

Beetlebrow gazed into her brown eyes. She saw Pook's wearied expression.

'You and me can do anything,' Beetlebrow said.

From *Beetlebrow the Thief* by Ben Parker (2018)

But perhaps Ada could help even now, after the disastrous meeting with Sir Robert Peel had irrevocably taken place?

The sole mention Charles makes of Ada in his autobiography is this:

Some time after the appearance of his memoir on the subject in the *Bibliothèque Universelle de Genève*, the late Countess of Lovelace informed me that she had translated the memoir of Menabrea. I asked why she had not herself written an original paper on a subject with which she was so intimately acquainted? To this Lady Lovelace replied that the thought had not occurred to her. I then suggested that she should add some notes to Menabrea's memoir: an idea which was immediately adopted.

We discussed together the various illustrations that might be introduced: I suggested several, but the selection was entirely her own. So also was the algebraic working out of the different problems, except, indeed, that relating to the numbers of Bernoulli, which I had offered to do to save Lady Lovelace the trouble. This she sent back to me for an amendment, having detected a grave mistake which I had made in the process.

The notes of the Countess of Lovelace extend to about three times the length of the original memoir. Their author has entered fully into almost all the very difficult and abstract questions connected with the subject.

The two memoirs taken together furnish, to those who are capable of understanding the reasoning, a complete demonstration – *That the whole of developments and operations of analysis are now capable of being executed by machinery* [Charles' italics].

It is a significant mention, though clearly Charles wants to avoid saying anything at all about Ada in a personal sense.

So if we can believe Charles' account, which there is no particular reason for not believing, Ada undertook the translation of Menabrea's memoir at her own initiative, and it was only after Charles made his suggestion that she added her own material to the translation. This material has come to be called Ada's *Notes*. They total about 20,000 words.

Ada was arguably the first person, apart from Charles himself, who understood the full importance of his work on calculating machinery in general and his invention of the Analytical Engine in particular. Ada's *Notes* were never completely forgotten by people who had a professional interest in the early history of the computer; for example, the great computer pioneer Alan Turing was aware of them. But it was only in the 1970s – thanks to the arduous efforts of the Australian computer historian Dr Allan G. Bromley, who conducted detailed research of Charles' books and documents – that Charles' work has received intense scrutiny, which in turn shone a new spotlight on Ada's own work.

From the 1970s until around the early years of the twenty-first century, Ada was seen by many male computer scientists, not including Dr Bromley, as an overrated aristocratic amateur who was little more than a painful thorn in Charles' side. Male computer scientists have frequently preferred to see Ada like this: the idea that a mere woman, twenty-four years his junior and born into privilege – and the daughter of a bisexual poet to boot – could possibly have added anything to

Charles' intellectual life is as much an anathema to them as the discovery of an impossible-to-remove bug at the heart of some pet software they've designed.

In fact, male computer scientists generally have a track record of disparaging the contribution women make to their profession, just as society has, both in the past and even now, regarded mathematics and science as areas in which women should not tread. Mary Somerville only became interested in mathematics when she enjoyed maths puzzles put into British embroidery magazines that wished to give their lady readers something else to think about other than needlework. More recently, Katherine Johnson, the African American mathematician whose calculations of orbital mechanics as a NASA employee during her thirty-five-year career were vital for the success of the first and subsequent US manned spaceflights, experienced great prejudice and misogyny among her male colleagues, chronicled in the book *Hidden Figures* (2016) and the movie of the same title which was released in the same year.

As regards Ada, the most virulent – and, frankly, obnoxious – criticism of her in any published work of which I'm aware is found in *The Little Engines That Could've* by the late Bruce Collier. This book contains much inspired technical material about Charles' machines of the mind. But when Collier writes about Ada, this is what he says:

> There is one subject ancillary to Babbage on which far too *much* has been written, and that is the contributions of Ada Lovelace … It is no exaggeration to say that she was a manic-depressive with the most amazing delusions about her own talents, and a rather shallow understanding of both Charles Babbage and the Analytical Engine … To me, this familiar material seems to make obvious once again that Ada was as mad as a hatter … I will retain an open mind on whether Ada was crazy because of her substance abuse … I guess *someone* has to be the most overrated figure in the history of computing.

What is especially interesting about this comment is why Collier is so willing to accept Charles' authority on matters to do directly with the Difference Engine and Analytical Engine but refuses to accept what

Charles says about Ada in his autobiography. Charles could certainly on occasion get into an irrational emotional state – he spent most of the meeting with Sir Robert Peel in one, for example – and his puns were often, as we've seen, rather feeble, but he wasn't a liar. There is absolutely no reason why we can't trust what Charles says in *Passages from the Life of a Philosopher* about the genesis of Ada's writing about the Analytical Engine.

After a few years of married happiness, Ada started to find her husband William annoying due to his lack of any tangible ambition. There is plenty of evidence that she enjoyed making love with him, and he was certainly her first serious sexual relationship, though despite the fling with her tutor apparently not leading to full 'connection' we can't, of course, be sure Ada was a virgin before she got married, and in any case that is surely her business rather than ours.

Yet one can't always be making love; it's also necessary to do some work in the world. Ada by now regarded her husband as very much a pointless person. Still, after hearing about the Peel debacle, which Charles must surely have told her about, perhaps she didn't really consider Charles much better. After all, Charles had made himself look like a total idiot to Sir Robert Peel and therefore to the government, and while there is no reference to that humiliation in any of the extant letters between Charles and Ada or vice versa, it's surely impossible not to believe that Ada, and presumably Lady Byron too, knew about what had happened. It's not difficult to imagine what Lady Byron thought when she learned about the interview, but more difficult to decide what Ada's inner reaction to it was. Annoyance with Charles' short-sightedness and impetuousness? Yes, at least if he gave her an emotionally accurate account of what had happened, which perhaps he did. Sympathy? Yes, surely. And is it in any way possible that her volunteering to translate Menabrea's article off her own bat, only telling Charles that she had done so after she had, was based, at least in part, on Ada wanting to help Charles after the disaster of the Peel interview?

During the first few years of Ada's marriage, Charles had often visited Ada and William at their home in Ockham in Surrey, and those were times when, if you visited rich friends in the country, you usually stayed with them for a week or more.

Ada certainly liked seeing Charles. In one brief letter written on 24 March, almost certainly in 1839, which would have meant she was writing on a Sunday, an especially plausible day for writing letters of invitation, she chastises Charles playfully: 'Sat[ur]d[a]y next will suit us perfectly, but we hope you will stay on as far into the following week, as possible. Surely the machine allows you a holiday sometimes.'

This note sets the tone for how their friendship developed in the late 1830s and the 1840s, with Ada often describing herself as 'a fairy', a word she loved to use whenever she wanted to write flirtatiously to Charles, which she often did. In November 1839, she writes to Charles to ask if he could help her find someone to teach her mathematics:

I have quite made up my mind to have some instruction next year in Town, but the difficulty is to find the *man*. *I* have a peculiar *way* of *learning*, & I think it must be a peculiar man to teach me successfully.–

Do not reckon me conceited, for I am sure I am the very last person to think over-highly of *myself*; but I believe I have the *power* of going just as far as I like in such pursuits, & where there is so very decided a taste, I should almost say a *passion*, as I have for them, I question if there is not always some portion of natural genius even. – At any rate the taste is such that it *must* be gratified. – I mention all this to you because I think you are or may be in the way of meeting with the right sort of person, & I am sure you have at any rate the *will* to give me any assistance in your power.

Lord L [Lovelace] desires all sorts of reminiscences, & that I am to take care & remind you about coming to Ockham. –

Yours most sincerely,
Ada Lovelace

When Charles replied on 29 November 1839, he did so with similar playful flirtatiousness:

Dear Lady Lovelace

I make no most ungrateful returns for your kind letter from London. I have lately been ever more than usually occupied by the Engine.

I allowed myself ten days in Cheshire and finding this did not do I was obliged to go to Brighton for five days which restored me to the calculating state and have been working very hard ever since.

I have just arrived at an improvement which will throw back all my drawings full six months unless I succeed in carrying out some new views which may shorten the labor.

I have now commenced the description of the Engine so that I am fully occupied.

I think your taste for mathematics is so decided that it ought not to be checked. I have been making enquiry but cannot find at present any one at all to recommend to assist you. I will however not forget the search.

The London World is very quiet at present. Mrs De Morgan has just added a new philosopher to its population and Mr Sheridan Knowles has written a most popular play called 'Love' to which I have been a frequent attendant. I met the author yesterday at a dinner at Mr Rogers'.

I could not by possibility have visited you this year in the West, but I cherish the hope of getting a few days at Ockham when I can indulge in a little recreation.

Pray forgive my epistolary negligence and believe me with best regards to Lord Lovelace.

> Ever very sincerely yours.
> C Babbage

So what does this letter tell us about Charles' feelings for Ada? It doesn't appear to be one from a man in love with the lady to whom it is addressed, though he hardly appears to be indifferent to her either. It is the letter of a respectful gentleman friend to a lady, but after all, the lady was married, and if a gentleman writes an ardent letter to a married lady in the hope that she may peruse it on the breakfast table, there is the very realistic danger that the husband may peruse it too, or instead of her.

Which is not to say that it is provable that Charles ever had any definite amorous designs on Ada – it simply isn't possible to demonstrate this from the extant documentary evidence. What is provable, though, and unquestionably the case, and indeed that letter just now quoted is a good example, is that as Charles' friendship with Ada progressed, he exposed himself emotionally to her more and more.

So in this letter Charles hints at despondency or even depression in relation to his time in Cheshire. He also makes clear how much he enjoys going to Ockham. Yet it is the reference to his 'frequent' visits to see the play *Love* (1839) that are surely most revealing here. They read like a discreet revelation from an emotionally hungry man to a woman whom he knows cares for him and who he is hoping will care for him more and more.

But what was this play that Charles was making such a fuss about? To the modern reader, Sheridan Knowles' play *Love* will seem mostly melodramatic twaddle, but it does have its moments, and the Shakespearean pastiche style in which it is mostly written occasionally soars into something memorable, such as the character Ulrick's paean to the eponymous 'Love' in Act 3, scene 1:

> O, never did achievement rival Love's
> For daring enterprise and execution!
> It will do miracles; attempt such things
> As make ambition, fiery at it is,
> Dull plodding tameness, in comparison.
> Talk of the miser's passion for his store –
> 'Tis milk and water to the lover's, which
> Defies the mines of earth and caves of ocean
> To match its treasure! Talk of height, breadth, depth –
> There is no measure for the lover's passion,
> No bounds to what 'twill do!

It's not known how often Charles went to see *Love*, but 'frequent' certainly means more than twice. Presumably he wouldn't have gone more than once had he not enjoyed lines like the above, and what they made him feel.

Charles' love of *Love* is pretty much the only evidence in the entire extant documentation about his life that gives us any indication of his fondness for something that is cultural in a dramatic and emotional, rather than scientific, way. This being so, it's surely worthwhile to consider at least one other perspective on *Love* in Charles' own day.

Buried in the 9 November 1839 issue of *The Spectator*, the weekly British magazine on politics first published on 6 July 1828, there is a highly articulate review of the play that takes us right back to a bustling autumn night in the theatre in that ostensibly remote, but actually oddly familiar time. This is an extract from the review:

> The first representation of Sheridan Knowles's new play, *Love*, filled Covent Garden with eager crowds, whose hushed attention through-out testified to its interest, and was the worthiest tribute that the author could desire: applause was not wanting either, but it was repressed as an interruption … Knowles was called for, as usual, but, with good taste, he left the theatre (in which he had not been visible to the audience) so soon as the success of his play was determined.
>
> *Love* is a drama of passion; character is only so far developed as the passion requires, and action there is little: everything tends to the main purpose of exhibiting the influence of love on human nature as exemplified by the principal character. These are the Countess Eppenstein, daughter of the Duke of Corinthia and her secretary Huon, her father's serf; between whom a mutual affection, unrecognised by either, has sprung up. In the struggle between love and pride in the breast of the Countess, and between love and duty on the part of the serf, is the source of the interest …
>
> The serious interest is relieved by a pleasant little underplot, wherein the everyday aspect of the tender passion is depicted. Catherine, a sprightly girl, with wit, sense and spirit, thus rallies her dull-souled swain – why, what a man you are, Sir Rupert! Fie! What! Not a word to say? Let's change the theme then: the argument shall be that you're in love; the which shall I affirm while you deny … Such materials as these in Knowles's hands promise a beautiful drama, happily blending the lively and pathetic: and such it is up to the end of the third act; but the last two 'drag their slow length along', weakening the interest, and wearying the patience of the audience.
>
> This is owing to two defects of construction. To make out five acts where three would have sufficed, the dialogue is expanded where it should have been compressed: four scenes occupy three acts, one of which (the fifth) would better be dispensed with altogether. Skilful pruning may lighten the heaviness of some scenes, but curtailment is a sorry substitute for condensation.
>
> […]

In spite of these faults, the inherent power of the writing is so strong, that not only is admiration compelled, but sympathy enlisted by the passionate earnestness of the dialogue: you feel that the author's heart is in his work; and nature as a voice speaks in the language of the characters, though the occasion is arbitrary and gratuitous. Nothing in the play is finer than many parts of the long scene in the fourth act between the Countess and Huon.

As *The Spectator* review is so fulsome in its praise of that scene, it would be churlish not to include an extract here. In some lines Huon speaks to the Countess in that scene, he seems to be speaking of a kind of general, comprehensive love of womankind. One is reminded of what Goethe has Faust say: '*Das Ewig-Weibliche zieht uns hinan*' ('eternal womanhood drives us forward'):

Huon. I loved thee once!
Oh, tell me, when was it I loved thee not?
Was't in my childhood, boyhood, manhood? Oh!
In all of them loved thee! And were I now
To live the span of my first life, twice told,
And then to wither, thou surviving me,
And yet I lived in my own sweet memory,
Then might's thou say of me, 'He loved me once;
But that was all his life!'

We're reminded of the misquotation referred to above which Charles appends to the start of his autobiography:

I'm a philosopher. Confound them all.
Birds, beasts and men; but no, not womankind.

Or perhaps Charles did not see this proclamation as being to all of womanhood – the womanhood that had in two instances ruined his life by dying. Perhaps, instead, in his imagination he regarded this proclamation as coming from within him, to Ada. For Charles, possibly his mention of the play *Love* in the letter he sent to Ada was the closest he dare get to telling her how much she meant to him.

15

ADA THE FAIRY

And those things do best please me
That befall preposterously.

> Puck, in *A Midsummer Night's Dream*,
> by William Shakespeare (1595 or 1596)

Ada Lovelace offered Charles charm, companionship, society, feminine graces and good looks (Ada was not a great beauty, but she was elegant and handsome) at a time when he very badly needed all those things. Ada was also endlessly friendly and supportive towards Charles, so often making suggestions to him that would bring him companionship and the chance for respite from his endless labours on his disappointing and expensive Engines.

Here, for example, is a letter Ada wrote to Charles on Tuesday, 12 January 1841:

My Dear Babbage.

If you will come by the *Railway* on Friday, we will send the carriage to meet you at *Weybridge*, for the Train that leaves Town about 4 o'clock & arrives at Weybridge a few minutes before 5 o'clock.

Bring warm coats or cloaks, as the carriage will be probably an open one.

If you are a *Skater*, pray bring *Skates* to Ockham; that being the fashionable occupation here now, & one *I* have much taken to.

I am very anxious to talk to you. I will give you a hint on *what*. It strikes me that at some future time, (it might be even within 3 or

4 years, or it might be *many* years hence), *my head* may be made by you subservient to some of *your* purposes & plans. If so, *if* ever I could be worthy or capable of being *used* by you, my head will be yours. And it is on this that I wish to speak most seriously to you. You have always been a kind and real & most invaluable friend to *me*; & I would that I could in any way repay it, though I scarcely dare so exalt myself as to hope however humbly, that I can ever be intellectually worthy to attempt serving *you*.

Yours most sincerely

A.A. Lovelace

You *must* stay some days with us. Now don't contradict me.

The tone of this letter is fairly typical of how Ada usually was when she wrote to Charles: slightly flirtatious, a bit forceful and with some intellectual humility, though on occasion she dispensed with the humility. She has often been criticised for being big-headed, and it's true that occasionally in her letters to Lady Byron, Charles and others she is conceited. But the fact is that the nature of her life, as a housewife and homemaker, denied the intellectual career she craved, and surrounded by people (including her husband) who didn't understand her very well, she had to, in effect, shout at herself in order to keep going intellectually.

Besides, people who blame Ada for being big-headed have perhaps never had to embark on a long and complex intellectual project such as writing a book or a complicated document such as Ada's remarkable *Notes*. Such projects require authorial confidence and optimism if the project is to be completed successfully. On the whole, I like the way Ada communicates with Charles. Her friendliness and hospitality must have made a big difference to him, a man whose life had been so plagued by disaster.

There is no record of Charles' visit to Ockham for that particular weekend, let alone any account of the great inventive analyst skating on the ice, which would surely have been quite a sight. If he *had* put skates on and ventured onto the ice, one imagines him subsequently declaiming to Ada about the phenomenon of friction (or lack of) while he was skating. But there is no reason to believe that he didn't visit Ada and William that weekend, even if he didn't, in the end, decide to skate.

Six weeks later, Ada returned to her fashionable, modern house on St James's Square. She urged Charles to visit at once and mentioned with mounting excitement that they would embark on a project together. On what would have been her father Lord Byron's fifty-third birthday, she wrote to her close friend:

Monday, 22 February,
Ockham Park

My Dear Mr Babbage

We are to move to Town on Thursday; & I hope to see you as soon afterwards as you like, – the sooner the better. Remember that *one* o'clock is the best hour for a call. –

I believe I shall perhaps pass Sunday Evening with Mr & Mrs De Morgan [Augustus and Sophia (Frend)]; but this is not yet quite fixed, & if it should not take place, will *you* come & spend it in St James' Sqre – You see I am determined to celebrate the Sabbath *Mathematically*, in one way or other. -

I have been at work very strenuously since I saw you, & quite as successfully as heretofore. I am now studying attentively the *Finite Differences* ... And in this I have more particular interest, because I know it bears directly on some of *your* business. – Altogether I am going on well, & just as we might have anticipated. –

I think I am more determined than ever in my future plans; and I have quite made up my mind that nothing must be suffered to inter-fere with them. – I intend to make such arrangements in Town as will secure me a couple of hours daily (with very few exceptions), for my studies.

I think much of the possible (I believe I may say the *probable*) future connection between *us*; and it is an anticipation I increasingly like to dwell on. I think great good may be the result to *both* of us; and I suspect that the idea, (which by the bye is one that I believe I have *long* entertained, in a vague and crude form), was one of those happy instincts which do occur to one sometimes so unaccountably & fortunately. At least, in my opinion, the results *may* ultimately prove it such. Believe me

Yours most sincerely
Ada Lovelace

We see very clearly here how, whatever emotional gratification Charles got from knowing Ada, she in turn found her friendship with him exciting for one major reason at least: that she hoped Charles would help to advance her own intellectual life. She found the job of translating Luigi Federico Menabrea's paper on the Analytical Engine utterly fascinating, but the task of adding her own *Notes* to it even more thrilling.

For Ada, the undertaking of writing her *Notes* was the highpoint in her life of intellectual achievement. When the *Notes* were published there was no great fuss made about them even in the scientific community, and how could there have been, when her thinking was maybe a century ahead of its time? But today, her *Notes* are recognised by the modern world as the extraordinarily brilliant thinking of a true genius.

Ada launched into her work on the translation with all her energy. We have no reason not to believe Charles' account in his autobiography that it was Ada's idea to produce the translation in the first place. On Sunday, 2 July 1843, he wrote a letter to her that included the following comment on a draft he had seen of some of her work:

There is still one trifling misapprehension about the Variable cards – a variable card may order any number of Variables to receive the same number upon theirs at the same instant of time – But a Variable card never can be directed to order more than one Variable to be given off at once because the mill could not receive it and the mechanism would not permit it. All this was impossible for you to know by an intuition and the more I read your Notes the more surprised I am at them and regret not having earlier explored so rich a vein of the noblest metal.

Charles had, in fact, misunderstood how Ada saw the Variable Cards. As she says:

> I cannot imagine what you mean about the Variable-Cards; since I never supposed in my own mind that one Variable-card *could* give off more than one Variable at a time; nor have (as far as I can make out) [I] expressed such an idea in any passage whatsoever.

This misconception by Charles appears to be the grave mistake to which he refers.

Yes, the Analytical Engine was Charles' idea, but Ada was not to be dominated by him intellectually. It is quite clear from reading the extant correspondence between them on the matter, that even though she was perfectly ready to seek advice from him when she felt she needed it, she was the mistress of the enterprise of writing the *Notes*, not him.

Some male computer scientists have suggested, though with less insistence and acerbity than was the case in the final decades of the twentieth century, that Ada's translation and notes were really the work of Charles. But again, this suggestion seems to spring from the same anti-Ada mindset that led to Bruce Collier calling her 'as mad as a hatter'. Besides, as Charles, who knew Ada and worked with her, very willingly reports to posterity that Ada's translation and *Notes* were her own work, what right has anyone from posterity, who didn't know Ada and never worked with her, to contradict him retrospectively? How would we feel about someone born about 200 years in the future telling posterity that we didn't actually carry out work we know we did, and which all our friends believed us to have carried out?

Here is an example of Ada's translation:

> The rigid exactness of those laws which regulate numerical calculations must frequently have suggested the employment of material instruments, either for executing the whole of such calculations or for abridging them; and thence have arisen several inventions having this object in view.
>
> For instance, the much-admired machine of Pascal is now simply an object of curiosity, which, whilst it displays the powerful intellect

of its inventor, is yet of little utility in itself. Its powers extended no further than the execution of the first four operations of arithmetic, and indeed were in reality confined to that of the first two, since multiplication and division were the result of a series of additions and subtractions.

The chief drawback hitherto on most of such machines is, that they require the continual intervention of a human agent to regulate their movements, and thence arises a source of errors; so that, if their use has not become general for large numerical calculations, it is because they have not in fact resolved the double problem which the question presents, that of *correctness* in the results, united with *economy* of time.

When, in his autobiography, Charles refers to the 'two memoirs taken together', he presumably means Ada's translation and also her *Notes*.

While Charles indeed only made the one reference to Ada in *Passages*, he also referred to Ada's achievement in a letter he wrote to Ada's son Byron Lovelace on 14 June 1857, seven years before *Passages* was published. In the letter Charles observed to the young man, who was then 21 years old: 'In the memoir of Mr Menabrea and still more in the excellent Notes appended by your mother you will find the only comprehensive view of the powers of the Analytical Engine which the mathematicians of the world have yet expressed.'

Male computer scientists who are still anti-Ada would do better to read the above paragraph by the remarkable genius who actually *knew* Ada, than condemn her because of their own misogynistic prejudice.

Ada wrote seven *Notes*, giving them the letters A to G. The *Notes* are, as we've seen, altogether about 20,000 words long, while her translation of the Menabrea article is about 8,000 words long.

While it is true that Ada's discursive remarks about the Analytical Engine in her *Notes* are what have established her fame today, in fact much of her *Notes* (the full text of which is readily available online) are highly technical mathematically. There is no reason to believe that she relied heavily on Charles to compose this technical material.

I provide a detailed analysis of the discursive content of the *Notes* in *Ada's Algorithm*. Here, it is only necessary to emphasise Ada's own genius and foresight in suggesting that the Analytical Engine – the world's first computer — need not, as Charles thought, merely be a calculating machine but could be a general-purpose device that could control pretty much any process it was desired for the machine to control. This insight went well beyond even Charles' conception of the potential of the machine.

In one especially extraordinary passage of her *Notes*, Ada in effect actually foresees the development in our own time of digitised music:

> In studying the action of the Analytical Engine, we find that the peculiar and independent nature of the considerations which in all mathematical analysis belong to *operations*, as distinguished from *the objects operated upon* and from the *results* of the operations performed upon those objects, is very strikingly defined and separated …
>
> The operating mechanism can even be thrown into action independently of any object to operate upon (although of course no *result* could then be developed).
>
> Again, it might act upon other things besides *number*, were objects found whose mutual fundamental relations could be expressed by those of the abstract science of operations, and which should be also susceptible of adaptations to the action of the operating notation and mechanism of the engine.
>
> Supposing, for instance, that the fundamental relations of pitched sounds in the science of harmony and of musical composition were susceptible of such expression and adaptations, the engine might compose elaborate and scientific pieces of music of any degree of complexity or extent.

We might very reasonably ask what Charles thought of this passage. The answer is that this simply isn't known. My own feeling is that he paid more attention to checking over the technical material than the discursive material, and may well have not paid much attention to Ada's great and profound thoughts about the Analytical Engine.

We need to remember (this can be very reasonably inferred from his extant correspondence with Ada and vice versa) that his motivation in suggesting to Ada that she write 'an original paper' (i.e. the *Notes*) on the Analytical Engine was *not* to set down insights that he, Charles, himself didn't have, but rather to publicise the Analytical Engine to the wider world. Charles used to like to refer to Ada as his 'Interpretress', not as someone who was actually adding to the insight of what the Analytical Engine really, at a very fundamental level, actually *was*. This, I believe, explains why Charles literally does not seem to have paid all that much attention to what Ada was actually *saying*: as if what mattered more to the subject of this biography was the number of column inches Ada was devoting to the Analytical Engine rather than the opinions she was expressing.

Similarly, for the same reason, he very likely didn't pay much attention to this momentous passage:

> The distinctive characteristic of the Analytical Engine, and that which has rendered it possible to endow mechanism with such extensive faculties as bid fair to make this engine the executive right-hand of abstract algebra, is the introduction into it of the principle which Jacquard devised for regulating, by means of punched cards, the most complicated patterns in the fabrication of brocaded stuffs.
>
> It is in this that the distinction between the two engines lies. Nothing of the sort exists in the Difference Engine. We may say most aptly, that the Analytical Engine *weaves algebraical patterns* just as the Jacquard-loom weaves flowers and leaves [Ada's italics].

As I suggest in *Ada's Algorithm*:

> This is the moment when Ada showed that her understanding of Babbage's Analytical Engine exceeded his. *He* saw both the Difference Engine and the Analytical Engine only as calculators, *she* saw that the Analytical Engine could be a general-purpose machine that could weave algebraical, numerical patterns and so could control any process, including music. This is how Ada's vision for what a computer — a mechanical computer — could be (though she never used the word in that sense) exceeded Babbage's. There are many other instances in her *Notes* that she had a more developed vision of the Analytical Engine than Babbage did, but this is the most obvious and clear example.

The year 1843, as we've seen, was the year with the largest number of surviving letters between Charles and Ada. Some of the content of these letters consists of Ada asking Charles' advice about technical aspects of her work on the *Notes*, though it is always clear that Ada is mistress of her work; she principally asks Charles for clarification.

Their correspondence in that year also reveals how close they were becoming emotionally; they were in many respects during that year developing a romantic friendship. Here, for example, is a letter Ada wrote to Charles on Wednesday, 5 July 1843, from Ockham. The salutation 'my dear Babbage', which sounds formal to us today, was actually quite an affectionate one in the 1840s.

This letter again emphasises how Ada, not Charles, was indeed the mistress of her work on her *Notes*:

My Dear Babbage

I am much obliged by the contents of your letter, in all respects. Should you find it expedient to substitute the amended passage about the Variable-Cards, there is also *one* other *short* sentence which must be altered similarly. This sentence precedes the passage I sent yesterday by perhaps half a page or more. It is where I explain that for every B after B_5, operations (13 ... 23) have to be repeated; & I believe it runs as follows:

'Not only are the *Operation* Cards precisely the same for the repetition, but the Variable Cards as well with the exception of one new one to introduce B_5 instead of Bs for operation 21 to act upon.'

I should wish to substitute what I enclose.

In the same letter there is a fascinating passage which seems very clearly to hint at their friendship having indeed developed an emotionally romantic dimension. The point is that Ada refers to a letter, presumably lost – at any rate, there is no indication that it is extant – which Charles sent to her, presumably not long before 5 July, and in which he asked the direct question: 'Why does my friend prefer *imaginary* roots for our friendship?'

It might very reasonably be asked what on earth Charles means by this.

The answer is that there isn't a definitive answer to this, and in the absence of any additional letter turning up to elucidate it, there never will be. One idea, suggested by businessman and chess player Chris Stampe in a Facebook posting in response to my own question soliciting ideas for what it might mean, is that Charles and Ada might have used the phrase '*imaginary* roots' to imply that their real meeting was in the realm of the mind rather than their literal physical meeting on 5 June 1833. It's an ingenuous idea, and could well be true.

Another friend, who prefers to remain anonymous, made the very interesting suggestion that the 'roots' might be imaginary roots in a mathematical sense, which is a more than reasonable idea for two people for whom mathematics was such a passion. There are indeed imaginary roots in mathematics (the square root of a negative number is what is known as an 'imaginary number', meaning that in itself it has no meaning or identity, although when it is squared it acquires a meaning again). But what exactly Charles or Ada might have meant in emotional and psychological terms by 'imaginary roots' will, unfortunately, most likely remain a mystery forever.

I do think it very likely that Ada, not Charles, said the phrase first: 'imaginary roots' does not sound like something Charles would originate. What is clear is that 'my friend' in 'Why does my friend prefer *imaginary* roots for our friendship?' is Ada; this is not, as we shall see, the first time Charles is definitely known to have referred to her gallantly in the third person, as men sometimes do when they feel shy of expressing things more directly to a woman they really like.

The meaning of 'imaginary roots' remains obscure. If Charles is not alluding to something Ada first said or wrote to *him*, perhaps he is simply saying that Ada likes to see their friendship as originating in the imagination, but we cannot know what exactly that means without discussing the matter with Charles and Ada themselves, which is unfortunately impossible, at least at the moment.

Let's look at the context of the remark in the letter of 5 July. In the very next paragraph after Ada wrote 'I should wish to substitute what I enclose', she says, changing the subject but without varying the pace:

'Why does my friend prefer *imaginary* roots for our friendship?' – Just because she happens to have some of that very imagination which *you* would deny her to possess; & therefore she enjoys a little *play* & *scope* for it now & then. Besides this, I deny the *Fairyism* to be entirely *imaginary*; (& it is to the *fairy* similes that I suppose you allude).

That *brain* of mine is something more than merely *mortal*; as time will show; (if only my *breathing* & some other et-ceteras do not make too rapid a progress *towards* instead of *from* mortality).-

Before ten years are over, the Devil's in it if I have not sucked out some of the life-blood from the mysteries of this universe, in a way that no purely mortal lips or brains could do.

No one knows what almost *awful* energy & power lie yet undeveloped [*sic*] in that *wiry* little system of mine. I say *awful*, because you may imagine that it *might* be under certain circumstances.

Another puzzle is what Ada means by 'the Fairyism'? Presumably this also comes from something Charles and Ada had discussed in private, and/or mentioned in letters that are now lost. They evidently saw a lot of each other around this time, and the whole imagination/Fairyism theme seems to be linked to flirtatious chats about what exactly Ada is to Charles, how she brings her womanly imagination and fairylike skills to his service. The same letter also contains an intriguing passage which most certainly indicates their emotional, and romantic, closeness. She instructs Charles when she would like him to be available if she has any questions about the Bernoulli numbers she is 'doggedly attacking and sifting to the very bottom'. As Ada writes later in the same letter:

I do not go to Town until Monday. Keep yourself open if you can for that day; in case there should be anything I wish to see you about, which is very likely. But the *evening* I think is most likely to be my time for you, as I rather expect to be engaged incessantly until after 6 o'clock.

I shall sleep in Town that night.–

At her own home in London presumably, but not necessarily …

It really is by no means impossible that there was a dimension to their relationship that is not recorded at all in the surviving correspondence.

At the very least, Ada was certainly on very familiar, cosy, emotional terms with Charles. For example, at the end of a letter she wrote to him the following day on Thursday, 6 July 1843, Ada, writing about a male friend of hers, observes to Charles: 'I see I am more his ladye-love [*sic*] than ever. He is an excellent creature, & deserves to have a ladye-love of his own.' This is hardly an observation Ada would have shared with Charles had she not known him very well, and been on emotionally intimate terms with him.

The point is, Ada's profound insights into Charles' work were not only confined to her understanding of what the Analytical Engine really was. She also understood Charles and, for all her affection and admiration for him, she knew that if his dreams were to come true, he needed help. And that was why, on Monday, 14 August 1843, she wrote one of the most poignant letters in the history of the computer. It is also one of the longest. Covering sixteen pages of her close handwriting, it runs to more than 2,000 words. The following is an edited version of it:

> My Dear Babbage. You would have heard from me several days ago, but for the *hot* work that has been going on between me & the printers. This is now happily concluded. I have endeavoured to work up everything to the utmost perfection, *as far as it goes;* & I am now well satisfied on the whole, since I think that *within the sphere of views* I set out with, & in accordance with which the whole contents & arrangement of the Notes are shaped, they are very complete, & even admirable. I could *now* do the thing *far better*; but this would be from setting out upon a wholly different *basis*.
>
> [...]
>
> As I know you will not be *explicit* enough to state the *real* state of your feelings respecting me at this time, I shall do so for you. You feel, my dear Babbage, that *I* have (tho' in a negative manner) *added* to the list of injuries & of disappointments & mis-comprehensions that you have already experienced in a life by no means smooth or fortunate. You *know* this is your feeling; & that you are deeply hurt about it; & you endeavour to derive a poor & sorry consolation from such

sentiments as 'Well, she don't *know* or *intend* the injury & mischief if she has done' &c.

[...]

I must now come to a practical question respecting the future. *Your* affairs have been, & are, deeply occupying both myself & Lord Lovelace. Our thoughts as well as our conversation have been earnest upon them. And the result is that I have plans for you, which I do not think fit at present to communicate to you; but which I shall either develop, or else throw my energies, my time & pen into the service of some other department of truth & science, according to the reply I receive from you to what I am now going to state. I do beseech you therefore deeply & seriously to ponder over the question how far you can subscribe to my conditions or not. I give to *you* the *first* choice & offer of my services & my intellect. Do not lightly reject them. I say this entirely for *your own* sake, believe me.

My channels for developping [*sic*] & training my scientific & literary powers, are various, & some of them very attractive. But I wish my old friend to have the *refusal.*

Firstly: I want to know whether if I continue to work *on* & *about* your own great subject, you will undertake to abide wholly by the judgement of myself (or of any persons whom you may *now* please to name as referees, whenever we may differ), on *all practical* matters relating to *whatever can involve relations with any fellow-creature or fellow-creatures.*

Secondly: can you undertake to give your mind *wholly* & *undividedly,* as a primary object that no engagement is to interfere with, to the consideration of all those matters in which I shall at times require your intellectual *assistance* & *supervision*; & can you promise not to *slur* & *hurry* things over; or to mislay, & allow confusion & mistakes to enter into documents, &c?

Thirdly: If I am able to lay before you in the course of a year or two, explicit & honorable propositions for *executing your engine,* (such as are approved by persons whom you may *now* name to be referred to for their approbation), would there be any chance of your allowing myself & such parties to conduct the business for you; your own *undivided* energies being devoted to the execution of the work; & all other matters being arranged for you on terms which your *own* friends should approve?

You will wonder over this last query. But, I strongly advise you not to reject it as chimerical. You do *not* know the grounds I have for believing that such a contingency may come within my power, & I wish to know before I allow my mind to employ its energies any further on the subject, that I shall not be wasting thought & power for no purpose or result.

At the same time, I must place the whole of your relations with me, in a fair & just light. Our motives, & ways of viewing things, are very widely apart; & it may be an anxious question for you to decide how for the advantages & expediency of enlisting a mind of my particular class, in your service, *can* over-balance the annoyance to you of that divergency on perhaps many occasions. My own uncompromising principle is to endeavour to love *truth* & *God before fame & glory or even just appreciation*; & to believe generously & unwaveringly in the *good* of human nature, (however dormant & latent it may often seem).

Yours is to love truth & God (yes, deeply & constantly); but to love *fame, glory, honours, yet more.* You will deny this; but in all your intercourse with *every* human being (as far as I know & see of it), it is a *practically paramount* sentiment. Mind, I am not *blaming* it. I simply state my belief in the *fact.* The fact may be a very *noble & beautiful* fact. *That* is another question.

Far be it from *me*, to disclaim the influence of *ambition & fame*. No living soul ever was more imbued with it than myself. And my own view of duty is, that it behoves me to place this *great & useful* quality in its *proper relations & subordination*; but I certainly would not deceive myself or others by pretending that it is other than a very important motive & ingredient in my character & nature.

I wish to add my mite towards *expounding & interpreting* the Almighty, & his laws & works, for the most effective use of mankind; and certainly, I should feel it no small *glory* if I were enabled to be one of his most noted prophets (using this word in my own peculiar sense) in this world. And I should undoubtedly prefer being *known* as a benefactor of this description, to *being* equally great in fact, but promulgating truths from obscurity & oblivion.

[…]

Will you come *here* for some days on Monday. I hope so. Lord L— is very anxious to see & converse with you; & was vexed that the Rail called him away on Tuesday before he had heard from yourself your own views about the recent affair.

I sadly want your *Calculus of Functions.* So *Pray* get it for me. I cannot understand the *Examples.*

I have ventured inserting to one passage of Note G a small Foot-Note, which I am sure is *quite tenable.* I say in it that the engine is remarkedly well adapted to include the *whole Calculus of Finite Differences,* & I allude to the computation of the *Bernoullian Numbers by means of the difference of Nothing,* as a beautiful example for its processes. I hope it *is* correctly the case.

This letter is sadly blotted & corrected. Never mind that however.

I wonder if you will choose to retain the lady-fairy in your service or not. Yours ever most sincerely.

A.A.L.

16

ENCHANTED

Bid me discourse, I will enchant thine ear,
Or like a fairy trip upon the green,
Or, like a nymph, with long dishevelled hair,
Dance on the sands, and yet no footing seen:
Love is a spirit all compact of fire,
Not gross to sink, but light, and will aspire.

Venus and Adonis, William Shakespeare (1593)

Make no mistake, Ada's letter to Charles was dynamite in the early history of the computer.

The letter constituted nothing less than an offer to handle, henceforth, what would most likely be regarded today as the management, political and public relations aspects of Charles' work on the Analytical Engine. Ada admired Charles, but by now she was certain that the ornery and undiplomatic aspects of his personality greatly handicapped him when it came to advancing the cause of his Engines. Ada was perceptive enough to understand something that Charles never saw: that advancing his project required not only technical wizardry, but also skill at dealing with influential and sceptical people.

Tragically, and the word 'tragically' is more than justified, Charles didn't accept the offer. He simply didn't have the sense to realise just how brilliant her understanding of his work really was, still less how deep her understanding of his personality was. One wonders how intently he had even read the discursive part of her *Notes*. The most likely scenario was that he did cast his eye over them but didn't get what Ada was talking about, or couldn't be bothered to work this out. If he had read them properly, wouldn't he have realised just how useful her insights were into the advancement of the Analytical Engine? Perhaps so, or perhaps not. After all, possibly Ada's insights were too profound and ahead of their time even for him.

Certainly, there is no surviving written evidence that Charles truly understood what Ada had written about the Analytical Engine. In reading her *Notes*, he may have focused merely on the complex mathematical material and attributed – or blamed – what he saw as its more discursive ideas on her 'fairy' imagination.

All we know is that the day after Ada wrote this letter, Charles said no to her without, apparently, giving much thought to the matter. At the top of the long letter that Ada sent him on 14 August and which is to be found in the Babbage papers, there appears a pencilled note in Charles' hand stating, simply, blatantly, brusquely and cruelly: 'Tuesday 15 saw AAL this morning and refused all the conditions.'

There is, alas, no record of what Ada thought of Charles' response. All we can be sure about is that Charles never grasped – or if he did, he never gave any indication of doing so – that Ada possessed an insight into his machines, and especially his Analytical Engine, that he himself did not have. The sad, sombre, dismal truth is that Charles did indeed, after all, only see Ada as his 'interpreter' or 'interpretess'. There is absolutely no evidence that, for all his genius, he ever had the insight to see just how inspired Ada's understanding of the Analytical Engine really was.

Would an Analytical Engine have been successfully completed if Charles had said yes to Ada's offer? It's impossible to know. At the very least, I think if he had said yes, the Analytical Engine project would have become much better known among influential people in Britain as a serious scientific project rather than an effusive notion of a man who was regarded as seriously eccentric; a man, moreover, whose machines were mostly famous for never being completed.

Gradually, the significance of the Analytical Engine would surely have become known around the world, especially in the United States, which even in the 1840s and 1850s was an astonishing and burgeoning hive of technological ingenuity and innovation. Studying Charles' life, it is almost impossible not to conclude that a hi-tech revolution in the 1840s or 1850s was definitely possible, and that if it had happened the entire history of the world since then would very likely have been different, perhaps even radically so, if that revolution had led to new levels of prosperity among nations.

Perhaps even the grinding poverty and economic collapse in much of Continental Europe that fostered the diabolical political development of the first forty-five years of the twentieth century might never have taken place if the world had been more prosperous. Who can tell what might have happened in that alternate reality? So often when we look at Charles' life, we are conscious of how close that alternative reality came to occurring. It's not just that our own world is a world of the fulfilment of much science fiction, but that our own world, our own time, might easily have embarked on that fulfilment more than a century before it did if Charles had been successful.

It is difficult not to conclude that Charles' disastrous handling of his meeting with Peel, coupled with his rejection of Ada's inspired and generous offer of help, were the two biggest mistakes of his life. The two errors very likely prevented a British information technology revolution happening in the mid–nineteenth century.

Ada's translation of Menabrea's paper on the Analytical Engine was published a few days later in September 1843, in the third number of *Taylor's Scientific Memoirs*. Entitled *Sketch of the Analytical Engine invented by Charles Babbage, Esq. (by L.F. Menabrea, with notes by Ada Lovelace)*, it was respectfully (but not enthusiastically) received by the scientific and mathematical community.

Strangely perhaps, Charles and Ada remained good friends even after he turned her down. Perhaps he turned her down in person less brusquely than in the note he wrote. In any event, he certainly remained enchanted by her.

That this was so is made clear in two remarkable, and indeed wonderful, letters Charles wrote at his London home on Saturday, 9 September 1843. By the time Charles wrote these letters Ada had finished a translation of an important paper, written in French, about Charles' work and was waiting for her paper and an even longer set of supplementary *Notes* she wrote (they are usually spelt with an initial capital letter in discussions of Ada) to be published. They were published the following month in the October issue of the journal *Taylor's Scientific Memoirs*.

On a Saturday morning which Sydney Padua – author of the highly entertaining and deeply informative graphic novel *The Thrilling Adventures of Lovelace and Babbage*, which also contains much excellent biographical material about Charles and Ada – has researched as having had 'fine' weather, Charles sat down to write letters which Padua not unreasonably describes as 'rather rambly'.

The crucial point is that Charles wrote the letters on the same morning. The first was to his friend Michael Faraday. The second, to Ada, contains the beguiling phrase 'Enchantress of Number'. For a long time the letter containing this phrase was well known whereas the Faraday letter was hardly known, and many people speculated on what Charles could possibly have meant by the phrase 'Enchantress of Number'. Incidentally, Charles writes the word 'Number' in the singular, although often it has been quoted as being in the plural.

Only the Faraday letter provides us with definite evidence that when Charles used the phrase 'Enchantress of Number' he was, in fact, referring to Ada. Otherwise, he might have meant mathematics in a generic sense, or he might even have meant the Analytical Engine. Padua's account of what it felt like for her to read the Faraday letter for the first time is so beautifully expressed that it's worth quoting here. As Padua says:

> Without the clarification of the Faraday letter, it has been argued by the anti-Lovelace faction that Babbage could not have been referring to the 'they claim' mathematically inept Lovelace as the 'Enchantress of Number' and he must be referring to some abstract personification of mathematics. Finding the Faraday letter opposite was my introduction to the very great thrill of throw-down victory in Combat Scholarship.

Padua is absolutely spot on that the anti-Ada faction never wanted to accept that Charles meant Ada when he used that phrase. The Faraday letter, however, provides proof beyond reasonable doubt that he did.

Here is the letter that Charles wrote to Faraday. It's not known which of the two letters he wrote first that Saturday, but I believe he penned the Faraday one before the other, because there is a sense that by the time he writes the second one he has established more comfortably in his mind his description of Ada, coined, I believe, in the first letter, as a special kind of enchantress:

My dear Faraday

I am not quite sure whether I thanked you for a kind note imputing to me unmeritedly the merit of a present you received I conjecture from Lady Lovelace.

I now send you what ought to have accompanied that Translation.

So you will now have to write another note to that Enchantress who has thrown her magical spell around the most abstract of sciences and has grasped it with a force which few masculine intellects (in our own country at least) could have exerted over it. I remember well your first interview with the youthful fairy which she herself has not forgotten and I am grateful to you both for making my drawing rooms the chateau d'eu of Science.

I am going for a short time to Lord Lovelace's place in Somerset. It is a romantic spot on the rocky coast called Ashley about 2 miles from the post town of Porlock.

I am my dear Faraday ever truly yours C Babbage

The 'present' which Charles refers to here was a copy of Ada's translation of the Menabrea article which she sent to Faraday. Incidentally, as Padua herself points out, Faraday was not an accomplished mathematician, despite his prodigious genius as an experimental scientist. The next letter – assuming my hypothesis that the Faraday one was the one Charles wrote first is correct – was to Ada herself:

My Dear Lady Lovelace

I find it quite in vain to wait until I have leisure so I have resolved that I will leave all other things undone and set out for Ashley taking with me papers enough to enable me to forget this world and all its troubles and if possible its multitudinous Charlatans – every thing in short but the Enchantress of Number.

My only impediment would be my mother's health which is not at this moment quite so good as I could wish.

Are you at Ashley? And is it still convenient with all your other arrangements that I should join you there? – and will next Wednesday or next Thursday or any other day suit you and shall I leave the iron-shod road at Thornton or at Bridgwater and have you got Arbogast Du Calcul des Derivations with you there? (i.e. at Ashley) I shall bring some books about that horrible problem – the three bodies which is almost as obscure as the existence of the celebrated book 'De Tribus Impostoribus'. So if you have Arbogast I shall bring something else. Farewell my dear and much admired interpretess.

Ever most truly yours

C. Babbage

The parentheses (i.e. at Ashley) are Charles'. The book Charles was referring to is by a French mathematician, Louis Arbogast. Ada and Charles liked exchanging books. As for the justly famous phrase 'everything in short but the Enchantress of Number', Charles is here unquestionably referring to Ada. The reference is, in all fairness, a little stilted and Charles' use again of the third person to refer to her carries a slight mawkishness along with the gallantry, but all the same, no one could doubt he meant what he said sincerely, and that it came from the heart.

Charles wrote the famous 'Enchantress of Number' letter to Ada just three weeks after so brusquely turned down her inspired offer.

So why was Ada not more hurt by his rejection of her offer? Perhaps she only expected it. Very likely she *was* deeply upset for a couple of weeks, but then got over it. In any event, she replied to him, flirtatiously and winningly the day after receiving the 'Enchantress of Number' letter, the one to which she is referring here:

Sunday, 10 September 1843

My Dear Babbage.

Your letter is *charming*, and Lord L— & I have smiled over it most *approbatively*. You must forgive me for showing it to him. It contains such *simple, honest, unfeigned* admiration for myself, that I could not resist giving him the pleasure of seeing it. I send you De Morgan's *kind & approving* letter about my article [i.e. her translation and *Notes*]. I never expected that *he* would view my crude young composition so favorably.

You understand that I send you his letter in strictest *confidence*. He might perhaps not like you to see his remarks about the relative *times* of the invention of the two engines. I am going to inform him of my grounds of feeling satisfied of the literal correctness of my statement on that point. I cannot say how much his letter has pleased me.

You are a brave man to give yourself wholly up to Fairy-Guidance! – I advise you to allow yourself to be unresistingly bewitched, neck, & crop, out & out, whole seas over &c, &c, &c, by that curious little being!

De Morgan's letter to Ada about her translation and *Notes* does not appear to have survived. There are letters from him to her in the Lovelace-Byron Papers at the Bodleian Library in Oxford, but the letter Ada mentions does not appear to be among them.

Charles' romantic friendship with Ada continued to be an important part of both their lives, and they evidently shared intimate confidence. In an undated letter most likely written in 1851, Charles even felt able to confide in Ada, self-pityingly but also movingly, about his loneliness. In those days, wives whose husbands had left the marital home would, with no other way of tracing their husband, often place advertisements in newspapers offering forgiveness and reconciliation if the husbands – their 'wandering lords', as Charles describes them – come home. The advertisements did not usually refer to the husbands by their names but by initials.

Charles, seeing some of these advertisements one day, was seized with a consciousness of his own loneliness:

My dear Lady Lovelace

I sat last night reading the advertisements of deserted wives to charm back their wandering lords.

I am not a wanderer though I had none to charm me.

Seeing the intimacy of this revelation surely justifies the belief that there were times when Charles and Ada were very close indeed, but that we have no choice but to be cautious about how close, because the extant correspondence does not, when all is said and done, reveal very much.

There is indeed abundant scope for speculation about what the true nature of that closeness might have been, but biographers should always use conjecture sparingly. All that can really be said about the relationship between Charles and Ada, in the absence of new documentary evidence appearing at some point, is that there is so much we don't know that what we imagine about it is inevitably likely to depend on how imaginative we allow ourselves to be in connection with these extraordinary human beings.

Charles went with Ada to the Great Exhibition, which took place at the Crystal Palace in Hyde Park in London, from 1 May to 15 October 1851. It was, at the time, the greatest exhibition of culture and industry that had ever taken place in Britain, and it was immensely popular and hugely profitable. It started a trend for such exhibitions that lasted for about a century. There was, for example, an *Exposition universelle* held in Paris in 1855 and four more during the later nineteenth century.

At around this time Ada unfortunately started to be unwell. She wrote to her son Byron from her London home at 6 Great Cumberland Place on Saturday, 15 November 1851, this time not leaving him under any illusions about her condition, though she starts the letter by reminding him that 'we have not heard from you for very many months': 'My health is at present very delicate and infirm, & I am obliged to be chiefly in Town; for surgical advice, & to lie up on the sofa almost entirely.'

Slowly but surely and inexorably, cancer took hold of Ada, causing her at first intermittent discomfort, then gradually worse and worse pain. For example, in a letter to her mother on Tuesday, 30 December 1851, Ada wrote:

> I am going on well, excepting that I had an *awful* night from pain. I am now obliged to give up sleeping in bed altogether, & *to be dressed*, & lie on a sofa or else *outside* my bed. In this way, I get *intervals* of sleep, from being able to rise & to move about freely, without risk of catching cold. I am going on perfectly well. It is *expected* there will be a great deal of trouble from pain.

By the end of 1851, though, there was nothing about Ada's health that she could be optimistic about. The pain from her cancer visited her more and more frequently, yet mercifully it was not continuous, and during her times of temporary remission from it she was almost back to her old optimistic and positive self, despite her feelings of physical weakness. By now Ada spent most of her time on the sofa in her London home and was pushed about by servants in her invalid chair when she wanted some fresh air. William was not often with her at this time but was away at Ockham or Ashley.

Writing to her mother Lady Byron on Sunday, 10 January 1852, Ada notes: 'It will be a long while before I shall have even average nervous energy. Everything is fatigue.' Yet in a burst of optimism, or perhaps to reassure Lady Byron, she adds: 'But I am never in bad spirits, which is surprising.'

On 28 February 1852, her illness again appears to be in remission but she adds:

> There is still some *uncertainty* forever, & possibility of relapse. As I am certain I could not get thro any more severe illness, I shall not feel confident just yet ...
>
> It has been a very bad case ... It is to me dreadful to know what the human frame *can* suffer, especially when I reflect there are even *worse* agonies than I have suffered.

The unavoidable truth was that Ada was fatally ill with uterine cancer. When writing to her mother, however, she tried at first to downplay it, partly because she knew how unsympathetic her mother could be towards illness suffered by anyone else. However, as she became more and more ill, which she did in the early months of 1852, there seemed little point concealing from her mother just how unwell she really was.

Charles was friends with her all this time, as he had been since they first met in 1833, and he was deeply concerned about her health and her prognosis: indeed, he was far more concerned than Lady Byron was.

In another letter to her mother which is undated, but was written on a Monday evening some time early in 1852, Ada wrote the following words about her terrible suffering:

> When I find that not only one's whole being can become merely one living *agony*, but that in that state, & *after* it, one's *mind* is gone more or less, – the impression of *mortality* become appalling; & not of mortality merely, but of mortality in an *agony* & *struggle* …
>
> The more one suffers, the more appalling is it to feel that it may all be only in order to '*die like a dog*' as they say …

Mary Somerville subsequently observed: 'I never knew of anyone who suffered such protracted intolerable agony.' Ada tried to use what drugs she could to relieve her condition. She may even have resorted to cannabis; she certainly mentioned it in a letter to Lady Byron. But the cancer continued inexorably to destroy her body. On Friday, 7 May 1852, Ada wrote to her son Byron:

> My dearest Son. I am quite a cripple & an *invalid* …
>
> I am sadly distressed to think that during the few weeks *you* are likely to be with us, you will have a *sick Mama*, whom I fear a handsome active young fellow like you, will regard as a bore. Yet I think you are too good, & too aware of my *affection for you* & of my anxiety to see you again to be otherwise than my *affectionate son*, whether I am ill or well. *I* resign myself to my present state & I trust will others.
>
> Your most *affectionate Mother*

Charles visited Ada one last time at Great Cumberland Place on Thursday, 12 August 1852. After this visit, Lady Byron did not allow Charles to visit her any more. Ada wanted Charles to be the executor of her will; he agreed, but Lady Byron was furious with both Ada and him for doing this.

Ada died, in great pain, of uterine cancer on 27 November 1852. The hypodermic needle had not yet been invented, and her only palliative was laudanum, a mixture of alcohol and morphine, which she could only take orally and which was therefore to some extent limited in its effectiveness by stomach acids.

On Wednesday, 25 August 1852, Charles Dickens had written a letter to his friend the wealthy philanthropist Angela Burdett-Coutts about a visit he had made to Ada six days earlier, when he read to her from his novel *Dombey & Son*. He'd read from the passage where little Paul Dombey dies, a passage that had caused comprehensive grief throughout Victorian Britain:

> The night before I left town (last Saturday) I had a note from Lord Lovelace to tell me that Lady Lovelace was dying, and that the death of the child in *Dombey* had been so much in her thoughts and had soothed her so, that she wished to see me once more if I could be found. I went, and sat alone with her for some time. It was very solemn and sad, but her fortitude was quite surprising; and her Conviction that all the agony she has suffered (which has been very great) had some good design in the goodness of God, impressed me very much.

On Friday, 3 December 1852, Ada was laid to rest in the Byron family tomb, next to her father, in St Mary Magdalene Church in the village of Hucknall Torkard, Nottinghamshire, which is a few miles from Lord Byron's ancestral home of Newstead Abbey. Ada and Lord Byron, who both passed away aged only 36, now lie side by side in a tomb that has been sealed since 1929. There are memorials to Byron, Ada and Byron's sister Augusta inside the church.

Charles, bereft of his great and dear friend, had almost two decades left to live.

17

LAST DAYS

A gull. Gulls. Far calls. Coming, far! End here. Us then. Finn, again! ...
A way a lone a last a loved a long the riverrun, past Eve and Adam's, from
swerve of shore to bend of bay, brings us by a commodius vicus of recirculation
back to ...

Finnegan's Wake, James Joyce (1939)

So now Ada, Charles' best friend, whose generous offer of help with his machines he foolishly rejected, was gone.

As I've suggested, it seems certain he told Ada about his disastrous interview with Peel, even though there is no definite primary source that confirms this. It seems very likely, too, that he told Charles Dickens, because subsequently Dickens appears to have drawn heavily on Charles' disappointment at the hands of the British government in his 1855 novel *Little Dorrit*, which is, among other things, a scathing indictment of the indifferent cruelty of official institutions.

Genius as he was, with a justifiably immortal reputation, Dickens was curiously technologically illiterate, and even in the last novel he completed, *Our Mutual Friend* (1865), he is strangely oblivious to the fact that by the time it was written, technology was making a considerable impact on Britain. *Our Mutual Friend* not only gives the impression of being set in about 1840 (at the very start Dickens describes the setting as in 'these times of ours, though of the exact year there is no need to be precise') but of having been written at about that time, too.

From 1839 to 1851, the two Charleses – Babbage and Dickens – lived only a few hundred yards from each other in London; Dickens on Devonshire Terrace in Marylebone Road, and Babbage at his home on Dorset Street. Dickens, born in 1812 (and who died the year before Charles did), was considerably the younger of the two; in fact, he was only about three years older than Ada.

It's not definitely known how Babbage met Dickens, but it was probably in 1838 through one of their mutual friends, the actor William Macready. Dickens was a writing prodigy; he became famous throughout Britain in his early twenties, under the pen-name 'Boz', with *The Pickwick Papers* (1837). The two men moved in similar circles, and were often guests at each other's dinner parties. Dickens was not, to put it mildly, of a scientific disposition or frame of mind, and had little or no technical knowledge of Charles' work. But Dickens had no problem understanding the benefit to mankind and freedom from mental drudgery that a calculation machine would bring. He tended to interpret and understand the world of industry in emotional, literary terms, and that's how he saw Babbage's plight, too. *Little Dorrit* is considerably more serious than his early works, although, like them, it contains an abundance of Dickens' social comment. It also contains a character who is almost certainly based on Charles Babbage. A major theme of the novel is how the chilly indifference of the law and government contribute heavily to human misery. The tenth chapter of the first part of the book, entitled ironically 'Containing the Whole Science of Government', depicts the 'Circumlocution Office', which devotes itself to never getting anything done. One of the most put-upon victims of the Circumlocution Office is an inventor called Daniel Doyce. As Dickens says in describing him:

He was not much to look at, either in point of size or in point of dress; being merely a short, square, practical looking man, whose hair had turned grey, and in whose face and forehead there were deep lines of cogitation, which looked as though they were carved in hard wood. He was dressed in decent black, a little rusty, and had the appearance of a sagacious master in some handicraft. He had a spectacle-case in his hand, which he turned over and over while he was thus in question, with a certain free use of the thumb that is never seen but in a hand accustomed to tools.

Apart from the spectacles – there is no evidence Charles wore them; none of the surviving photographs of him show him wearing spectacles, though it is perfectly possible he sometimes used them for close work – and the thumb movement (which Charles may have had but which is not documented anywhere) this is a fairly accurate description of our man.

While there is no incontrovertible evidence that Dickens based the character of Daniel Doyce on Charles, it certainly seems plausible given their enduring friendship. The connection was first suggested by Anthony Hyman. In *Little Dorrit*, the character Mr Meagles – a jovial, convivial self-made businessman, who likes to think of himself as practical – introduces Doyce to Arthur Clennam, the hero of the novel, who is trying to make a new life for himself in England after spending much of his life abroad:

> 'This Doyce,' said Mr Meagles, 'is a smith and engineer. He is not in a large way, but he is well known as a very ingenious man. A dozen years ago, he perfects an invention (involving a very curious secret process) of great importance to his country and his fellow-creatures. I won't say how much money it cost him, or how many years of his life he had been about it, but he brought it to perfection a dozen years ago … He is the most exasperating man in the world; he never complains!'

Charles certainly complained to Peel, as we've seen, but generally he was renowned for his great patience.

George Orwell, in his long and brilliant essay 'Charles Dickens' (1940), which I think is one of the very best things that Orwell ever wrote, points to the lack of detail given about Doyce's work and actually uses this as an example of Dickens's relative lack of interest in writing about work:

> Nothing is queerer than the vagueness with which he [Dickens] speaks of Doyce's 'invention' in *Little Dorrit*. It is represented as some-thing extremely ingenious and revolutionary, 'of great importance to

his country and his fellow creatures'… yet we are never told what the 'invention' is! On the other hand, Doyce's physical appearance is hit off with the typical Dickens touch; he has a peculiar way of moving his thumb, a way characteristic of engineers. After that, Doyce is firmly anchored in one's memory, but as usual, Dickens has done it by fastening on something external.

Of course, it is likely Dickens may have avoided being specific about the invention as a deliberate ploy to avoid linking Doyce too specifically to Charles, but most likely Dickens knew little or nothing about the technical aspects of Charles' project and was even less interested in them. Still, it is known that Dickens was aware of what Charles was trying to do.

A chance remark by Dickens in a letter some eight years after the Peel/Babbage debacle makes it clear that Dickens certainly knew about Charles' work, which he could hardly have done unless Charles (or possibly Charles and Ada together) had told him about it. Writing from Broadstairs, Kent, to his brother Henry Austin on 20 December 1851 about the soaring costs of the modifications to his new house in London's Tavistock Place, Dickens was ruefully and ironically to comment that the bill submitted by the builder was 'too long to be added up, until Babbage's Calculating Machine shall be improved and finished … there is not paper enough ready-made, to carry it over and bring it forward again'.

'A dozen years ago', to use Mr Meagles' words, is certainly a good fit to 1842, given *Little Dorrit*'s publication in 1855, and in 1854 Dickens was been hard at work writing it. After all, there was no reason why Dickens needed to choose the dozen years time frame if he hadn't specifically wanted to.

As well as the close fit of the time frame, Doyce's physical appearance, and the fact of Dickens' close friendship with Charles, suggests that he did indeed base Doyce on Charles. I also even wonder whether Dickens, who liked word-play when naming his characters – he created the name 'Oliver Twist' as a punning comment on the Poor Laws of the time being 'all of a twist', and he gave his hero David Copperfield his own initials, but reversed – may possibly have composed Daniel Doyce's name by taking the letters 'bb' in the middle of Babbage's name and reversing them.

Mr Meagles tells Clennam how Doyce has been castigated by the government for having sought its help, and had been considered by the government as a 'public offender' for merely having approached them, and is now seen by officialdom as a 'man who has done some infernal action' and is 'to be worn out by all possible means':

> Well, Mr Clennam, he addresses himself to the Government. The moment he addresses himself to the Government, he becomes a public offender! … he ceases to be an innocent citizen, and becomes a culprit. He is treated from that instant as a man who has done some infernal action. He is a man to be shirked, put off, brow-beaten, sneered at, handed over by this highly-connected young or old gentleman, to that highly-connected young or old gentleman, and dodged back again; he is a man with no rights in his own time, or his own property; a mere outlaw, whom it is justifiable to get rid of anyhow; a man to be worn out by all possible means.

This is so close a reflection of what happened to Charles when he went to see Robert Peel that it really is difficult to believe otherwise than that he gave Dickens a full account of what had happened during that fateful meeting. Certainly, what Doyce says about how inventors such as he are treated at home compared with abroad could easily have been words taken down pretty much verbatim from some lament Charles might, in a self-pitying mood, have made at one of Dickens' numerous dinner parties at Devonshire Terrace:

> 'Yes. No doubt I am disappointed. Hurt? Yes. No doubt I am hurt. That's only natural. But what I mean, when I say that people who put themselves in the same position, are mostly used in the same way —'
>
> 'In England,' said Mr Meagles.
>
> 'Oh!' [said Doyce], 'of course I mean in England. When they take their inventions into foreign countries, that's quite different. And that's the reason why so many go there.'

In *Little Dorrit,* Daniel Doyce is, in fact, quite an important character and plays a crucial role in the happy ending. Before this, Doyce goes into partnership with Clennam, though Dickens is – typically, for in his entire *oeuvre* he rarely writes much in detail about specific professions, with the exception of Mr Venus in *Our Mutual Friend*, whose profession of taxidermist clearly fascinated him – disappointingly vague about what specific expertise Clennam contributes to the partnership. Doyce finally recovers his fortunes by accepting a post with an unspecified foreign nation (Orwell believed Dickens was referring to Russia). As Dickens writes:

> A certain barbaric Power with valuable possessions on the map of the world, had occasion for the services of one or two engineers, quick in invention and determined in execution: practical men ... who were as bold and fertile in the adaptation of such materials to their purpose, as in the conception of their purpose itself. This Power, being a barbaric one, had no idea of stowing away a great national object in a Circumlocution Office, as strong wine is hidden from the light in a cellar until its fire and youth are gone, and the laborers who worked in the vineyard and pressed the grapes are dust. With characteristic ignorance, it acted on the most decided and energetic notions of How to do it; and never showed the least respect for, or gave any quarter to, the great political science, How not to do it. Indeed it had a barbarous way of striking the latter art and mystery dead, in the person of any enlightened subject who practised it.

Generally, Daniel Doyce is depicted as a wise and good man, who works hard in comparative solitude. Very likely Dickens saw Charles in much the same way. Yet Charles craved success in the real world, not in the world of his friend's imagination. The sombre truth is that the rest of Charles' life, which lasted another thirty-eight years, was a complete failure as far as his machines of the mind were concerned. He never completed more than the one-seventh portion of a Difference Engine, and the Analytical Engine never amounted to anything more than notes and incomplete plans.

Mrs Annie Crosse, in her book *Red-Letter Days of My Life* (1892), includes a section about her personal knowledge of Charles, evidently focusing on his later life:

From Sir Andrew Ramsay I gathered several anecdotes about Babbage. It chanced, some years since, that one day when Ramsay was walking leisurely along Piccadilly, he met De Fitton, the well-known geologist. 'Where are you going?' said the latter.

'I am going to the Athenaeum to dine.'

'By yourself?'

'Yes.'

'Then come with me,' said Fitton; 'I want to see Babbage, and we will get him to dine with us.'

They called on Babbage and found the philosopher and his calculating machine together. Sir Andrew then went on to describe that Babbage gave them a learned disquisition on his machine, explaining by the aid of numbers and certain curious laws of variation belonging thereto his theory of the miracles.

'We could hardly get him away from his subject,' said Ramsay; 'but he agreed to dine with us, and on our way down to the Athenaeum we met William Brown, the botanist; he said that he too would join us, making a party of four. The conversation at dinner was very original and amusing; afterwards we sat down to whist and played on till long after midnight. Babbage was a first-rate player.'

From Sir Andrew I heard the story, which I believe has been told elsewhere, of Whewell, Peacock, and Babbage walking together across the quadrangle of Trinity, when Peacock observed, 'Well, I think we can boast that we are the three ugliest fellows in the University.'

'Speak for yourself, Mr. Peacock,' retorted Whewell in evident annoyance, and, turning round, left his friends to the consideration of 'how in minutiae the character peeps out.'

Babbage was a plain man, I must allow, the plainest of the three, I think, but he wore well; in the quarter of a century that I knew him he had scarcely altered at all. Early in the Sixties Miss Kinglake and I went one evening to take tea with Mr. Babbage. He had promised to show us some interesting papers respecting Lady Lovelace's mathematical studies, and by arrangement there were no other guests. Mr. Babbage's house in Dorset Street, Manchester Square, was the same that had long been occupied by Dr. Wollaston.

It was large and rambling for a London house, having several spacious sitting-rooms, all of which, with the exception of the drawing-room, were crammed with books, papers, and apparatus in apparent confusion, but the philosopher knew where to put his hand on everything.

He received us in his unused drawing-room, which looked dreary in the extreme; the furniture had the stiff primness of age and pretension, without a trace of homely use and custom.

[...]

He told us that not only had he crippled his private fortune by his devotion to his calculating machine, but for this idol of his brain he had given up all the pleasures and comforts of domestic life. He married early, but his wife died while he was a young man. With an amount of feeling that I had never associated with a philosopher who wore the armour of cynicism, he pathetically lamented the dreary isolation of his lot, 'for, of course,' said he, 'fond as I am of domestic life, I should have married again if it had not been for my machine.'

[...]

His father, a well-to-do banker, was nicknamed by his townsfolk 'Old Five Per Cents', he talked so constantly about money matters [Mrs Crosse is, as far as I'm aware, the only source for Benjamin being given this nickname, but it seems believable enough].

The eminent mathematician's mother lived to a great age; and I have heard from those who remembered earlier times that she was occasionally to be seen at the brilliant receptions Babbage used to give in the Forties, in this same dreary, ghost-haunted room where we then sat, surrounded by faded hanging and tarnished gilding. In the old days it was the son's greatest pleasure to bring up his most distinguished guests to be introduced to his mother, the homely old lady seated on the stiff-backed sofa, the place of honour [Charles Babbage's mother Elizabeth (Betty) died on 5 December 1844, aged 84, a grand old age indeed at the time].

He spoke of his mother on this memorable evening, repeating to us her reply when it became a question whether he should make further outlay respecting the machine, which had already cost his private purse £20,000.

The old lady said, with a large-mindedness rare in our thrifty sex, 'My dear son, you have a great object in view worthy of your ambition; my advice is, pursue it, even if it should oblige you to live on bread and cheese.' Babbage mentions the fact, I believe, in his 'Passages in the Life of a Philosopher.'

I well remember Sir Andrew Ramsay praising this book very highly, as being an autobiography of permanent interest, and he added that the world often owes more to the impetus given to progress by a man's mind than to his completed work. This was said, of course, in reference to the calculating machine, which seems to me to have been the bane of his life. I speak as a non-mathematician, and am therefore unworthy to speak; but with Babbage's great powers and practical capacity, his country would gladly have associated his name with something other than a magnificent failure. His conversation on the evening in question made me aware how deeply the disappointment about his work had bitten into the very core of his spirit.

Charles continued to labour on his dream of cogwheel computation to the very end. In 1867, *Alice in Wonderland* creator Lewis Carroll (Charles Dodgson) apparently paid a visit to Charles; they were respectively 35 and 76 at the time. In a disappointingly brief diary entry, Carroll remarks:

Then I called on Mr Babbage, to ask whether any of his calculating machines are to be had. I find they are not. He received me most kindly, and I spent a very pleasant three-quarters of an hour with him, while he showed me over his workshops etc.

There is not, as far as I'm aware, any other source that corroborates this, and so it is possible that Carroll, who was not after all a man devoid of imagination, set this entry down as about an imaginary visit, but the visit seems plausible enough.

In his last years, Charles was unfortunately plagued by headaches and the noise of urban life. He loathed street musicians, who often played deafening barrel-organs at night (this was not illegal at the time) as a form of blackmail, to get irate and sleepless householders to pay them to shut up or to go and make their racket somewhere else. Often unable to sleep due to the noise outside or, perhaps, the oppression of his own thoughts, he socialised little, spending much time alone in his London home, living among the ghosts of his dreams.

A precious but tragic insight into Charles' forlorn later life was provided to a mathematical conference in July 1914 by the statesman, mathematician, scientific adviser and judge Lord Moulton, who was born on 18 November 1844 and lived until 1921. Recalling a visit he had made to Charles many years earlier, most likely in the late 1860s, Moulton painted a dismal picture of the price the gods had extracted from Charles for having bestowed on him a vision of a computer, without granting him the tools – technological, financial and diplomatic – to make his dreams come true:

> One of the sad memories of my life is a visit to the celebrated mathematician and inventor, Mr Babbage. He was far advanced in age, but his mind was still as vigorous as ever. He took me through his work rooms. In the first room I saw the parts of the original Calculating Machine, which had been shown in an incomplete state many years before. I asked him about its present form.
>
> 'I have not finished it because in working at it I came on the idea of my Analytical Machine, which would do all that it was capable of doing and much more. Indeed, the idea was so much simpler that it would have taken more work to complete the Calculating Machine than to design and construct the other in its entirety, so I turned my attention to the Analytical Machine.'
>
> After a few minutes' talk we went into the next work-room, where he showed and explained to me the working of the elements of the Analytical Machine. I asked if I could see it.

'I have never completed it,' he said, 'because I hit upon an idea of doing the same thing by a different and far more effective method, and this rendered it useless to proceed on the old lines.' Then we went into the third room. There lay scattered bits of mechanism but I saw no trace of any working machine.

Very cautiously I approached the subject, and received the dreaded answer, 'It is not constructed yet, but I am working at it, and it will take less time to construct it altogether than it would have taken to complete the Analytical Machine from the stage in which I left it.'

I took leave of the old man with a heavy heart. When he died a few years later, not only had he constructed no machine, but the verdict of a jury of kind and sympathetic scientific men who were deputed to pronounce upon what he had left behind him, either in papers or mechanism, was that everything was too incomplete to be capable of being put to any useful purpose.

Charles was still working on designs for the Analytical Engine when, after a short illness, he died on 18 October 1871, seventy-one days short of his eightieth birthday. He'd lived for 29,149 days, and he made an indelible impression on the world and the human imagination.

His obituary was published in *The Times* of London for Monday, 23 October 1871. It is a useful source, though it contains many inaccuracies. This is an edited version of the original; I have left out most of the sections that contain inaccuracies, and any remaining ones I indicate with a '*sic*':

THE LATE MR. CHARLES BABBAGE

Our obituary column on Saturday contained the name of one of the most active and original thinkers, and his name has been known through the length and breadth of the kingdom for nearly half a century as a practical mathematician – we mean Mr. Charles Babbage. He died at his residence in Dorset-street, Marylebone, the close of last week, at an age, spite of organ-grinding persecutors, little short of eighty years.

Little is known of Mr. Babbage's parentage and early youth, except that he was born on 26th December 1792 [*sic*] and was educated privately. During the whole of his long life, even when he had won for himself fame and reputation, he was always extremely reticent on that subject, and, in reply to questions, he would uniformly express an opinion that the only biography of living personages was to be found, or, at all events, ought to be found, in the list of their published works.

As this list, in Mr. Babbage's own case, extended to upwards of 60 productions, there ought to be no dearth of materials for the biographer; but these materials, after all, as a matter of fact, are scanty, in spite of an autobiographical work which he gave to the world about seven years ago, entitled *Passages in the Life of a Philosopher* …

His achievements here were twofold; he constructed what he called a Difference Engine, and he planned and demonstrated the practicability of an Analytical Engine also. It is difficult, perhaps, to make the nature of such abstruse inventions at all clear to the popular and untechnical reader, since Dr. Lardner, no unskilful hand at mechanical description, filled no less than twenty-five pages of the *Edinburgh Review* with but part of an account of its action, confessing that there were many features which it was hopeless to describe effectively without the aid of a mass of diagrams.

All that can be said of the machine is that the process of addition automatically performed is at the root of it. In nearly all tables of numbers there will be a law or order in the differences between each number and the next. For instance, in a column of square numbers – say 9, 16, 25, 36, 49, 64, 81 &c – the successive differences will be 7, 9, 11, 13, 15, 17, &c. These are differences of the first order. If, then, the process of differencing be repeated with these, we arrive at a remarkably simply series of numbers – to wit 2, 2, 2, 2 &c and into some such simple series most tables resolve themselves when they are analyzed into orders of differences: an element – an atom, so to speak – is arrived at, from which by constant addition the numbers in the table may be formed. It was the function of Mr. Babbage's machine to perform this addition of differences by combinations of wheels acting upon each other in an order determined by a preliminary adjustment. This working by differences gave it the name of the 'Difference Engine'.

[…]

Mr. Babbage was the author of published works to the extent of some 60 volumes. A full list of these, however, would not interest or edify the general reader, and those who wished to study their names can see them recorded at full length at the new library catalogue at the British Museum. Further information respecting them will be found in the twelfth chapter of Mr. Wald's *History of the Royal Society*, which we have already quoted. One or two of these, however, we should specify. The best known of them all, perhaps, is his *Ninth Bridgewater Treatise*, a work designed by him at once to refute the opinion supposed to be implied and encouraged in the first volume of that learned series, that an ardent devotion to mathematical studies is unfavourable to a real religious faith, and also to give specimens of the defensive aid which the evidences of Christianity may receive from the science of numbers, if studied in a proper spirit.

Another of his works which has found a celebrity of its own is a volume called, *The Decline of Science* [sic] both the title and the contents of which give us reason to believe that its author looked somewhat despondingly of the scientific attainments of the present age. The same opinion was further worked out by Mr. Babbage in a book on the first Great Exhibition, which he published 20 years ago. Another of his works which deserve mention here is one on *The Economy of Manufactures* [sic], which was one result of a tour of inspection which he made through England and upon the continent in search of mechanical principles for the formulation of Logarithmic Tables ...

Mr. Babbage was one of the oldest members of the Royal Society at the time of his death; he was also more than 50 years ago one of the founders of the Astronomical Society, and he and Sir John Herschel were the last survivors of that body [as the Royal Astronomical Society is still running today, this is obviously not true]. He [Babbage] was also an active and zealous member of many of the leading learning societies of London and Edinburgh, and in former years at least an extensive contributor to their published *Transactions*. His last important publication was the amusing and only too characteristic autobiographical work to which we have already referred as *Passages in the Life of a Philosopher*.

With some exceptions, such as the obituarist getting the year of Charles' birth wrong, and some other minor errors, it is a full and reasonable account of Charles' life, though – needless to say, one might add – it fails to mention anything about Ada and her enormous contribution.

The obituary also says nothing about the Analytical Engine, although it is highly unlikely that any useful information about that would have been available to the obituary writer, as nothing was available in any detail for about another ninety years. In fairness to the writer of the obituary, the account of the ideas behind the Difference Engine and the way the Difference Engine works are extremely accurate and still reliable today as source information about Charles.

It is of course particularly interesting that the writer speaks of Charles' fame. This may not be easily comprehensible to the modern reader. After all, didn't Charles fail at his two projects of building the Difference Engine and the Analytical Engine? Furthermore, when all is said and done he didn't really make an enormous contribution to mathematical thinking.

Yet we must remember that he was one of the richest men in Britain and had many distinguished friends, including many aristocrats; and in the nineteenth century in Britain, anyone who socialised with aristocrats had some of aristocratic magic rub off on them; they were seen as being of a different order from normal human beings.

So Charles was famous for his wealth and his calculating machines that never quite seemed to get completed. It is significant, unquestionably, that there is a photograph of a newspaper hoarding in London, with the newspaper seller standing next it, which has the headline 'Death of Mr Babbage' on the hoarding, which clearly shows that Charles was indeed a celebrity in his day, despite his failure.

18

SO WHY DID CHARLES AND ADA FAIL?

LORD BYRON'S GHOST
What a wonderful daughter she was! How proud I'll always be
That Ada and I now lie side-by-side in the family tomb for eternity!
Dear future dwellers, let me tell you about dear Ada:
Today, in your world, she's seen as a crusader
For understanding, better than Babbage, the potential of the computer,
Today, a billion Ada fans eternally salute her!

From *Ada Lovelace: The Musical*
Libretto and lyrics by J. Essinger

The reasons for Charles' failure have been suggested above at various junctures, but it is worthwhile to summarise them here. The reasons can, I think, be said to be:

- The high cost of making identical cogwheels in Charles' day. Again, he did not have access to the level of precision he needed.
- Charles' comparatively limited financial resources. Yes, he was an extremely wealthy man by the standards of his time or ours, but even he was not wealthy enough to found a new industry without external assistance.
- Charles' stubbornness in thinking that he could do everything necessary for his project's success himself.

- Charles' inability to charm people he needed to charm, especially Sir Robert Peel.
- Charles' folly in not fully appreciating the contribution Ada Lovelace could have made to the project both conceptually and at a practical level when it came to wooing influential people. Charles was much too ready to see Ada as merely his interpreter, or publicist, rather than as a colleague. He never stopped greatly liking her, loving her even, but he was handicapped by his epoch in not seeing women as the equals of men. It is a great pity he lived too early to meet the Nobel Prize-winning novelist William Golding, who once observed that women were not only the equals of men but superior to them.

As for Ada's global and iconic reputation today, Lord Byron's Ghost sums it up reasonably well in the quotation at the start of this chapter. Today, Ada's reputation soars around the world, and she is certainly more famous than Charles.

But while Charles and Ada both went to their graves as failures, the success of the London Science Museum team in building a working, full-scale Difference Engine in 1991 using Charles' plans – and only the materials and levels of precision available to him – and the subsequent completion by the same team of a Babbage-specified printer, was a glorious vindication of Charles' ideas and plans for the Difference Engine.

Today, in our world, Charles' and Ada's dreams have not only come true, but have been taken to new heights that very possibly not even they would have been able to imagine. We live at a time when our electronic companions are so reliable, and offer us such a multitudinous range of enjoyable features, that for many of us an arguably significant problem is that we actually spend too much time in our virtual electronic worlds and not enough in the real one that we inhabit.

Certainly, Ada was a most remarkable genius. Yet let's not be too hard on Charles. For all his faults, he was one of the most brilliant inventors of all time, and it was only his inventiveness that gave Ada the opportunity to show what a genius she was.

Charles had the most eclectic of minds, yet posterity remembers him because of one of the dreams at the heart of his genius: a dream that in some ways was a dream a child might have – that of making a machine that will let you do sums more easily and more quickly, so you can get on with other things; a childhood dream that stayed with him all his life.

If Charles could somehow see our world, he would, I think, smile.

As these wondrous times of ours – these days in which we are indeed living so many of our science-fiction dreams – take us forwards to ever greater technological achievements, Charles Babbage and his friend Ada Lovelace will always be there with us. Charles will be striding by our side, in his Victorian morning coat and heavy boots, attempting puns, not all of which come off, but which endear him to us nonetheless. Ada will smile at him, and sometimes feel she needs to apologise for him, but she'll always be fond of him.

Yes, Charles and Ada will be there with us – encouraging us, our inspirations and mentors – as we march onwards to our technological destiny.

ACKNOWLEDGEMENTS

My thanks to Margaret Dowley MBE for her excellent work on transcribing numerous Dictaphone tapes and for being such an excellent colleague on our visit to 'meet' Babbage and Ada. Thanks also for formatting the draft index with such meticulous care.

My thanks to Francesca Garratt for checking the index and for her friendship generally, especially during the time in 2016 when I was making regular visits from Canterbury to the British Library to research original sources.

My thanks also to Annelisa Christensen for her absolutely first-class research and for our many discussions about Charles and Ada. I am especially grateful to Annelisa for her arduous work to successfully ascertain and prove the precise date of the death of Charles' wife Georgiana and daughter Georgiana. Neither of these dates have been given before in any biography of Babbage.

My gratitude also to Doron Swade MBE and Betty Toole, to Jeff Kattenhorn and Khondaker Ahmed of the British Library and to Brenda Hockley and her colleagues in the Manuscripts Room at the British Library; to Oliver House and to Colin Harris of the Special Collections department at the Bodleian Library; to Dr Sian Prosser of the Royal Astronomical Society in London; and to the writer Amy Licence for her help generally and for her no doubt accurate suggestion for the decipherment of the word 'jury' in 'jury mad' in Lunn's letter to Babbage of 8 September 1830.

My great gratitude to Ada's descendant, the late Earl of Lytton, for granting me access to the Lovelace-Byron Collection at the Bodleian Library, Oxford, and for permission to reproduce material from it. My thanks also to the Earl of Lytton's literary executors, Laurence Pollinger Limited.

My sincere thanks as well to Briony Kapoor; Helen Komatsu; Maria Calo; Francesca Garratt; the late Rupert Essinger; Chris Stampe; Fred Watler; Yang Seungman; the highly talented radio journalist Hanna Wick of SRF; Rudolf Matter, director of SRF; Dr Laurence Green; Zoe Stansell from the British Library's Manuscripts Reference Service; Virginia Mills, archivist of the Royal Society; Fenya Sharkey; and to Richard Palliser IM, Matt Read and John Saunders for finding out the correct spelling of the surname of Babbage's Trinity College chess opponent, John Brand.

APPENDIX

INFORMATION ON SOURCES

The first and most fundamental point to make about researching the lives of Charles Babbage and Ada Lovelace is that there are relatively few original sources; that is, either statements by Charles or Ada themselves or by people who knew them. There is a considerable amount of secondary material, much of which, naturally enough, is based on similar primary sources but comments on the sources in different ways. Here, I provide a fairly concise guide to the primary sources I used for this book. In the bibliography I include primary source books and secondary sources that I find helpful, and also other books that may be of interest to the reader.

Source Notes for the Preface

Unquestionably the most important source for the life of Charles Babbage is the Babbage Archive in the British Library in London. The Babbage Archive consists of twenty-four volumes under the classification Add MS 37182–37205. Add MS 37182–37201 are twenty volumes of correspondence, and Add MS 37202–37205 are four volumes of scientific papers. The classification 'Add MS' is the abbreviation for 'Additional Manuscript'.

It is no exaggeration to say that studying the Babbage Archive not only requires a tremendous amount of dedication and application, but ideally would need several years of study. I did not have that time, though I made altogether about twenty visits to the British Library from my home town of Canterbury, Kent. I knew from the beginning that in the time available for researching the Archive, I would need to be strict with myself in order to focus on material of maximum utility. I made those visits during 2016, but I had already inspected the Babbage Archive fairly extensively about fifteen years earlier when I was researching my book *Jacquard's Web*. I was also careful to avoid repetition of material of that book in this new one.

Ironically, the task of researching the vast Babbage Archive was made simpler by the fact that the great majority of letters are either wholly illegible, or substantially so, and so either are not available for study at all, or only parts of them are. Moreover, most of them – by definition really as, after all, this was Charles' personal archive – are written from other people to Charles and so don't necessarily contain material by Charles himself.

Also, much of the correspondence and other documents is mundane and of no significant interest to posterity from a historical point of view. That said, there is also a tantalisingly large amount of material which appears to be of considerable interest, or at least there are sufficient legible glimpses in the material for us to guess that the whole letter or document in question would have been a fount of information.

In any event, the nineteenth century was not an era of clearly readable handwriting and I often wondered whether letters sent to Charles and now in the Archive were ever seriously expected to be read by anyone, because I don't see why Charles would necessarily be any better at deciphering them than I was.

Fortunately, as I've said, Charles himself was in the habit of keeping copies of letters he wrote to third parties, and these copies remain in the Archive. We can be extremely grateful to Charles for this, because without his careful husbanding of documents and letters he felt were particularly important, posterity would have lost them.

He also sometimes wrote notes himself about matters that had upset him or that he particularly cared about, and these notes also remain in the Archive: perhaps the best example is the remarkable document he wrote after getting home from his agonising and painful meeting with prime minister Sir Robert Peel, in which Charles, as I suggest in the text, scratched his frustration into the pages such that one can often see the very blots of ink that he made in his frustration and despair.

In the preface I also draw on Charles' autobiography *Passages from the Life of a Philosopher* (1864) and also from Lord Byron's *Don Juan* (1824). Generally, in the text I make clear what my sources are and I don't see the point of repeating that here, I just use this note on sources to clarify what my sources were when this is not clear.

The Sirens of Machinery

My source here is the Babbage Archive generally in which I pieced together Charles' story and retold it in my own way. The material by Charles Lyell about his times with Babbage and their friends Fitton and Conypeare is from Sir Charles Lyell, *Letters and Journals*, Volume 1, (1881).

Again, in this section I draw from Charles' autobiography and from a much more recent book *Zen and the Art of Motorcycle Maintenance* (1974), by Robert Pirsig.

1. Britain Transformed

My source for this chapter is general reading about the nineteenth century and I found *The Encyclopaedia Britannica* particularly helpful.

Like all historians, my work derives from my general reading, specific reading, and also from reasonable guesswork.

2. Boyhood

Again, the relative paucity of original sources for the lives of Charles and Ada is shown by the inevitability with which anyone writing about Charles' life (and especially the early part) has to rely on *Passages from the Life of a Philosopher*. In fact, his autobiography is particularly useful for his early life, but is much less useful later on. Indeed it is rather a poor autobiography, with its great absence of detail for his life beyond his childhood and with the idiosyncratic and sometimes weirdly opinionated comments he brings into it.

The material about Totnes derives substantially from my visit there in the early years of the twenty-first century. Totnes is a town I grew to love and I spent several nights there. The great thing about it, like many of the other locations mentioned in the book, is that the locations have not really changed much since Charles' day and when you walk you can easily envision Charles coming out of a shop or perambulating along the high street, albeit that he would wear rather different clothes to what you would wear.

I pieced together his story from disparate sources and from general reading, but again, his autobiography was by far my main source for this chapter. It is in now tragic that Charles did not write about his adult life with the same level of detail that he did his childhood. I would gladly exchange any of his anecdotes about his boyhood life at school for more information about conversations with Ada and more details about their friendship, which I've had to piece together from largely – though not entirely – inadequate primary source material.

3. Cambridge Days, and Ada is Born

This chapter is based on my general research about Cambridge and again, on Charles' autobiography. I was lucky enough to obtain an examination paper from Trinity College, from which I derived what seems to be one of the most interesting pieces in the whole book: the detail of the mathematical puzzles which the unfortunate candidates had to answer as part of the maths Tripos.

This chapter also introduces Ada's story. By far the most important sources for Ada Lovelace's life are the Lovelace-Byron papers, held in the Special Collection department of the Bodleian Library in Oxford. This is glorious original source material: unlike the Babbage Archive, it is not pasted up into ledger books but instead is loose leaf in numerous boxes. There are altogether about 1,000 letters written by Ada of which I have only perused a relatively small number, but fortunately Betty Toole has studied them all and the fruit of her work is found in her book *Ada, the Enchantress of Numbers* (1992). I do not believe that there is any significant letter written by Ada of which I am unaware.

The poem I quote in this chapter can be found in any general collection of Byron's work.

Again, I make use of Charles' autobiography to a considerable extent here.

4. Family Matters

The two most valuable secondary sources for my book are Anthony Hyman's remarkable *Charles Babbage, Pioneer of the Computer* (1982), which is the first scholarly biography of Charles, and Doron Swade's *The Cogwheel Brain* (2000). I must acknowledge a significant debt to Anthony Hyman; he often pointed me in the direction of a particular letter which I was able to find in the Babbage Archive and I tended to quote more from the significant letters than Hyman did himself. The Archive was particularly useful for this chapter in providing letters that had never been published before and which give, I think, considerable information about Charles' feelings as a young man trying to make his way in the world with a dominant and wilful father who not only controlled his purse-strings, but who was also never particularly sympathetic to Charles and his dreams. Some of the information about the French element of Charles' inspiration derives from research I undertook at the start of the twenty-first century for my book *Jacquard's Web*.

5. The Epiphany that Changed Charles' and Ada's Lives

Some of the research here derives from a visit I made to the Royal Astronomical Society near the start of the twenty-first century. The autobiography was very useful here in this chapter, as elsewhere, as was Doron Swade's *The Cogwheel Brain*.

6. 1827: Charles' Year of Disaster

Georgiana's letter to John Herschel about Benjamin's death is quoted by Anthony Hyman and is also found in the Archive. The other letters quoted there I have found myself from the same Archive and this chapter is also derived from research I undertook at Totnes.

7. Ada Dreams of a Flying Machine

We now switch to the first major chapter in the book about Ada Lovelace. The main sources for this chapter are the Lovelace-Byron papers, in which fortunately many explicit letters by Ada to her mother about her (Ada's) intellectual plans survive. Moreover, Ada and

Charles had in common that their handwriting was relatively legible and there have only been a few occasions where I wasn't able to decipher words. Incidentally, this was not true at all of Ada's husband Lord Lovelace, whose handwriting defies the eye and it also defies belief that a nobleman of his calibre could get away with writing so unclearly, although perhaps he regarded his readers as being responsible for reading his handwriting rather than him for making it legible.

8. The Solitary Widower

Writing the entire book demanded much detective work but especially in this chapter, where it's often the case that one has to infer Charles' emotional state from the absence of information about his family life, for example, after Georgiana's death; it is clear that when she died he lost much of his interest in his family. He became more withdrawn and focused even more on his work.

Sometimes, inevitably perhaps, when one examines a substantial part of a long archive collection, one enjoys surprise victories and perhaps the most exciting of all in the entire research was the reference to Charles having considered suicide when his wife died. This is the letter to Medley which is in ledger book 37184, folio 233 of the Archive. Similarly, finding the letter from Edward Tenceley to Charles was also a great delight.

I relied on Hyman to some extent for the account of Charles travelling abroad.

The letter from Lunn to Babbage about the apparently feeble attempt to find Charles a new wife is also in the Babbage Archive: ledger book 37185, folio 310.

9. *On the Economy of Machinery and Manufactures*

My source for this chapter is of course Charles' wonderful book itself.

10. Charles and Ada Meet

The first stanza of Canto Three of Byron's *Childe Harolde's Pilgrimage* has been much-quoted whenever Ada Lovelace is in discussion. It is an admirable stanza and beautifully written with the way it rises in the middle rather like a wave itself before the cadences of the verses dissipate. Let's remember, though, that Byron was never much of a father and was better at being sentimental about it than becoming involved in practicalities. In this chapter I draw heavily on the Lovelace-Byron papers and especially Lady Byron's letter to Dr William King which is, as I say in the text, the only primary source about the meeting between Charles and Ada, of which we would like to know so much more, but of which there is so little information available.

11. The Remarkable Ada Byron

Lady Byron is also the source of much of this chapter; her letter to King explains the impact Charles had on Ada.

In this chapter I have drawn heavily also on the surviving correspondence between Charles and Ada, which consists of eighty-five letters from Ada to Charles and twenty-five letters from Charles to Ada. As I mentioned in the text, it is quite clear that many letters they wrote to each other have not survived, either by accident or because they were deliberately destroyed.

12. A Fresh Tragedy; the Analytical Engine; and Ada's Marriage

In this chapter I have drawn from primary sources, including the listing on the death of Georgiana, Charles' daughter. This is in the *Standard* for 30 September 1834. The letters from Herschel to Charles are found in the John Herschel papers held at the Royal Society in London. The catalogue number is HS; the papers cover the years 1812–65.

I also rely here on a private conversation with Doron Swade (which he has given me permission to mention) which seems to me to provide some of the really powerful evidence about the dreadful impact on Charles of the death of his daughter Georgiana.

Again, Lady Byron is a crucial source here for what happened on the evening, 15 December 1834, when Charles went public on the Analytical Engine invention.

My own book *Jacquard's Web* is a source for my discussion here of Jacquard and the implications of Jacquard's invention for Charles' work. Charles' own sketchbooks, currently in the Science Museum archives in London, are also a crucial source here, as is Charles' autobiography.

Ada's letter to William on 28 June 1835 is found in the Lovelace-Byron papers. Obviously, many letters Ada sent in her life are no longer extant because – unlike Charles – she does not seem to have habitually made copies of important letters she wrote. We are, in fact, extremely fortunate that so many of Ada's letters survive because they were to other members of the Byron family, such as her mother and also to her husband Lord Lovelace, and so they are still to be found in the Lovelace-Byron Archive.

13. Dabbling in Politics

The main source for this chapter is letters from the Babbage Archive at the British Library and also the major document that Charles wrote when he returned home after the disastrous interview with Robert Peel.

Nathan Myhrvold's observations about Charles were made at a Computer History Museum event – Myhrvold & Swade Discuss Babbage's Difference Engine – a video of which can be seen on the Computer History Museum website.

14. A Stage Play that Held Up a Mirror to Charles' Heart

The initial quotation here comes from Charles' autobiography, as is made clear in the text. Much of the other material in this chapter is based on my own research into Charles and Ada, which began in 1997 and has so far (I am writing in 2019) not stopped.

Charles and Ada's correspondence is also a key source here. Charles' letter of 29 November 1839, mentioning Sheridan Knowles's play *Love*, sent me on a trail to find this play and to read it, inasmuch as it is feasible to read a play that for the most part is of a very low and melo dramatic standard.

I was also lucky enough to find a review of the play in a contemporary edition of *The Spectator*.

15. Ada the Fairy

As the text makes clear, I consider Charles and Ada's correspondence as the key source for information about their friendship, although there is considerable additional circumstantial evidence. How I regard the code and tenor of this correspondence is clear from the text, but reading it I was repeatedly struck by a belief that there were other, much more intimate, letters that have never survived and that someone, possibly Lady Byron, had been at pains to ensure the intimate letters never did survive. The ones that did are more about Charles and Ada's working relationship, although there is plenty of personal material as well.

As far as Ada's *Notes* are concerned (I follow what seems to me a sensible convention and give the word 'notes' an initial capital letter when mentioning them here) these were first published, as an accompaniment to Ada's translation of translation of Menabrea's article, in September 1843 in the third number of a journal called *Scientific Memoirs*. They are entitled *Sketch of the Analytical Engine invented by Charles Babbage Esq*, which is the title of Menabrea's article. They have been republished since, such as in *Science and Reform: Selected Works of Charles Babbage* (1989), which has that title despite Ada's *Notes* being a large part of the book. However, Ada's translation and *Notes* are readily available online, and yielded by a search for the title, in English, of Menabrea's article.

Ada's letter to Charles of 15 August 1843 is, I believe, the key letter of their personal and professional relationship. The offer which Ada made to Charles is momentous and historic.

16. Enchanted

Charles' letters to Ada and vice versa are crucial source material in this chapter, as is the letter which Charles wrote to Faraday about Ada. Until this letter became widely known in about 2014, it was believed by Babbage scholars that Charles was referring to the Analytical Engine itself by the phrase 'Enchantress of Number' in his letter to Ada of 9 September 1843. It is now known that he was in fact referring to Ada herself.

17. Last Days

Charles Dickens' novel *Little Dorrit* (1855) is the principal source in this chapter. The possibility that Dickens based the character Daniel Doyce on Charles is not provable but there is so much circumstantial evidence for his having done so that I think any other conclusion is rather precious and not very reasonable. The reminiscence by John Fletcher, Lord Moulton, about having met Charles in the late 1860s, is found in an address he made in 1914 to a conference celebrating the tercentenary of the invention of Napier's logarithmic tables.

Charles' obituary was published in *The Times* of London on Monday, 23 October 1871.

18. So Why Did Charles and Ada Fail?

The sources for this chapter are generally my overall research into the lives of Charles and Ada.

SELECT BIBLIOGRAPHY

Selected Works by Charles Babbage

Babbage, Charles. *On the Economy of Machinery and Manufactures.* London: Charles Knight, 1832.

Babbage, Charles. *On the Principles and Development of the Calculator.* New York: Dover Publications, 1961.

Babbage, Charles. *Passages from the Life of a Philosopher.* New Brunswick: Rutgers University Press, and Piscataway: IEEE Press, 1994.

Babbage, Charles. *Science and Reform, Selected Works of Charles Babbage.* Cambridge: Cambridge University Press, 1989.

Secondary Sources

Aspray, William (ed.). *Computing Before Computers.* Ames: Iowa State University Press, 1990.

Bromley, Allan. *The Babbage Papers in the Science Museum.* London: The Science Museum, 1991.

Brown, Donald. *Charles Babbage – The Man and his Machine.* Totnes: The Totnes Museum Study Centre, 1992.

Byron, Lord. *The Works of Lord Byron.* London: Wordsworth Editions, 1994.

Buxton, H.W. *Memoir of the Life and Labours of the Late Charles Babbage Esq. F.R.S.* Cambridge, MA: MIT Press and Tomash Publishers, 1988.

Campbell-Kelly, Martin and William Aspray. *Computer: A History of the Information Machine.* New York: HarperCollins, 1986.

Collier, Bruce. *The Little Engines that Could've.* New York and London: Garland Publishing, 1990.

Crosse, Annie. *Red-Letter Days of My Life.* London: Bentley, 1892.

Dickens, Charles. *The Letters of Charles Dickens: 1820–1870* (2nd release). Electronic edition.

Dickens, Charles. *Little Dorrit*. London: Chapman & Hall, 1855.

Eisler, Benita. *Byron*. London: Hamish Hamilton, 1999.

Essinger, James. *Ada's Algorithm*. London: Gibson Square, 2013.

Essinger, James. *Jacquard's Web*. Oxford: Oxford University Press, 2004.

Grosskurth, Phyllis. *Byron, The Flawed Angel*. London: Hodder and Stoughton, 1997.

Hyman, Anthony. *Charles Babbage, Pioneer of the Computer*. Oxford: Oxford University Press, 1982.

King-Hele, D.G. (ed.). *John Herschel 1792–1871: A Bicentennial Commemoration*. London: The Royal Society, 1992.

Knowles, James Sheridan. *Love, A Play in Five Acts*. Baltimore: H.A. Turner, *c*.1840.

Lethbridge, Lucy. *Ada Lovelace, Computer Wizard of Victorian England*. London: Short Books, 2004.

Maddox, Brenda. *Rosalind Franklin, the Dark Lady of DNA*. London: Harper Collins, 2002.

Moore, Doris Langley. *Ada: Countess of Lovelace: Byron's Legitimate Daughter*. London: John Murray, 1977.

Moseley, Maboth. *Irascible Genius: A Life of Charles Babbage, Inventor*. London: Hutchinson, 1964.

Snyder, Laura J. *The Philosophical Breakfast Club*. New York: Random House, 2011.

Stein, Dorothy. *Ada: A Life and Legacy*. Cambridge, MA: MIT Press, 1985.

Swade, Doron. *Charles Babbage and his Calculating Engines*. London: The Science Museum, 1991.

Swade, Doron. *The Cogwheel Brain*. London: Little, Brown and Co., 2000.

Ticknor, George. *The Life, Letters and Journals of George Ticknor*. Boston and New York: Houghton Mifflin Co., 1909.

Toole, Betty. *Ada, the Enchantress of Numbers*. Mill Valley: Strawberry Press, 1992.

Woolley, Benjamin. *The Bride of Science*. London: Macmillan, 1999.

INDEX